LEE vs. McCLELLAN

Lee vs. McClellan

The First Campaign

Clayton R. Newell

REGNERY PUBLISHING, INC.
Washington, D.C.

Library of Congress Cataloging-in-Publication Data
Newell, Clayton R., 1942–
    Lee vs. McClellan : the first campaign / Clayton R. Newell.
        p.   cm.
    Includes bibliographical references and index.
    ISBN 0-89526-452-8
    1. West Virginia Campaign, 1861.   2. West Virginia–History–Civil
War, 1861–1865.   3. Lee, Robert E. (Robert Edward), 1807–1870.
4. McClellan, George Brinton, 1826–1885.   I. Title.
E472.17.N49   1996   96-30748
973.7'31–dc20   CIP

Published in the United States by
Regnery Publishing, Inc.
An Eagle Publishing Company
422 First Street, SE
Washington, DC 20003

Distributed to the trade by
National Book Network
4720-A Boston Way
Lanham, MD 20706

Designed by Dori Miller
Maps by XNR Productions, Inc.

Printed on acid-free paper.
Manufactured in the United States of America

10 9 8 7 6 5 4 3 2 1

Books are available in quantity for promotional or premium use. Write to
Director of Special Sales, Regnery Publishing, Inc., 422 First Street, SE, Suite
300, Washington, DC 20003, for information on discounts and terms or call
(202) 546–5005.

For my father:
Reverend Wendell R. Newell
A man of peace.

CONTENTS

MAPS AND ILLUSTRATIONS

MAPS

ILLUSTRATIONS

Frontispiece:
A cannon from Brigadier John B. Floyd's Confederate brigade emplaced on Cotton Hill prepares to open fire on the Federal supply depot in the town of Gauley Bridge on November 1, 1861. The attack came as a complete surprise to Brigadier General William Rosecrans, who had neglected to occupy the mountain that overlooked the Federal position.

Front Endpapers:
Two six-pounder cannons of Barrett's Ohio Battery under the direction of Colonel Frederick W. Lander open the first battle of the campaign in western Virginia by firing on the town of Philippi on June 3, 1861. Their aiming point was the neatly aligned white tents of the Upshur

Grays, part of Colonel George Alexander Porterfield's Confederate forces holding the town.

Back Endpapers:
Troops of the First Georgia from Brigadier General Robert Garnett's Confederate command on Laurel Hill advance toward the Ninth Indiana and Fourteenth Ohio of Brigadier General Thomas Morris's brigade (foreground) near Belington on July 5, 1861. The skirmish preceded by five days the Federal attack on the Confederate position at nearby Rich Mountain.

ACKNOWLEDGMENTS

E.B. VANDIVER, a long-time student of the Civil War, provided the inspiration for this book. He did the initial work on the military operations conducted in western Virginia in 1861. When I expressed an interest in pursuing a book on the subject, he very generously shared his ideas and research with me. He followed the erratic progress of my research and writing, provided interest and enthusiasm along the way, and twice read the manuscript in draft, correcting errors and offering suggestions. E.B. did his part to make the book better; any flaws that remain are my responsibility.

Many individuals provided support and background information on the Civil War and West Virginia history that helped shape the book. Bobbi Rogers created the maps. Susan Crites helped me understand how residents of West Virginia view the Civil War. Louise Arnold-Friend at the U.S. Army Military History Institute cheerfully guided me through the extensive holdings there. The staff at the Ruth Scarborough Library at Shepherd College in Shepherdstown, West Virginia, was most helpful as they patiently retrieved book after book from the West Virginia Collection. The historian at Fort Myer, Virginia, Kim Holien also provided timely information. My thanks to Daniel W. Strauss, Anne Marie Price at the Virginia Historical Society, Corrie Hudgins at the Museum of the Confederacy, Debra

Basham at the West Virginia Division of Culture, and the Military History Institute for their help with photographs.

This book would not have been possible without the faith of my agent, Jane Dystel who accepted the idea before seeing anything in writing. At Regnery Publishing I had the help of Richard Vigilante who provided encouragement, Charlotte Hays who smoothed out the rough edges of the manuscript, and Christopher Briggs who guided it skillfully throught the production maze.

On the home front my loyal companions, M.I. Grant and his associate, Henry Reginald, were always ready for a research trip, and they patiently listened to me while I explained yet another battle to them. As always, the most important person in my writing is my wife, Gwendolyn. For this book she spent countless hours reading draft chapters, providing key insights for the manuscript, and procuring photographs and maps.

INTRODUCTION

THIS BOOK EXAMINES the first campaign of the Civil War in terms of its strategic objective, western Virginia. Earlier historical interpretations of the military operations in western Virginia in 1861 have generally described a variety of campaigns in the region. Articles in *West Virginia History,* for example, include "General R. E. Lee's Northwest Virginia Campaign,"[1] "Campaigns of Generals McClellan and Rosecrans in Western Virginia, 1861–1862,"[2] and "General John B. Floyd and the West Virginia Campaigns of 1861."[3] Other titles include *R. E. Lee's Cheat Mountain Campaign,*[4] "The First West Virginia Campaigns,"[5] and "The Northwestern Virginia Campaign of 1861."[6] As evidenced by the titles, these treatments examine only a portion of the larger campaign by focusing on a specific personality or area. McClellan identified the strategic objective in May 1861 when he wrote to Lincoln that it was his intent "to secure Western Virginia to the Union."[7] The objective had both a military and a political component. Attainment of the former–military control of the western counties of Virginia– laid the foundation for the latter, a state government that desired to remain in the Union.

Wars are the result of political actions; they are fought to attain political goals. When peaceful means of solving problems fail, political entities turn to force to attain the desired goals. The role of a military force is to produce a situation favorable to achieving the desired political objectives. Without a clear and direct relationship between the political goals and military operations, battle is an exercise in futility and an irresponsible waste of men and material. War's potential devastation demands close coordination between political and military objectives before, during, and after the fighting. The strategic objectives set forth for military forces must be attainable within the constraints of available resources and contribute to producing a favorable political situation. Unfortunately, political and military leaders frequently must spend considerable blood and treasure to learn that relatively simple concept. All too often the political leadership abdicates responsibility for its actions at the outbreak of war, while the military leadership, for its part, sees political constraints and guidance during the war as interference.

Ideally, political and military leaders work together to establish strategic military objectives that will contribute to the political objectives of the war. In the words of a well-known nineteenth-century military philosopher: "No one starts a war—or rather, no one in his senses ought to do so—without first being clear in his mind what he intends to achieve by that war and how he intends to conduct it. The former is its political purpose; the latter is its operational objective."[8] Once the desired political objectives are clear, military leaders can plan the necessary campaigns that will attain the desired strategic military objectives that will result in the conditions necessary for attaining the political objectives.

Wars are fought for political reasons. They begin and end based on the activities and decisions of politicians. Military campaigns are conducted, or at least they should be, to attain a strategic objective that will contribute to the political goal of the war. Like war, a military campaign can start as the result of political activity, and the results of a campaign can have significant political repercussions. Indeed, it is entirely possible that the ultimate political results of a campaign may not be fully known for some time after military operations cease. That was true in the case of the Civil War's first campaign.

A military campaign is a connected series of battles that form a distinct phase of a war. In the course of a campaign one or more battles will be fought. Historically, campaigns have been defined by time, by location, or even by associating them with a particular commander. While all of those methods can define a distinct phase of a war, a campaign can be more clearly defined by determining the strategic objective it sought to attain. The battles that comprise a campaign can then be examined for tactical objectives, each of which should have contributed to progress in the larger strategic objective. Campaigns take place in a theater of operations. According to a prominent early nineteenth-century interpreter of Napoleon's campaigns, a military campaign takes place in a theater of operations that "embraces all the territory it may desire to invade and all that it may be necessary to defend."[9] In the first campaign, the theater of operations and the strategic objectives were the same, the western counties of Virginia between the Shenandoah Valley and the Ohio River.

Without understanding the political objectives of war, military history can become a simple recitation of battles apparently fought for the sake of fighting. Battles thus fought are futile exercises in wasted lives and treasure. The ultimate objective in war is to attain a political situation that furthers the interests of the political entity waging the war. Strategy seeks to establish a military situation that contributes to attaining the political goals, while tactics considers the maneuver of forces in battle. The study of one can easily, and frequently does, exclude the consideration of the other. Strategic studies of a lengthy conflict such as the Civil War tend not to get bogged down in the details of battle, while the tactical examination of a particular engagement concentrates on the immediate event. Using a campaign for the framework of analysis offers the opportunity to relate it to the war's strategic situation while examining battles at the tactical level. In the 1980s the U.S. armed forces began

using the term "operational art" to describe planning and conducting campaigns. Although it is a relatively new addition to the American military lexicon, the concept of operational art has its roots in
the nineteenth century.[10]

The most prominent figures in the first campaign, Robert E. Lee
and George B. McClellan, never met in 1861 in western Virginia.
But the plans they made and their conduct of operations when they
were personally commanding forces in the theater of operations
made the first campaign of the Civil War a battle of minds between
two generals who gained their lasting reputations for actions later in
the war. The campaign began in May 1861 when McClellan
ordered Federal troops into western Virginia; it ended with the battle at Camp Allegheny in December. McClellan was in the theater
for just over thirty days in June and July, and shortly after he
departed, Lee arrived and remained there about ninety days. More
than any other factor, their preparations before the campaign and
their actions while commanding on the battlefield contributed
directly to the results of the first campaign.

The Civil War lasted more than four years, and the truly cata-
clysmic battles that followed the first campaign continue to have a
profound effect on the history of the United States. Those years also
had an effect on many of the men who played an active role in the
campaign. So as not to interrupt the flow of the narrative, the epi-
logue summarizes how some of them fared for the remainder of the
Civil War. As with the campaign, their later accomplishments and
disappointments have largely overshadowed what they did in western Virginia, for better or worse.

This book is about the first campaign of the Civil War, the Federal invasion of western Virginia. In 1861, as both sides struggled to
mobilize armies and put them in the field, a small Federal army conducted a remarkable campaign that had long-standing and tangible
results. That first campaign, overshadowed by the four years of war
that followed, stands as a model of how political goals can be

attained by military operations. One reason the first campaign has been largely overlooked is that the battles fought in western Virginia were small affairs with few casualties that were forgotten in the wake of the later bloodbaths of the big battles that dominated most of the war.

CHAPTER ONE

Lee's Virginia on the Brink of War

A PALE GREEN haze covered the western mountains of Virginia as spring, the season of renewal, made its appearance in 1861. In the mixed forests of deciduous and evergreen trees, the light new leaves contrasted with the stands of darker pine needles. Here and there redbud and white dogwood flowers lent a bit of color, giving the hillsides a whimsical air. In normal years the people would be preparing the ground for planting and looking forward to the long warm days of summer that would make for a productive harvest in the fall. But 1861 was not going to be a normal year. The seeds of secession had been sown in Richmond, and no one could predict what harvest the autumn might bring to western Virginia.

Abraham Lincoln's election as the sixteenth president of the United States in November 1860 had touched a raw nerve in the South. For years emotions between the North and the South had been building. The national election had been conducted along regional lines, and the results reflected the strong feelings of sectionalism in the country. In the four-way presidential race Lincoln, the Republican party candidate running on a platform designed to win both radicals from the eastern and western parts of the country, led the popular vote and received a majority of electorate votes with 180, all from free states. Democratic party candidate Stephen A. Douglas, running on a platform that supported the territorial right to choose slavery without reference to Congress, was second in the popular vote, but garnered only twelve electoral votes. John C. Breckinridge, candidate of the Southern faction of the Democratic party that supported territorial slavery, placed third in the popular vote but collected seventy-two electoral votes from the slave states. The fourth candidate, John Bell of the Constitutional Union party, was fourth in the popular vote, but third in the electoral count with thirty-nine votes from three border slave states, including Virginia.

Lincoln's victory over the Southern candidates provoked a crisis of a magnitude never before faced by the young nation. Throughout the South angry citizens held rallies and mass meetings to express their displeasure with Lincoln's position on slavery, the "peculiar institution" upon which much of the region's economy depended. Within days of the election, the South Carolina legislature called a special state convention to meet on December 20. President James Buchanan, aware of the high passions over the election results, was determined to keep the possibility of civil war in check until Lincoln's inauguration in March 1861. In his December 3 State of the Union message, Buchanan attempted to find a middle ground to avert war, at least until he left office. He voiced his disapproval of breaking up the Union, but he also expressed the opinion that the Federal government had no legal power to prevent a state's leaving the United States.

The crisis deepened when South Carolina's special convention voted unanimously on December 20 to secede from the Union.

Secession fever spread quickly through the deep South. Before Lincoln's inauguration, six more slave states had followed South Carolina's lead. The debate over whether to leave the Union raged through Virginia. But in Virginia, the Old Dominion, the question of secession was more than a difference between North and South; it threatened to aggravate long-standing east-west issues that had the potential to tear the state apart. In the 1860 national election Virginia voters expressed a moderate mood by evenly splitting between Breckinridge and Bell, each of whom received about 44 percent of the popular vote. Douglas and Lincoln trailed badly, the former receiving less than 10 percent and the latter less than 1 percent.[1]

Virginia governor John Letcher, in office less than a year, reflected the state's moderate mood in the closing months of 1860. He sought a national convention to work out a peaceful solution to the nation's divisiveness and delayed a call for a special session of the Old Dominion's legislature until January 1861 when he hoped it would be able to "determine calmly and wisely what action is necessary in this emergency."[2]

In spite of the winter cold in January 1861, Richmond burned hot with excitement as residents watched the members of the General Assembly gather in the capital city for the special session. When they convened in Richmond on January 7, the members of the legislature acted as though war were imminent. They voted to improve the state's military preparedness by issuing $2,000,000 in treasury notes, authorizing the sale of bonds to support militia companies, and sending a commission to England to buy arms. Their belligerent mood was evident in the tone of the resolution the delegates passed on January 21 declaring that should the differences between North and South prove irreconcilable, then "every consideration of honor and interest demands that Virginia shall unite her destiny with the Slave holding States of the South."[3] One member wrote home that "[t]imes are wild and revolutionary beyond description," and went on to express his "fear [that] the Union is irretrievably gone."[4]

While the Virginia General Assembly went about its work, six more states, Mississippi, Florida, Alabama, Georgia, Louisiana, and Texas, left the Union. As the delegates pondered over possible courses of action for the Old Dominion at the special session, the debate took on a distinctly regional flavor. The eastern section of the state generally supported secession, but in the western counties there was considerable pro-Union sympathy. As the session went on, these differences tended to polarize the delegates and erode the feelings of moderation.

The differences between the two sections of the state did not really surprise anyone. For thirty years leading to the 1861 secession crisis, the internal conflict had festered in a complex variety of geographical, cultural, and political issues that had long pitted the western portion of the state against the east. Virginia's first constitution, written in 1776, gave the eastern counties a disproportionate share of the legislature and allowed only landowners to vote. As the population increased in the western portions of the state, there was a demand for a constitutional convention to redress the legislative representation and equalize the tax burden. In 1828 the question of constitutional reform finally went before the voters who approved a convention by a majority of more than five thousand votes. In October 1829 the long-awaited convention assembled. But the constitution the delegates produced in January 1830 simply allocated legislative representation to specific geographical areas of the state rather than basing it on population, thus assuring that the eastern portion of the state would always hold a majority of votes. Although a majority of the state's voters approved the constitution in a referendum, the eastern counties gave it more support than those in the west. The new constitution did little to quell the east-west conflict in the state. In the years between 1830 and 1861 there were a variety of predictions that the Old Dominion might be split along east-west lines. In the 1861 crisis the larger national issue of North versus South received most of the attention at the special legislative session, but that issue was also stretching the ties between eastern and western Virginia close to the breaking point.[5]

As the secession crisis deepened in both Virginia and the nation, the legislature called for a state convention to determine the state's future course. Members of the General Assembly, however, could not be delegates to the convention, since the legislature planned to stay in session during the crisis. Any actions taken by the state convention had to be approved by the state's voters in a special referendum before they became effective. Delegates to the convention were selected in a special election on February 4, and they convened in Richmond nine days later.

At the same time the General Assembly was laying the groundwork for secession in Virginia, the search for a compromise that could avert the crisis went on. Letcher was finally able to hold the national convention he hoped would provide a peaceful solution. On February 4, the same day Old Dominion voters were selecting their delegates to the state convention, representatives of twenty one states, including six slave-holding states, met at a peace conference in Washington, D.C., in the hope of finding a compromise that would avert a civil war. But the conference was doomed to failure before it began. On the same day it opened, delegates from the seven seceded states were meeting in Montgomery, Alabama, to form a new government, the Confederate States of America. Since those states sent no representatives to Washington, there was no way to forge any sort of compromise. In the end, the best the delegates meeting in Washington could do was agree on a modified version of the Crittenden Compromise, a proposal by Senator John J. Crittenden that called for recognition of slavery across the nation south of the 36° 30′ line established in the Missouri Compromise of 1820. But that idea, at President-elect Lincoln's urging, had already been rejected by a special Senate committee in December. The conference's proposal met the same fate.

In spite of the warlike mood of the General Assembly and the futile efforts of the peace conference, when the 152 representatives to the Virginia Convention gathered in Richmond on February 13, the Old Dominion's secession from the Union was not a foregone conclusion. By no means were all the delegates in favor of the state leaving the United States to join the Confederacy. Initially, the convention was hopeful of compromise and spent its days listening to various delegates present proposals and outline positions while it waited for the outcome of the peace conference in Washington. As the convention began its work, representatives from South Carolina, Mississippi, and Georgia addressed the delegates, trying to convince them of the need for Virginia to join with her Southern brethren in the cause of states' rights and generally increasing the pressure for secession. For weeks the convention seemed to be marking time, as if reluctant to come to grips with the terrible question of whether to leave the Union. The editor of *The Western Virginia Star* reported to his readers that he had "been waiting and waiting for something tangible to be done by this Convention." He had arrived in Richmond hopeful "that something would be done to relieve the anxiety and suspense of the people of Virginia," but that hope had soon "been doomed to disappointment."[6]

Virtually all of the convention's delegates were seasoned politicians, and it was not long before leaders of the various factions began to emerge and line up supporters for their points of view. The most prominent leader of the secessionists was the outspoken Henry A. Wise, Letcher's immediate predecessor as governor of Virginia. The Unionists looked to John S. Carlile, a lawyer who had been elected to his second term in Congress in the 1860 national election, and Waitman T. Willey, who had been a delegate to the Constitutional Union convention that had nominated Bell. Both men represented the northwestern region of the state and staunchly opposed secession. Willey was especially worried about western Virginia's exposed strategic position in the event of war. The region's proximity to the northern states of Ohio and Pennsylvania could make it an early casualty of Federal occupation.[7]

At the beginning of the convention the estimates of how the delegates felt about the issue of secession varied widely. The editor of the *Southern Literary Messenger* thought there were ninety Unionists, fifty secessionists, and twelve doubtful. Ironically, he listed Wise among the doubtful. Another estimate of the composition of the delegates who gathered in Richmond "approximated thirty secessionists, seventy moderates, and fifty Unionists." A contemporary observer, perhaps anticipating the outcome of the convention, categorized the delegates as "one hundred ultimate secessionists, forty-one instant secessionists, and ten unconditional Union men." With no one to unite the moderates, however, the convention began to polarize, making the debate less one of seeking compromise than an issue of whether the state would leave the Union.[8]

The move to support secession grew stronger as time went on. As the options became fewer, more moderates moved toward the idea of joining other Southern states as part of the Confederacy. Unionists and moderates struggled for conciliation, while the secessionists used delaying tactics to increase their strength. As the convention dragged on, the crisis exacerbated Virginia's old east-west sectional grievances. A Morgantown editorial clearly expressed the mood of many in the northwestern part of the state: "We have been 'hewers of wood and drawers of water' for Eastern Virginia long enough, and it is time that that section understood it. . . ." In spite of the tension among the delegates, the stimulus that galvanized the convention into action came from outside Virginia.[9]

While Virginia had been trying to determine a course of action, events in other parts of the country had brought the secession crisis to a head in South Carolina. Most of the Federal property in the seceded states had been quickly occupied by militia forces. Fort Sumter, however, in Charleston harbor remained in Federal hands. President Buchanan attempted to resupply the garrison in January using the unarmed transport, *Star of the West,* but shore batteries in the harbor, now manned by South Carolina troops, drove

her off. Major Robert Anderson, an 1825 graduate of the U.S. Military Academy at West Point, commanding the Federal forces holding Sumter, did not answer the shore batteries in the hope of
avoiding war. After the failed resupply mission, the fort, still occupied by Federal troops, received no fire from the shore. The men
of the garrison, however, were not allowed to go out of the fort
to purchase supplies, leaving them to rely on existing stocks.
Buchanan, a lame-duck president not anxious to rock the ship of
state any further before he left office, left the problem for his
successor, Lincoln.

On March 5, one day after Lincoln's inauguration, Major Anderson notified Washington that he had provisions for less than six
weeks. The new president hesitated. The national situation had
changed significantly since the failed January resupply effort. In
February, delegates from the seven seceded states had met in Montgomery, Alabama, to establish a provisional government for the
Confederate States of America. For a month Lincoln considered
risking war with the newly created Southern government by launch-
ing another attempt to resupply the fort or, by doing nothing,
admitting that the Federal government could not muster enough
force to prevent the rebel states from leaving the Union. Finally,
after a month of contemplation, Lincoln acted. On April 8 he sent
an envoy to notify the governor of South Carolina that the Federal
government planned "to supply Fort Sumter with provisions only,
and that if such an attempt be not resisted, no effort to throw in
men, arms, or ammunition will be made without further notice, or
in case of an attack upon the fort."[10]

Jefferson Davis, president of the Confederate States of America,
upon learning of the planned resupply effort, ordered Brigadier
General P. G. T. Beauregard, commander of Charleston's Confederate defenses, to demand the fort's immediate evacuation. Should
the garrison fail to comply, Davis instructed Beauregard to "proceed in such a manner as you may determine to reduce it."[11] On

April 11 Beauregard sent a delegation to notify Anderson, who had once been his gunnery instructor at West Point, to evacuate the fort or be fired upon. Anderson refused, but he commented to Beauregard's representatives that his men would be starved out in a few days if the fort were not battered to pieces. For a brief moment there loomed the possibility that the South could gain the fort without having to fire the first shot of the war, but with the impending arrival of the Federal relief force, Beauregard decided he could wait no longer. On April 12 the Confederate barrage opened at 4:30 A.M. and "continued without intermission" until the Federal garrison surrendered on April 13. The next day Anderson, carrying a sense of failure that he had been unable to prevent the outbreak of war, led his weary soldiers out of the fort and onto a waiting Confederate steamer that took them to a U.S. navy ship from the Federal relief force standing outside the harbor.[12]

In Virginia, the events at Sumter captured the attention of both the public and the convention delegates. News of the fort's surrender brought crowds of demonstrators carrying Confederate flags into the streets of Richmond to celebrate the victory. Any hope the remaining Unionist delegates to the Virginia Convention may have held of preventing secession faded on April 15 when Lincoln issued a call for 75,000 militia troops to suppress the insurrection. In spite of Letcher's moderate stance and hopes for a peaceful resolution to the crisis, he could not abide Federal interference by force of arms with Virginia's internal affairs. He immediately notified Washington that because Lincoln had "chosen to inaugurate civil war," Virginia would provide no troops for the Federal government's use.[13]

With feelings running high, the delegates to the Virginia Convention voted to go into secret session, and the secessionists took control. Their most outspoken leader, Wise, a longtime proponent of slavery, had already taken it upon himself to take the first steps toward secession by moving to seize Federal property in Virginia. Meeting secretly with a group of militia officers in his room at the

Exchange Hotel in Richmond during the night of April 16, Wise, who had no military experience himself, urged them to move against the Federal armory at Harpers Ferry and the U.S. Navy Yard at Norfolk as soon as possible. Wise also sent a delegation to Governor Letcher to sanction his actions, but the governor demanded official notification from the convention that it had voted for secession before he would take any precipitous action. In spite of Letcher's position, Wise acted. Wise wanted to present the convention with a *fait accompli*. Working frantically through the night with the help of sympathetic railroad officials who routed trains to carry troops, Virginia militia forces began moving on April 17. When Wise, a slightly built man with long hair and angular features, rose to address the delegates in the secret session, he paused briefly to ensure that all eyes were on him; he was a fine public speaker, accustomed to having people listen when he had something to say. When he had everyone's attention, he began a fiery speech, delivered "with glaring eyes and bated breath," in which he announced that even as they were debating in Richmond, members of the Virginia militia were on the way to capture the Federal garrisons at Harpers Ferry and Norfolk.[14]

Caught up in the excitement of the moment, the delegates passed the ordinance of secession on April 17 by a vote of eighty-eight to fifty-five, although it still had to be ratified by a popular vote on May 23 before it could officially take effect. A majority of the delegates had approved secession, but the pattern of votes reflected the state's east-west conflict with forty-two of the "no" votes coming from western Virginia, while that area cast only twenty votes in favor of the ordinance. While about two-thirds of all the delegates to the convention favored secession, roughly that same percentage of representatives from the western part of the state opposed it. But the western opposition was lost in the excitement. The news of the decision spread rapidly through the city. Richmond was soon rampant with talk of secession from the Union, and many residents eagerly anticipated the great adventure of war. "Schools were broken up, and knots of excited men gathered at every street corner," recalled Sallie Hunt, a young schoolgirl at the time.[15]

The delegates to the convention had struggled with multiple issues during their long deliberations. The larger problem facing them was the North-South dilemma, which they believed had been resolved with the vote for secession, but within the state, the long-standing east-west question was part of the secession crisis. Most of the western pro-Union delegates simply refused to accept the vote of the convention. Their feelings for the Union, combined with the pent-up antagonism directed toward the eastern part of the state, provided the impetus for an active political movement to form a separate state. The intrastate issue of the western counties seceding to become a state, debated for years among Virginia politicians, was directly related to the geography of the Old Dominion.

In 1861 Virginia was one of the largest states in the Union. It stretched 425 miles from the Atlantic Ocean to the Ohio River, and 300 miles north from North Carolina to Pennsylvania, encompassing 67,230 square miles of territory, an area about the size of New England. Geographical features divided it into two north-south planes that sloped in opposite directions, with a broad, fertile valley between them. The eastern plane rose gently from the Chesapeake Bay west to the mountains of the Blue Ridge. An imaginary fall line of the rivers in the area divided it into two parallel regions, the coastal Tidewater and the Piedmont, just east of the Blue Ridge. The western plane, the Trans-Allegheny region, sloped downward from the Allegheny Mountains to the Ohio River. Between the two planes lay the Valley of Virginia with the Blue Ridge marking its eastern edge and the Allegheny Mountains defining the western side. The Shenandoah River, flowing from south to north, where it emptied into the Potomac River at Harpers Ferry, frequently lent its name to the famous valley.

Tidewater, along the eastern seaboard, was the earliest part of the state to be occupied by immigrants. It was settled with Europeans arriving from across the Atlantic. Over time, residents began to move west into the Piedmont, and as that region became more populated, the two areas became virtually identical in social and political outlook. With the mountains of the Blue Ridge barring easy movement further west out of the Piedmont, the Valley of Virginia was settled mainly by immigrants moving south from Pennsylvania and Maryland in search of cheap land. About a third of the state lay west of the Valley. The long mountain range of the Trans-Allegheny region was part of the vast Appalachian system. The main ridge of the range averaged about 2,500 feet above sea level, but its highest point stood almost 4,500 feet. This formidable barrier had a pronounced effect on settlers in the region. Some of the more adventurous of the Valley settlers eventually moved west along the Great Kanawha River to make significant inroads into the Trans-Allegheny region, but the easier route along the Ohio River had been the choice of most immigrants into the mountainous region of western Virginia. This pattern of settlement shaped the political sympathies of the area.

The majority of the first settlers in the Valley and Trans-Allegheny regions were German or Scotch-Irish who did not necessarily sympathize with the political and social views of Tidewater and Piedmont residents in eastern Virginia. The independently minded Virginians living west of the Blue Ridge did not initially embrace the concept of slavery. Slave labor lends itself to a mild climate with fertile soil where agricultural production centers on a staple crop, such as cotton, that requires simple, routine, labor -intensive operations. The agriculture of the regions west of the Blue Ridge, small-unit subsistence family farming, contrasted sharply with the highly organized and socially regimented plantation-slavery system in Tidewater and the Piedmont. During the early part of the nineteenth century, however, slavery had become economical in the Valley. With the rise of proslavery sentiment there,

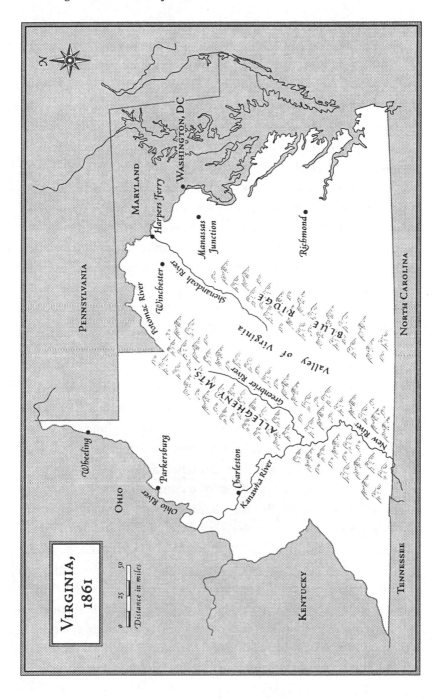

VIRGINIA, 1861

Distance in miles
0   25   50

the Trans-Allegheny became the only region of Virginia that did not hold large numbers of slaves. Farming in the rugged hill country that comprised most of western Virginia remained unsuitable to the slave system, although a substantial number of slaves were held in the Kanawha Valley.

Before 1830 the residents of the Shenandoah Valley and the Allegheny Mountain regions had been generally agreed in their complaints against the dominant eastern part of the state. But by 1830 the counties in the Valley and their counterparts in the Alleghenies no longer shared a common view, and by 1861 the residents in the mountains were divided in their opinions. This change in attitude in the Valley toward slavery fostered further feelings of isolation by the residents of Trans-Allegheny. Slavery, the South's "peculiar institution," had become prevalent in Valley agriculture, but in the heavily wooded mountains to the east the small patches of farmland that could be cleared did not lend themselves to the system.

Before 1830, western Virginia included both the Valley and Trans-Allegheny regions. But that changed as a result of the 1830 constitution. The most contentious question before the constitutional convention had been representation in the legislature. The white population west of the Blue Ridge was fast approaching that of the eastern portion of the state, and western reformers who had long wanted to change a number of elements of the state constitution were finally able to gain approval of a constitutional convention to address their concerns. But the increased importance of slavery in the Valley made the area more receptive to the conservative views of the eastern establishment, and the traditional western alliance unraveled. The constitution that resulted from the convention's efforts was a compromise that pleased the conservatives but left Trans-Allegheny largely unsatisfied. Voting patterns in the 1830 referendum that approved the new constitution reflected the sectional character of the state with most of the counties in Trans-Allegheny rejecting it. By 1861 the Allegheny Mountains were considered the dividing line between eastern and western Virginia, a boundary that could easily be defended should it become necessary.[16]

In 1861 the geographical and cultural differences between eastern and western Virginia made them strikingly dissimilar in outlook. The residents of the western counties, especially those located in the northwest, were separated by mountains from the rest of Virginia and had more in common with the more accessible states of Ohio and Pennsylvania. Transportation and communications in the area generally ran north and south along the Ohio River and further encouraged economic and political ties to the non-slave-holding states that bordered northwestern Virginia.

The residents of the western counties were separated from the eastern population by more than geographic factors, however. The ethnic, social, cultural, and ideological backgrounds of the settlers tended to encourage Unionist loyalties. Where the dominant stock in eastern Virginia was English, large numbers of Scotch-Irish, Germans, and Welsh immigrants settled the western counties. Also, dissidents from eastern Virginia along with hunters, trappers, small farmers, factory workers, lawyers, merchants, and ministers who had no use for or no contact with slavery found the northwest part of the state a good place to settle down. Most of the western population made a frugal living on small farms, and slavery was practically nonexistent in the northwestern part of the region. The social structure tended to be more egalitarian in the west than in the east with its long-standing plantation aristocracy.

In spite of the long-standing differences between eastern and western Virginia, in early 1861 pro-Union sentiment was confined largely to the northwestern counties clustered along the banks of the Ohio River and the Pennsylvania border. These pro-Union counties contained a white population of about 210,000. Another twenty-four western counties, further south along the Kanawha Valley, with 145,000 white inhabitants, generally opposed breaking up Virginia and supported the Confederacy. Of the thirty-one delegates to the

Virginia Convention that represented the counties in the north-western part of the state, twenty-four voted against secession, five voted for it, and two abstained.

After the Richmond convention reached its climax with the secession, the pro-Unionist northwestern delegates conferred at the Powhatan Hotel. Fearing for their safety and seeing no reason to remain in Richmond, they soon obtained safe conduct passes from Governor Letcher and departed Richmond. On their return home they found the resistance movement to secession well under way. Carlile, leader of the Unionist political movement in the northwest part of the state, left Richmond on April 19, traveling by way of Washington, D.C., where he probably provided the first information to Lincoln that the Virginia Convention had indeed passed the secession ordinance. Carlile, one of the most popular political leaders in northwest Virginia in early 1861, was described by the Wheeling *Intelligencer* as "a ready, keen, solid, and impressive man" who was "somewhat singular looking, being very sallow and angular in his face, flat on his head, compact and well-knit in framework," and he delivered his speeches in a "rich, deep voice."[17]

Upon his return to his home in Harrison County, Carlile directed an enthusiastic meeting of "nearly twelve hundred citizens." Under Carlile's leadership the meeting unanimously adopted the "Clarksburg Resolutions." The resolutions called for a general convention of five of the "wisest, best, and discreetest men" in each northwest county to meet at Wheeling on May 13 to determine what measures "the people of Northwest Virginia should take in the present fearful emergency." The resolutions were published as part of an extra edition of the *Western Virginia Guard* on the evening of April 22, and the paper was distributed by "messengers mounted on horse-back" to the surrounding counties and along the railroads west to Wheeling and Parkersburg on the Ohio River and east to Martinsburg in the Valley of Virginia.[18]

The Clarksburg Resolutions sparked a series of mass meetings in the northwest, during which Francis H. Pierpont, a well-known northwestern leader, became a popular public speaker. Pierpont was born in Monongalia County and attended Allegheny College in Meadville, Pennsylvania. After a brief sojourn in Mississippi where he taught school, he returned home in 1842 to open a law practice in Fairmont and became an outspoken critic of slavery. He had not been a delegate to the Virginia Convention, but he had exchanged letters with Willey and was bitterly opposed to Virginia's secession. The Wheeling *Intelligencer* credited him with having "that incisiveness of speech and that indomitable will and courage that carries the people with him." At Clarksburg on May 3 he delivered a two-and-one-half hour speech to "an unwearied audience."[19]

Carlile's Clarksburg Resolutions were not the only reaction to the secession vote. Having long chafed at the policies of a state government far away in Richmond, the northwestern counties reacted to the idea of Virginia's impending departure from the Union with thoughts of their own secession from the Old Dominion. News of the convention's vote preceded the returning delegates, and even before they arrived home, local leaders were holding rallies and mass meetings to proclaim their loyalty to the Constitution of the United States. Many town meetings took place in Unionist communities in the western counties. For years western residents had been angered at Richmond's authority, "believing that the state was run by tidewater folk for tidewater's benefit." Within days of the secession ordinance there was serious talk in the west of forming a new state, with proclamations that Virginia's connection with the Confederacy would be "fatal to her credit, her prosperity, and the happiness of her people."[20]

The secession ordinance that met with wide approval in eastern Virginia provided the spark that ignited divided loyalties that had long been smoldering in the mountains. Residents of the northwestern counties had little in common with the more prosperous east and generally favored staying with the Union. But with the question of whether or not to follow the Old Dominion into the Confederate States fueling emotions, many pro-Union supporters in the western counties were reluctant to make their positions public, fearing retaliation from secessionists. The editor of the Wheeling *Intelligencer* expressed the view of many when he wrote to Governor William Dennison of Ohio to encourage occupying the border with Virginia as soon as possible. "Secession is creeping up," he wrote, and went on to express his fear that "Union men in Western Virginia will shortly all be slaughtered."[21]

On the other side of the question, Governor Letcher in Richmond received numerous letters from western residents warning him that pro-Union sentiments were running strong. "The Secessionists . . . are in a bad predicament here–and [we] know not what moment we may grace a lampost," wrote one. Another wrote that "two-thirds of the people West of Barbour favor the movement" for division. A writer from Mason County warned Letcher that "treason against the State is advocated here with perfect impunity."[22]

By April 18 Virginia was rapidly arming and organizing state troops to defend its territory from the widely anticipated Federal occupation even though it was not yet officially part of the Confederacy, that question having been deferred to the May referendum. For his part, Lincoln would not send any Federal forces into Virginia until the secession question had been referred to the popular vote, leaving the state a month to get ready for the possibility of war. With Richmond only one hundred miles from Washington, D.C., and exposed to invasion by Federal forces, military preparation in the Old Dominion focused on protecting the state capital. For the moment, the problems in the western counties remained far away from Richmond as the state government, assuming the populace would approve the secession ordinance, prepared to defend the Old Dominion from Federal invasion. But ignoring a problem does not solve it, and in western Virginia the question of secession remained open. Pro-Unionist politicians there would soon welcome Federal assistance to help the area remain part of the United States.

Two Armies

D URING APRIL 1861 political and military preparations
moved quickly. Two days after Carlile published the
Clarksburg Resolutions calling for a convention in Wheeling to consider the implications of the Richmond secession vote, the
governors of Ohio and Virginia named the men who would command their militia forces. Dennison of Ohio selected a railroad
man, George B. McClellan; Letcher tapped Robert E. Lee, a professional soldier who had just resigned from the U.S. army. Both
men were on the job before the end of April, making the plans that
would take them both to western Virginia where they would ultimately make their first reputations in the war.

The two men who would determine the fate of the western counties would never face each other on the battlefield during the first
campaign. But the plans each made in the spring of 1861 provided

the foundation for that campaign. The first campaign was a battle
for the political minds of the population. Its outcome depended on
the military plans that originated in the minds of two generals who
assumed their first position at high command on opposite sides of
the theater of operations where they would take the first steps
toward building lasting reputations as senior commanders.
Although they did not know it, their initial preparations would
largely decide the outcome of the first campaign.

When Lincoln called for 75,000 militia on April 15, war preparations on both sides accelerated. The call for troops galvanized the
people; the North was delighted, the South appalled as hopes for a
peaceful resolution of the crisis ended abruptly. Northern states
wired their immediate acceptance of Lincoln's call to protect the
Union and promised troops, while the remaining Southern states,
Virginia among them, refused just as rapidly. On both sides, men
and boys scrambled to join local militia forces, and prospective
colonels began to raise regiments of volunteers. Whether motivated
by a wish to preserve the Union, protect a Southern way of life, support states' rights, or simply to experience the great adventure, the
general reaction to the threat of war was the armies that began to
appear. Southerners rallied to fight for independence from what
they viewed as Yankee oppression; they saw the coming war as
another American war of independence. Northerners felt it their
duty to preserve the Union; they sought to protect the republic their
forefathers had built and passed to them.[1]

In April 1861, having made the decision to leave the Union, Virginia's political leadership faced the possibility of a Federal invasion. Indeed, in some ways military preparations anticipated
political decisions. Even before the Virginia Convention's vote on
secession, the impetuous Wise, acting as though he were still governor, had directed elements of Virginia's militia forces to conduct
preemptive military operations against the Federal arsenal at
Harpers Ferry and the Gosport Navy Yard in Norfolk. Once the

convention voted to secede, state officials began to mobilize Virginia's militia forces and cast about for qualified officers to lead them without waiting for the results of the popular referendum scheduled for May 23.

With the news of the firing on Fort Sumter and Lincoln's subsequent call for troops, Ohio, a state that shared a 256-mile river border with the Old Dominion, found men crowding into recruiting stations to "enlist for the defense of the national flag and the national union." Ohio's Governor William Dennison, a Republican elected in 1859, was concerned that his state might present a tempting target to Confederate forces operating out of western Virginia. He responded to Washington's quota of thirteen regiments by wiring Lincoln that he could "hardly stop short of twenty." As in Virginia, political decisions made in response to Lincoln's call for troops initiated the preparations for war in Ohio.[2]

In 1861 two countries with a common heritage of revolution rushed headlong to commit the flower of their manhood to attain diametrically opposed political objectives by force of arms. The United States of America sought to prevent the dissolution of the Union formed as a result of a rebellion against English authority, while the Confederate States of America saw themselves defending the American tradition of revolt against tyranny. The political leaders on both sides enjoyed considerable support from their respective national populations as men flocked to the colors in support of the political goals. Beyond defending the national capitals, however, neither side initially thought much about how their rapidly growing armies could best be used on the strategic level to gain their political goals. The strategic military objectives that would produce a favorable political situation were yet to be determined by either side at the national level in early 1861. The Confederate states saw the threat of Federal invasion as the primary military problem facing them and began sending forces north to defend the new nation where it bounded the Union in Virginia. From the Union point of view, the only way to prevent the new Southern nation from becoming a reality was to invade and occupy its territory, but initially there was more concern about defending the national capital, Washington, D.C. With Virginia's decision to leave the Union, Washington had become dangerously vulnerable to the Confederate forces assembling in northern Virginia.

In Virginia the military situation, like the political crisis, had both a North-South and an east-west dimension. The military preparations had to center on defense against a possible Federal invasion from the north, thus coinciding with the overall strategy of the Confederacy. But the state of Ohio, spurred on by the perception of a possible threat from western Virginia, was raising forces faster than the Federal government could use them. By concentrating on the larger, more visible, Northern threat, the state government in Richmond overlooked the potential military threat that Ohio posed to Virginia's western flank. For pro-Union politicians in the western part of the state, however, Ohio's military buildup offered a potential solution to their desire for Virginia, or at least part of it, to remain in the Union.

As war preparations got under way, the United States had a small regular army with only a thousand or so professional officers on active service to call on, and they were scattered across thousands of square miles of American soil. The South had an even smaller number of men with military experience on which to build its preparations for war. The Congress of the Confederate States had authorized a regular army on March 6, but it still remained only a paper force in April. In both the North and the South military experience in virtually any form was suddenly in great demand as political decisions made war highly probable. Federal law allowed U.S. army officers to resign their commissions at their pleasure, and many from Southern states opted to do so, leavening, to a large extent, the experienced, professional military leadership available to each side as war preparations moved forward in earnest.

Although political differences were pulling the North and South apart, the officers who would lead both armies shared a common military heritage. The men who would soon be commanding generals on both sides brought the same military education and experience to the war.

In 1861 the U.S. army was led by Lieutenant General Winfield Scott who, at the age of nearly seventy-five, had held the post of general in chief for the past twenty years. His successful campaign to capture Mexico City in 1847 had made him a national hero whose opinions still carried considerable influence in the North and the South. As a result of his experience in the Mexican War, he was the only officer of any grade on either side with experience maneuvering military formations numbering more than five thousand troops. Indeed, there were few officers, active or resigned, who could claim to have anything but a theoretical knowledge of maneuvering anything larger than a regiment. Advancing age and ill health prevented Scott from duty in the field, but he remained intellectually capable.

The Mexican War that made Scott a nationally known military figure also provided practical experience in planning and conducting warfare for many officers destined to play an early role in the Civil War. For officers serving close to Scott, the campaign to capture Mexico City confirmed the widely held nineteenth-century concept that offensive action on the battlefield was essential to success in war. Scott's daring thrust from Vera Cruz exemplified offensive maneuver warfare. At Cerro Gordo in April 1847, for example, he took advantage of the information his engineers had gathered from an extensive reconnaissance of possible routes around the flanks of the Mexican defensive positions to maneuver his forces to victory, rather than attempt a costly frontal assault. Despite poor execution of an excellent plan by volunteer general officers, Scott won a decisive victory when the Mexicans fled the field as U.S. forces appeared on both flanks.

Scott's offensive action in Mexico was successful because his forces were better trained and had superior officers, enabling them to prevail over the larger, but less able Mexican forces. Also, the primary infantry weapon for both sides was the musket, a generally inaccurate, short-range, hard-to-load weapon. In an assault, if the attacking forces could close before the defenders could fire more than one or two rounds, the bayonet would likely carry the day, giving well-trained, well-led troops a distinct advantage. But, by 1861, technology had changed the face of war. In the Civil War the rifle, although initially in short supply, was the infantry weapon of choice, and with its greater range and accuracy much of the tactical advantage went to the defender. It would take time and large, bloody battles before the generals learned that lesson, however. In 1861, as both Northern and Southern officers prepared for battle, the lessons of Mexico remained America's most recent example of how to conduct war.

After the war with Mexico, in the years immediately preceding the Civil War, the U.S. army had only conducted small land operations. At the end of 1860 it had a total strength of slightly more than 16,000 officers and men. The vast majority of the army was stationed west of the Mississippi River in company size or smaller units. While that army had served the country well until 1860, it was not up to the task of dealing with the crisis facing the nation in 1861. With the regular army scattered across the country, and with no realistic chance of its being assembled into a cohesive force in a timely manner, Lincoln resorted to calling up the militia. As Northern states raised their initial quotas, they turned to the numerous graduates of West Point who had left the army to pursue civilian careers in the years building up to the crisis, offering them volunteer commissions as general officers in their militia forces. Southern states drew on the same pool of officers, but they also had the graduates of military schools such as the Virginia Military Institute, the South Carolina Military College, and the Citadel, which would provide excellent leadership at both the tactical and strategic levels during the Civil War.

In spite of the U.S. army's paucity of recent experience with maneuvering large forces in battle, the officers educated at the U.S. Military Academy at West Point, New York, had been exposed to European theories on conducting a new style of warfare. Since 1832 Dennis Hart Mahan had been the professor of military and civil engineering. Mahan, an 1824 graduate of the academy, spent four years studying the art of war in France before joining the faculty. It was but a small part of the academy's four-year curriculum, but Mahan's course, Military and Civil Engineering and the Science of War, provided an introduction to the art and science of war for cadets. For some students he was an inspiration, for others an instructor to be feared and endured. In either case, his ideas on the art and science of war were an important part of a cadet's last year at West Point.

Mahan taught his theory of strategy to America's future Civil War generals using his interpretation of European military thought, particularly as it applied to what he perceived as the genius of Napoleon. Baron Henri Jomini, a Swiss officer who had served on Napoleon's staff and was the best-known interpreter of Napoleonic warfare at the time, influenced much of Mahan's writing. Through Mahan, Jomini became a popular source of military theory for American officers interested in pursuing the study of war. Mahan extolled the offensive warfare conducted by Napoleon and advocated by Jomini, but he also cautioned "great prudence . . . in advancing; as the troops engaged are liable at any moment to an attack on their flank." He also advocated the indirect approach of maneuver and deception against an entrenched defensive position. The Mahanian interpretation of warfare, an offensive attitude combined with a healthy respect for the defense, fit well with Scott's campaign in Mexico, giving the many West Point graduates who participated in that war theoretical and practical approaches to war that were mutually reinforcing. Newly promoted generals on both sides heeded their experience in Mexico as they prepared to wage their first campaigns of the Civil War.[3]

The success of armies on both sides depended largely on the capabilities of the generals who led them. In the spring of 1861 both sides selected and fielded senior officers with high hopes of success. In some cases early success begat further hopes and led to rapid promotion, while in others great expectations met with dismal failure and diminished faith.

The first step in preparing for war in April 1861–raising regiments of privates–was easier than finding the generals who could organize them into effective armies. Because of the shared military heritage in the U.S. army, the infantry regiment became the basic maneuver unit for both armies. At the time, an army regiment at full strength had just over one thousand officers and men organized into ten companies, although the actual number of men available at any one time might vary widely. The infantry regiment formed the building blocks for the larger formations that would be needed to fight the war. During the course of the war, as armies on both sides grew in size, regiments were organized into larger units of brigades, divisions, and corps to facilitate handling ever-larger numbers of troops in the chaos of battle. But the first campaign of the war in western Virginia did not have the benefit of any formal organization larger than a regiment, although both sides soon found it expedient to form brigades of two or more regiments under a single commander to facilitate command and control in the mountains. In the absence of a brigadier general, the colonel of one of the regiments usually assumed command of the brigade.

The first federal call for troops reflected the hope of a short war as it required only a three-month enlistment for the new regiments. As the government came to realize that this was not going to be the short war it had wanted, the duration of regimental enlistments increased. In the North, three years became the standard term of regimental enlistments, while the South raised regiments for three years or for the duration of the war. But in the initial encounters of the war, senior Federal officers had to contend with three-month regiments that exercised their right to disband and go home at the end of their enlistments, regardless of the status of the campaign.

Regiments were commanded by colonels who were usually appointed by the governor of the state where the regiment was raised. Political connections, more than military experience or education, gained many of the colonels their commissions. Men of the regiment elected their company officers. As result, officers had little more than a vague idea of how an infantry regiment should behave in combat. In nineteenth-century warfare, an infantry regiment was expected to perform intricate maneuvers on the battlefield to bring effective volley fire to bear on an opponent. The first Federal regiments were raised for three months, hardly enough time to learn the basic drills required for even the most fundamental battle maneuvers. In the opening months of the war, regiments were frequently formed by throwing together individually raised militia companies whose officers may not have ever met the regimental commander. With hundreds of regiments in the formative stages, newly elected officers sought guidance on how to conduct basic drill. It was not unusual for officers to drill their new charges while reading the manual. Due to the rapid pace of events leading to war, when the first regiments marched off to fight, they could hardly be called well trained.[4]

In the mid-nineteenth century, armies relied on muscle power to move them. Infantry regiments, the bulk of an army's size, used men's muscles and walked virtually everywhere they went. Their logistics support system used the muscles of horses and mules to carry supplies, ammunition, cannons, and equipment. Orders in battle were passed by word of mouth or by the sounds of bugles and drums. At the tactical level of the regiment, movement and communications remained largely unchanged from what they had been in Napoleon's day, so old training manuals were generally adequate

to needs, and commercial publishers rushed them into new print-
ings to meet the demands of aspiring new officers in both armies.

Above the regimental level of command, however, technology
provided significant advances in movement and communications.
The rifle was the technological innovation that changed war at the
tactical level, but steam and electricity had a much more profound
influence on war at the operational and strategic levels. The steam-
powered locomotives of the railroad on land and the steamboat on
rivers, although not developed primarily for military operations,
allowed commanders to concentrate their combat power rapidly at
a decisive point. The electricity that carried messages across the
telegraph lines allowed commanders to coordinate their campaigns
across long distances. Infantry forces could move by train and
steamboat and arrive in close proximity to the battlefield, allowing
for a faster concentration of forces with the troops in better condition. With the telegraph, senior commanders had the capability to
plan and direct strategic operations without actually being on the
battlefield in person, and they could effectively coordinate military
activities over large geographic areas. Steam and electricity
changed warfare, making the Civil War the first modern war. Both
played significant roles in the first campaign of the war.

As states along the boundary between the North and the South
prepared for war, the usual course of action was to designate an officer to command all of the militia forces in the state. Along with command of the militia, these officers became responsible for defending
the state. Preparations for that defense centered on geographical
considerations. Geography dictates the conduct of most campaigns,
and significant terrain features, especially the man-made ones such
as roads and railroads, frequently guide the course of strategic military operations in modern warfare. Large rivers affect military campaigns because they can provide either a barrier to attack or an
avenue for logistics supporting an invading force. Roads, railroads,
and rivers all influenced the military campaign in western Virginia.

In 1861, the Valley of Virginia was the most important strategic geographical feature in the Old Dominion. It offered a line of communications that ran southwest from Maryland into Tennessee. Two east-west railroads crossed the Valley with strategic implications. Crossing its northern, or lower end, the Baltimore and Ohio Railroad linked the eastern and western portions of the Union, while across its southern, or upper end, the Virginia and Tennessee Railroad provided communications between Richmond and the western portions of the Confederacy. Confederate control of the lower Valley would restrict Northern lines of communication to the rail lines in Pennsylvania and the western states of the Union. Similarly, the South faced lengthy rail detours through the Carolinas and Georgia should the railroad across the upper Valley fall to Union forces.

The Valley was the key to holding the state of Virginia together in 1861. A good road network connected the Alleghenies on the west to the Blue Ridge on the east and provided good movement up and down the Valley. In Confederate hands the Alleghenies provided a barrier into the Valley to Union forces operating out of Ohio. However, with Federal forces holding the western mountains, the Valley would be vulnerable to invasion. Should Union forces gain control of the Valley, they would have access to the many gaps in the Blue Ridge that provided access to the routes into Richmond. The Shenandoah Valley could then become a base of operations for Federal forces to threaten the vulnerable Piedmont, which had few natural defenses. The South needed to hold the Shenandoah Valley, so it could fight a war in Virginia. The Valley provided a means to move forces rapidly and securely, and its vast acreage of grain easily fed the forces operating along its length. However, the northeast-southwest orientation of the Valley made it more important to the South than to the North. A Confederate army moving northeast down the Valley would pose a threat to the prominent Northern cities of Philadelphia, Baltimore, and Washington, D.C., but a Federal army using the same route would find itself moving southwest,

THEATER OF
OPERATIONS

away from Richmond and other significant strategic military objectives. Additionally, the Confederate army, inferior in size to Federal forces, needed the food the Valley provided.

The best way for Virginia and the Confederacy to defend the Valley was to hold the western counties, an area offering considerable advantages to the defender and posing difficult challenges to a potential invader. The mountainous region of western Virginia is a vast wooded area between the Ohio River on the west and the Valley of Virginia on the east. It is compartmentalized into canyon-like valleys oriented generally north-south with swift flowing streams and rivers making east-west movement difficult, although the Great Kanawha River offered access to the Ohio River, and that river had for many years provided good transportation north and south for goods and people. In 1861 the roads and rail lines in the theater were few, offering an invading force little choice as it advanced east from the Ohio River into the interior of Virginia. Control of the limited transportation network through the mountains was the key to defending the area.

The Kanawha River in the southern portion of the theater offered limited east-west transportation opportunities, but it was navigable by light craft only. The earliest road in the theater, the James River and Kanawha Turnpike, was completed in the 1830s. It ran east from Guyandotte on the Ohio River to Charleston where it then followed the Kanawha River to Gauley Bridge. From there it crossed the Alleghenies, passing through White Sulphur Springs on its way to the town of Lexington on the western edge of the Valley. The route was used by cattle and hog drivers to move their products on the hoof to eastern markets. It was also a popular mail and passenger route that connected the region to the Valley. In 1861 the population living in the area along the turnpike with its greater access to the Valley showed greater sympathy for holding the Old Dominion together than did the northwestern corner of the state where the transportation systems allowed residents to maintain closer economic ties with Ohio and Pennsylvania.

In the northern part of the theater, two principal roads ran east-west through the mountains. The northernmost was the Northwestern Turnpike. It connected Winchester, a prominent town in the northern part of the Valley of Virginia, with Parkersburg on the Ohio River. From Winchester it ran west through Romney, Grafton, and Clarksburg. However, in 1861 it was not in good repair as a result of heavy flooding in 1852 and 1853. The second major route, the Staunton-Parkersburg Turnpike, ran west and north from Staunton in the Valley, crossed the Alleghenies at Cheat Mountain, and passed through Huttonsville. At Huttonsville the Huntersville Pike ran south to the town of the same name while the turnpike turned north to Beverly. From there the turnpike continued west to Parkersburg on the Ohio River, passing through Buckhannon and Weston. It was partly macadamized and had bridges over the larger streams. In 1861 it too was in bad repair in places because of the heavy flooding in previous years. The Weston and Gauley Bridge Pike provided a north-south link between the towns of Weston on the Staunton-Parkersburg Turnpike and Gauley Bridge on the James River and Kanawha Turnpike in the southern portion of the theater. The north-south Beverly-Fairmont Pike, taking its name from the two towns it joined, provided a road between the two northern turnpikes. This pike ran from Beverly, through Philippi, and crossed Laurel Hill, the northward extension of Rich Mountain. It then followed the Tygart's Valley River north and crossed the Northwestern Turnpike at the village of Pruntytown, near Grafton, finally terminating at Fairmont on the Baltimore and Ohio Railroad.[5]

By 1861 repair costs for the turnpikes had risen so far above the tolls collected that they were frequently in a state of considerable disrepair. As railroads were built in the area, it became more economical to move goods and people by rail, and that resulted in further neglect of the turnpikes. In spite of the roads' generally neglected state, however, the terrain in the theater of operations was so difficult that even a bad road was better than no road at all. Consequently, most military operations in the area tended to follow the turnpikes.

There were secondary roads in abundance throughout the mountains. From late November until April, however, most were not passable for large bodies of men or wagons unless the deep mud was frozen. In May, spring rains could turn the winding roads into mud slides. In summer, when the roads were characterized by thick dust, a thunderstorm could make them impassable for twenty-four hours. Without maps, travelers unfamiliar with the broken terrain could easily become confused by the numerous roads that led seemingly nowhere. To make up for the lack of maps, military commanders frequently relied on local residents to help them sort out the road networks, but this system had its pitfalls because it was not always possible to determine accurately the political leanings of a particular guide. More than one commander in western Virginia found himself in the wrong place at the wrong time because he had misjudged the loyalties of a local guide.

In the first half of the nineteenth century railroads began to replace roads for moving goods and people. The Baltimore and Ohio Railroad moved west into western Virginia in 1827, prompting population growth along the right of way and making it easier for residents to trade with Maryland and Pennsylvania than eastern Virginia. In 1861 the railroad crossed the Potomac River at Harpers Ferry and crossed the northern part of Virginia by way of Grafton to Wheeling, a distance of 188 miles. Grafton, an important rail center in the area, was located at the intersection of the Baltimore and Ohio Railroad and the Northwestern Virginia Railroad that ran the 104 miles from Grafton to Parkersburg on the Ohio River.

Most of western Virginia was rural in 1861, and some parts remained virtually empty of human habitation. The area south of the Kanawha River was thinly populated, although in some areas there was a fairly heavy concentration of people. The Virginia side of the Ohio River, between Moundsville and Wheeling in the northern panhandle, had a large population, while the Tygart's Valley River further to the east had considerable agricultural activity. Economically, western Virginia was predominantly agricultural, corn raised for livestock being the most important crop. Livestock grazing was found on virtually every farm. Coal mining was an important commercial enterprise in many counties. Western Virginia produced approximately one-third of the manufactured goods produced in the state and more than one-third of that came from Ohio County in the northern panhandle between the states of Ohio and Pennsylvania. The Kanawha Valley was the major producer of salt in the South, and in 1861 coal-oil production was also beginning to become a major industry in the area. All in all, with war on the horizon, the area represented a valuable source of men and natural resources for the South.

The city of Wheeling, county seat of Ohio County, boasted 14,000 residents and was the major population center in northwestern Virginia. Its location in the northern panhandle put it between Ohio and Pennsylvania, making it more of a Northern city than a Southern one. The Cumberland Road, or National Pike, completed in 1818, connected the city with eastern markets in Maryland and Pennsylvania and channeled trade from Wheeling toward Philadelphia and Baltimore. The city's position at the head of low-level navigation on the Ohio River made it a major trading center in the Ohio Valley. Eastern trade increased when the Baltimore and Ohio Railroad reached nearby Benwood in 1853, and Wheeling's position as a major transportation center for Northern states was further enhanced when a ferry connected the city with the terminus of the Central Ohio Railroad at Bellaire on the western side of the Ohio River.

Wheeling developed an industrial capability as a result of abundant coal in the area. Industrial facilities included nail factories, rolling mills, foundries, machine shops, tanneries, and paper mills. Industry and manufacturing attracted Northern capital and workmen to Wheeling. The workers and factory owners certainly did not think of Wheeling as a Southern city. They had moved to the city from Northern free states and maintained strong economic ties with the eastern and midwest states. For them the city occupied a geographic position between Ohio and Pennsylvania that was better suited to east-west than north-south commerce. On the land between Fairmont and Wheeling, a number of villages had developed as a result of the Baltimore and Ohio Railroad right of way. In 1861 Wheeling, far away from possible reprisals from the government in Richmond and with close ties to Ohio and Pennsylvania, soon emerged as a major political center for pro-Union sympathizers who eventually rejected eastern control of the state.

In addition to Wheeling, western Virginia boasted two other large population centers, Parkersburg and Charleston. South of Wheeling on the Ohio River, Parkersburg, at the western end of both the Northwestern and the Staunton-Parkersburg Turnpikes, was much smaller than Wheeling, but still important to the region. In 1857 the Northwestern Railroad reached the town, and the 1858 oil boom made it one of the most promising economic areas in all of Virginia. Charleston, on the Kanawha River, was the principal economic center in the southern part of western Virginia. It had no railroad, but it did maintain significant trade along the river with Cincinnati and Louisville and was the major town on the James River and Kanawha Turnpike that provided communications to the east with the Valley of Virginia and west to Guyandotte on the Ohio River.

The course of the military campaign in western Virginia would be dictated by a variety of factors. In the first few months of the war, leaders on both sides struggled to field armies and understand how they could be used to attain the desired political goals. The strategic objectives that emerged for military operations in the area were as much political as territorial. The objectives for both sides in the first campaign were understandably similar. Both wanted to create a military situation so favorable as to allow their supporters to take political control of the area included in the theater of operations. At the theater level, pro-Union sympathizers needed Federal forces to protect their antisecession activities, and Confederate supporters wanted military resources to defend against an invasion from Ohio. Strategically, the Union sought to keep at least part of Virginia in the fold, while Virginia and the Confederacy could ill afford to lose such a lucrative source of manpower and resources.

Union tactical objectives were to push any Confederate forces out of the area and occupy the theater of operations. The objectives of the Confederates were to block the lines of communications through the theater to prevent a Federal advance to the Shenandoah Valley. At the tactical level, opposing military commanders sought to control territory, but the real strategic goal was controlling the population. Ultimately, military occupation of the theater by one side or the other would dictate political control of the area.

There were two transportation hubs in western Virginia in 1861 that would play key roles in the first campaign. In the southern portion of the theater of operations, the town of Gauley Bridge lay at the confluence of the New and Gauley Rivers where they combine their flows to become the Kanawha River, and small steamboats could navigate up the river to the town. Gauley Bridge was also on the James River and Kanawha Turnpike and was the southern terminus of the Weston and Gauley Bridge Pike, a north-south road along the western edge of the Allegheny Mountains. Control of the intersection of those two roads and the Great Kanawha River would allow military forces concentrated at Gauley Bridge to move north, east, or west as operational requirements dictated. In the north, Grafton, where the Northwestern Railroad intersected with the Baltimore and Ohio Railroad, was the critical hub. Along with being at a key rail intersection, Grafton was located on the Northwestern Turnpike, and the Beverly-Fairmont Pike crossed the Northwestern Turnpike at nearby Pruntytown. The Beverly-Fairmont Pike intersected with the Staunton-Parkersburg Turnpike south of Prunty-town at Beverly. Control of Grafton, therefore, provided access to railroad lines and roads for troop movement throughout the northern part of the theater of operations.

CHAPTER THREE

Lee and McClellan

ROBERT E. LEE and George B. McClellan had much in common. They both graduated from the U.S. Military Academy at West Point in New York second in their class, although sixteen years apart: Lee in 1829, McClellan in 1845. As a result of their high academic standing, both received commissions into the army's elite Corps of Engineers. Both had their first taste of war in Mexico with General Winfield Scott's successful Vera Cruz campaign where they undoubtedly knew each other. They each received praise from Scott for their performance in the Battle of Cerro Gordo, and that battle made a lasting impression on both men, especially the poor performance of the American volunteer troops. After the Mexican War, they each served at West Point, although not at the same time, and both were acquainted with Professor Dennis Hart Mahan, the preeminent American military theorist of the time.

In the years before the Civil War, Lee and McClellan pursued different careers. Both transferred to the cavalry in 1855. Lee reported to the newly formed Second Cavalry in Texas where he would serve until 1861. McClellan went to Europe for a year as a member of a military commission to study European armies, after which he resigned to work in railroading until 1861. With the secession crisis both men received a call to high command. Lee chose to offer his services to his home state of Virginia, while McClellan sought to defend the Union. On April 23 both men received commissions as major generals in state forces on opposite sides of the Ohio River, Lee in Virginia and McClellan in Ohio.

When called to war, Robert E. Lee was a highly respected U.S. army colonel well versed in military matters, although he was largely unknown outside military circles. His army reputation and famous family name, however, promised great potential. General Winfield Scott, the senior general in the U.S. army, had expressed great faith in Lee's abilities, but in April 1861 Lee had not led great numbers of men in battle nor organized large forces for war. Nonetheless, when Virginia called, he answered.

Lee came from a prominent and distinguished Virginia family. For generations the Lee family had served in Virginia's House of Delegates, and the Lees represented the best of the Southern aristocracy. His mother was also from an old Virginia family, the Carters, a large wealthy clan that shared the Lee family values and even ran their own schools, one for boys and another for girls, to ensure the children received a proper preparation for the positions of responsibility they would surely hold. Lee spent much of his youth in the company of Carters and received his first formal education in the Carter's boys school.

Along with developing strong feelings for the Old Dominion, Lee grew up surrounded by the reputation of a highly visible hero of the American Revolutionary War. His father, Henry "Light Horse Harry" Lee, had fought with great distinction with George Washington. After the war, however, Henry Lee did not fare well. He squandered the family fortune and eventually exiled himself to the West Indies to avoid creditors, leaving Robert's mother to care for the family in Arlington, Virginia. The decision to attend West Point was partly the result of the Lee tradition of arms, and partly economic—there was no money for Robert's education, and there were no tuition costs at the Military Academy. The combination of his father's heroic military reputation and well-known economic failures made Lee a familiar name in the South. Robert received endorsements from five senators and three representatives to accompany his request to the secretary of war, John C. Calhoun, for an appointment to West Point. Although competition for an appointment was so stiff in 1824 that Calhoun had to turn down twenty-five applicants from Virginia, Lee was accepted. He received an appointment to the academy in March 1824, but, because of the unusually large number of cadets entering the academy, he did not begin until July 1825.[1]

Lee entered West Point in 1825 and completed his studies in 1829. He stood second academically in his class all four years. Ahead of Lee at the end of each year was Charles Mason of New York, a man whose subsequent military career was rather limited. After graduation Mason served one year on the faculty at West Point and then resigned to settle in Burlington, Iowa. Lee was one of the six cadets in the graduating class who had received no demerits during their tenure at the academy. When he left West Point, Lee had a military bearing and looked like a soldier. He stood almost six feet with dark brown eyes and thick black wavy hair, and was referred to as the "Marble Model" by his classmates. His high class standing gave him his choice of branches, and, as was usual for cadets given the opportunity to choose, he selected the Corps of Engineers, long considered the elite service in the army.[2]

Lee entered active duty with the army as a brevet, or temporary, second lieutenant in the Corps of Engineers. While Lee awaited orders for his first assignment, he spent the summer of 1829 in

northern Virginia getting reacquainted with family and friends he
had not seen since his one leave from West Point two years earlier.
One of those was Mary Ann Randolph Custis. Like Lee, Mary
Custis came from a prominent Virginia family. Mary's father,
George Washington Parke Custis, was Martha Washington's grand-
son from her earlier marriage. George Washington had adopted
Custis and the youngster grew up at Mount Vernon where he developed something of a hero worship for his step-grandfather. Custis
began building Arlington House in 1803 on an 1,100-acre tract of
land he inherited along the Potomac River. The entire house took
fifteen years to complete, and it became a virtual museum to
George Washington, containing many items Custis had acquired
from Mount Vernon.[3]

Perhaps not surprisingly, Lee proposed to Mary Custis in 1830,
and they wed the next year at Arlington. After they were married,
they moved into the house at Arlington where Lee found himself
surrounded by items that had belonged to, or were used by, Washington, thus strengthening Lee's feelings for the man whose name
had become synonymous with revolution against tyranny. The
Custis and Lee family associations with Washington made the first
president one of Robert E. Lee's personal heroes.

For seventeen years Lee worked on various engineering projects
around the nation, establishing a solid professional standing in the
Corps of Engineers as a competent engineer who could get things
done. In 1844, as a member of the Board of Visitors to the Military
Academy, he made the acquaintance of Winfield Scott, who was
already general-in-chief of the United States army. Scott was also a
Virginian and an American hero as a result of his service in the War
of 1812. Lee admired Scott, and, as subsequent events would show,
the feeling appears to have been mutual.[4]

A year after the two men met, the U.S. boundary dispute with
Mexico developed. Lee asked the chief of engineers for a field
assignment should hostilities develop, even if it meant leaving the

Corps of Engineers. Finally, in August 1846, after fretting that the war would pass him by, Captain Lee received orders to join the staff of Brigadier General John E. Wool in San Antonio, Texas. It was an indication of his eagerness to be a part of the war that it took him only a month and two days from the day he received his orders at Fort Hamilton, New York, to report for duty in San Antonio–a very fast journey for those days.[5]

With Wool, Lee spent most of his time scouting on horseback. On more than one occasion he spent several days and nights in the saddle, testifying to his high state of physical fitness and stamina. After four months with Wool's expedition in Mexico, Lee received orders to report to General Scott's headquarters in Texas, where the commanding general was preparing to conduct an amphibious landing at Vera Cruz on the Mexican coast that would initiate a campaign to capture Mexico City. Lee served in Scott's "little cabinet," a select group of engineer officers that Scott relied on for accurate information and sound advice. Two others in that group, Lieutenants P. G. T. Beauregard and George B. McClellan, would also play roles in the first campaign of the Civil War. Lee watched Scott conduct a successful campaign to capture Mexico City by thrusting straight toward the strategic objective, while avoiding peripheral battles. As a member of Scott's headquarters, Lee learned from the experience of preparing and conducting a successful offensive campaign of maneuver against a larger army.[6]

Scott expected great things from his cabinet of selected engineers, and Lee received appropriate recognition for his actions during the campaign. At Cerro Gordo in April 1847, Lee, participating in his first battle, received glowing mentions in dispatches as being once "again indefatigable" in finding the route that allowed the Americans to flank the Mexican position. The battle made a lasting impression on Lee not only because it was his first taste of combat, but because he saw the benefits of attacking an entrenched foe from an exposed flank. The action also earned him a brevet promotion to major that entitled him to wear the higher rank and use the title even though his permanent grade remained that of captain. Officers who performed well in combat frequently received a brevet as recognition of their accomplishments. Consistent high performance could result in multiple brevets. Lee would eventually receive three brevets for his service in the Mexican War. But along with the glory he also saw the grimmer side of war. The dead and dying Mexican soldiers he had seen strewn about the battlefield prompted him to write to his son Custis after Cerro Gordo: "You have no idea what a horrible sight a field of battle is." He then described how he had aided a young girl trying to save a small boy who was pinned under a wounded Mexican soldier.[7]

Lee, after working in close association with Scott and his staff, took a number of lessons away from his experiences in Mexico. He learned to appreciate the value of audacity, a trained staff, careful reconnaissance, fortifications, flank movements, and the relationship between lines of communications and strategy. As he watched Scott during the campaign, Lee concluded that the primary function of the theater commander is to plan the campaign, communicate the plan to subordinate commanders, and bring together the resources necessary to carry out the plan, but that the actual conduct of the battles should be left to subordinates. That method of conducting a campaign, however, requires competent subordinates who understand and can carry out the desires of the theater commander.[8]

In Mexico Lee developed confidence in his abilities as a soldier. He understood the military value of terrain, how to associate one feature with another and to take advantage of them. His physical fitness and oft-mentioned "indefatigable" stamina contributed to his success. From Scott he learned that a smaller army can defeat a larger one with offensive action, but that lesson carried a hidden danger. Offensive action in the Napoleonic mold was certainly in the forefront of military thinking in the mid-nineteenth century, and in Mexico, American attacks against fortified positions were successful.

The smoothbore muskets used by both armies were effective only to about one hundred meters, which allowed the attackers to come very close to the defenses before taking casualties. The Mexican army also had low morale, little training, and poor leadership, all of which lowered the effectiveness of their defensive capabilities. Lee and other American officers who participated in the campaign took the success as confirmation of the efficacy of Napoleonic warfare.[9]

In 1848, shortly after the treaty ending hostilities in Mexico was signed at Guadalupe Hidalgo, Lee returned to the United States after two years of war. Breveted three times during the war and now referred to as Colonel Lee, he returned to duties with the Board of Engineers for Atlantic Coast Defenses. Lee had learned much from his wartime experience, and his reputation as a soldier had been greatly enhanced. No less a figure than Winfield Scott considered him a "military genius . . . far above that of any other officer of the army."[10]

For three years Lee labored at various engineering projects along the Atlantic seaboard until he received orders making him the superintendent of the Military Academy, a job he accepted with something less than complete enthusiasm. Indeed, before his arrival, he wrote to Professor Mahan, a prominent member of the Academic Board, that he was reluctant to take the position at all. Even though Mahan had not been a professor during Lee's student years, Lee, now superintendent, had the opportunity to absorb Mahan's theories of Napoleonic warfare. While at West Point, Lee also took advantage of the library to read French military histories and manuals and study Napoleon's campaigns as interpreted by Baron Henri Jomini, a Swiss officer who had served on the emperor's staff.[11]

In 1855, during Lee's tenure as superintendent of the Military Academy, Congress approved an expansion of the army and added two new regiments, the First and Second Cavalry. Lee had not sought an appointment in the new regiments, but the secretary of war, Jefferson Davis, who had graduated from West Point one year before

Lee but had resigned from the army in 1835 to pursue a career as a planter and politician, announced that Lee was to be the lieutenant colonel of the Second Cavalry, stationed in Texas. Although surprised by the appointment, Lee was ready for a line assignment; he had for some time been reading more about how to conduct war than engineering. He accepted the assignment and, leaving his wife and children at Arlington, reported to his new regiment in April. In Texas, Lee experienced army life on the frontier and gained an insight into how men reacted to the rigors of soldiering.[12]

The death of his father-in-law, George Washington Parke Custis, in October 1857, prompted Lee's return to Arlington. Upon his arrival in Virginia, he discovered that Custis had died heavily in debt and for some time had neglected his properties. Lee needed considerable time to get the Custis estates in order. The added difficulties of handling the Custis will caused Lee to request that his leave be extended until December 1858. Scott would grant further requests for extensions to May, and finally to October 1859 as Lee tried to deal with the Custis properties.[13]

On October 17, as Lee was finally preparing to return to his regiment in Texas, Lieutenant J. E. B. Stuart arrived at Arlington with a message from the secretary of war, John B. Floyd. Floyd, a native Virginian and former governor of the state, had been Buchanan's secretary of war since 1857, but his mishandling of government contracts had given him an unsavory reputation. When he arrived at the War Department, Lee learned that there was trouble in Harpers Ferry, and that Floyd wanted Lee to lead a contingent of troops to regain order. During the evening of October 16 John Brown, an antislavery fanatic, had occupied the Federal arsenal at Harpers Ferry with a force of twenty-one men. Brown was well known. In 1856, with four of his sons and three other men, he had murdered five innocent farmers at Pottawatomie Creek in Kansas. He was admired by some Eastern abolitionists, but his announced intention of freeing slaves and establishing a free state for blacks in the hills of

Virginia and Maryland had raised Southern fears of a widespread uprising among the slave population.

So rapidly did Lee report to the War Department that he was still in civilian clothes when he accompanied the secretary to the White House for orders from the president. At the White House Buchanan gave Lee his instructions. A contingent of marines had already been dispatched by rail. Lee was to take command of them and resolve the potentially explosive situation as soon as possible. By the morning of the 18th, with an audience of some two thousand people looking on, Lee and his marines prepared to assault the building housing the arsenal's fire engines where Brown and his followers, holding thirteen local hostages, had taken refuge. After offering the terms of surrender that Brown refused, Lee ordered the marines forward, the first command in his long army career that encountered firing weapons. Stuart, who had accompanied Lee on his mission, read the ultimatum to Brown and led the assault into the engine house. In three minutes it was all over. The hostages were freed unharmed, four of Brown's followers were dead, and Brown himself was wounded and in custody.

By early afternoon Henry A. Wise, the governor of Virginia, was on the scene, eager to interrogate Brown and gain what political advantage he could from the situation. Wise had been appalled when he learned that his Virginia militia had been unable to handle the situation by themselves, and that Federal forces had to be dispatched from Washington to take control of the situation. Before he left Richmond, Wise, in an attempt to assert his authority as governor over the Federal military forces at Harpers Ferry, had sent Lee a telegram advising him to "make no terms with the insurgents before I reach you." Although it is not clear that Lee even received the message, Wise, always ready to believe in his ability to take control of events, assumed that Lee had conducted himself in accordance with the governor's telegram and had therefore been under his command.[14]

With Brown in custody, Wise insisted that the state of Virginia conduct his trial. After a brief trial, a court in nearby Charles Town convicted Brown of treason, murder, and inciting slave insurrection and sentenced him to die by hanging on December 2. Wise, as governor, could have commuted the sentence to life imprisonment, but, as an unwavering supporter of slavery, he ordered the execution to proceed. Brown's death prompted an emotional debate over the slavery issue. In death John Brown became a martyr for Northern abolitionists, while the spread of his fanatic antislavery views heightened Southern concerns about their future as part of the United States. For Lee, Brown's raid was a small military affair, but it had directly involved him with Floyd and Wise, two political rivals whose animosity would come back to haunt him within two years of the events at Harpers Ferry.

Lee was able to return to his regiment in Texas in early 1860. By now he was fifty-three years old, and his health was not as good as it once had been. His letters home complained of various ailments. He suffered from a cold in April, a fever confined him to his room in July, and a lingering pain in his right arm was attributed to rheumatism. From Texas, Lee followed the growing secession crisis, and in February 1861 received orders to report to Scott in Washington. Upon his arrival in Washington in March, Lee learned from the old general that he was to be promoted to colonel of the First Cavalry. While he was happy finally to receive a command, he was concerned about the secession crisis and fearful that he might have to take up arms against his native Virginia should the state resolve to leave the Union.[15]

Lee anxiously followed events in Richmond from his home in Arlington. When the results of the convention's secession vote reached him, family tradition dictated that he follow his ancestors' footsteps in declaring allegiance to Virginia over the United States. In studying his family history, he had learned that in six instances where there was a question of pursuing a new allegiance or staying with Virginia, the Lees had opted for supporting a new order only in the case of the American Revolution. Every other time they had followed tradition and remained loyal to Virginia. When Lee faced that question in 1861, he believed he had no choice but to support Virginia. On April 20 he presented his resignation to General Scott, writing that he had no desire ever to draw his sword again, "save in defense of my native state. . . ." When Letcher sent for him the next day, Lee made good on these words and accepted command of the state militia.[16]

Virginia handed command of its militia to Lee on April 23. Even though the popular vote for secession was a month away, the state government assumed that the people would ratify the convention's vote, leaving Virginia, with its proximity to Washington, D.C., and its long common borders with the staunchly Union states of Ohio and Pennsylvania, to become the front line of the Confederacy. On April 24 Lee began his duties as "commander of the military and naval forces of Virginia" with the rank of major general in the Virginia militia. Although his knowledge of tactics was limited, Lee was well read in theoretical strategy, and he drew on that knowledge as he organized the defenses of the Old Dominion to head off the much anticipated Federal invasion.[17]

Lee knew that there were four potential invasion routes into Virginia from Union-controlled territory. The shortest route led from Washington, D.C., where Federal troops were gradually assembling in response to Lincoln's April 15 call, south to Manassas, and then to Richmond, a distance of about one hundred miles. Two other routes also offered Federal armies the opportunity to threaten the state capital: one led south from Maryland into the lower end of the Shenandoah Valley, the other led from Hampton Roads up the peninsula between the James and York Rivers to Richmond. Loss of the lower Shenandoah would not only threaten Richmond from the west, it would deprive Virginia of the food produced there, while Federal control of the peninsula and rivers would pose a danger to

Richmond from the east. The fourth and longest route to the heart of Virginia led from the Ohio Valley through the rugged western portion of the state.

In April, two of the routes were under Southern control. By holding Harpers Ferry, Virginia could block an invasion through the Shenandoah, and the Confederate government was already sending troops into the Old Dominion to counter the Federal buildup in Washington. However, additional Union troops had moved into Fort Monroe on Hampton Roads after the Virginia militia had seized the Gosport Navy Yard, thereby giving Federal forces a foothold that could be used to mount an invasion up the peninsula to Richmond, and the western counties lay open to invasion from Ohio. As he began to organize the defenses of the Old Dominion, Lee concentrated on protecting the three avenues of approach that posed the greatest immediate threat to Richmond and took steps to ensure that he had reliable commanders working for him. Lee's defense plans called for five regiments to be stationed in the western counties, but he did not anticipate an early threat there and assumed local commanders would be able to recruit the necessary defense forces. In relying on local commanders, however, Lee failed to consider the entire western portion of the state as a single theater of operations and did not provide for one overall commander who could coordinate the activities of the various forces he envisioned operating in the area. This oversight would have tragic consequences in the first campaign.

In his assumption that local forces would be willing and able to defend the western counties, Lee did not understand the great differences that existed in the Old Dominion between him, holder of a great eastern Virginia name, and the residents of the northwest. Where Lee and his family tradition put the state ahead of the nation, the more egalitarian westerners sought to stay with the Union in 1861. Lee's values were those of the Tidewater aristocracy that had for generations controlled the destiny of Virginia from Richmond.

His privileged background blinded him to the more democratic view of life that typified western Virginia, where one's accomplishments counted for more than a proud name. That the people of the western counties were not inclined to defend a state government that many believed had not treated them fairly was something Lee did not understand as he prepared his strategic defense of Virginia. By the time he realized his error, the strategic advantage had passed to Federal forces.

Lee initially estimated a need for 51,000 troops to defend the state, and on May 3, he sent out his first call for volunteers. He was heartened by the strong response to recruiting efforts in most areas of the state. Stories of disaffection in the western counties reached Richmond, but since the threat there did not appear imminent, little was done. Lee believed that the western residents held the same strong feelings for Virginia he did, and that they would rally in time to defend their state from the Federal forces assembling just across the river in Ohio. Lee's assessment, however, did not take into consideration the ambition and abilities of the man who had just been named commander of the Department of the Ohio, an area that initially included the states of Illinois, Indiana, and Ohio.

Lincoln's call for militia to preserve the Union did not surprise the superintendent of the Ohio and Mississippi Railroad, George B. McClellan. Although he had resigned from the U.S. army in 1857 to embark on a railroad career, he had remained interested in the army's activities and was highly regarded as a military intellectual. As war fever swept the nation, McClellan became the most sought-after former officer in the Union. Although a native of Pennsylvania, McClellan had no strong state ties; his loyalty lay with the nation. As he expressed his reaction to the secession of the Southern states from the Union to a friend, "the government is in danger, our flag insulted, and we must stand by it."[18]

McClellan had no real family history of military service. A great-grandfather, Samuel McClellan, had served in the militia during the

American Revolution, but that was the extent of his military heritage. George McClellan was born in Philadelphia December 3, 1826, the son of a prominent doctor. He attended the U.S. Military Academy at West Point at least in part for financial reasons; McClellan's father had assumed considerable debt from his father and had paid for a medical education for George's older brother, making the free education available from West Point a desirable prospect for the family. In the spring of 1842 the senior McClellan wrote the secretary of war requesting an appointment for George.[19]

McClellan entered the academy in 1842, and four years later he graduated second in his class. The top man academically in 1846 was Charles Seaforth Stewart, but McClellan was universally thought of by the cadets as the real star of the class. Classmates "predicted real military fame for McClellan," while Stewart, in spite of his class standing, made little impression on his fellow cadets. Stewart's unremarkable military career saw him finally promoted to colonel of engineers at the end of the Civil War.[20]

McClellan was also well thought of by his instructors, one of whom recalled that "a pleasanter pupil was never called to the blackboard." At West Point McClellan had been exposed to the concept of Napoleonic warfare under the tutelage of Mahan, and he led his class in Mahan's department. In a letter to his mother, an enthusiastic Cadet McClellan expressed a "passionate fondness for Military Engineering, & Military Tactics." Years later, when McClellan became a general, Mahan remembered his former student and wrote him to say that "some of you turn[ed] up as I hoped for." During his final year at West Point McClellan was president of the Dialectic Society, the intellectual cream of the crop of upperclassmen, which offered membership by invitation only. In his final address as president, McClellan referred to Napoleon's "thrilling proclamations which imposed new ardor into the worn out frames of his troops." In the same speech he expressed his support of the Union should increasing sectionalism lead to civil war.[21]

Although he was disappointed in not attaining the top spot in his class, McClellan's high standing earned him a commission in the Corps of Engineers on July 1, 1846. Shortly thereafter McClellan received orders to join the Company of Engineers at West Point, a newly formed organization slated for duty in the recently declared war with Mexico. After less than three months of training, the unit was on its way to Texas. On September 26 McClellan sailed out of New York with the company and arrived in Texas two weeks later. After a long march to Tampico, the company became part of Scott's expeditionary force that was assembling for the Vera Cruz campaign. When the amphibious assault went ashore on March 9, McClellan and the Company of Engineers were in the first wave of boats to hit the Mexican beach.[22]

As a junior officer, McClellan was not particularly close to Scott, but he was occasionally part of the "little cabinet" that advised Scott. McClellan learned a lot about war from watching Scott in Mexico. He was especially impressed with how Scott avoided frontal assaults whenever possible; how he used turning movements to take fortified positions; how he carefully prepared before taking the offensive; and how he elicited considerable affection from the troops. McClellan was an active participant in Scott's successful campaign to capture Mexico City by maneuver. The offensive spirit of the campaign corresponded to what McClellan had learned of Napoleonic warfare at West Point, and Scott's success with flank attacks reinforced Mahan's admonition to avoid frontal assaults in favor of the indirect approach whenever possible. McClellan received recognition for his actions during the campaign. The battle of Cerro Gordo in April 1847 impressed him, and he was cited there for courageous action while under fire. He would long remember Scott's flanking maneuver, which brought a clear victory with a low price in American lives, as a tactical masterpiece. At the same battle he also gained a distinctly unfavorable impression of volunteer troops; in his journal he recorded Brigadier General

Gideon Pillow's "folly, his worse than puerile imbecility ..." in carrying out the volunteers' part of the attack.[23]

Shortly after the end of hostilities in Mexico, McClellan returned to West Point with the Company of Engineers holding the brevet rank of captain. His Mexico experience had given him a taste of the excitement and chaos of combat and provided him a rapid advancement in rank unusual for the period. While stationed at West Point he had taken advantage of the opportunity to continue his study of the art and science of war. He had been an active member of Mahan's Napoleon Club where faculty members and other officers stationed at West Point discussed and analyzed the Corsican's military campaigns. McClellan wrote two papers for the club, one of them a 111-page analysis of the Russian campaign that had been well received by the club's membership. He also studied other European writers in an effort to widen his understanding of planning and conducting warfare.[24]

McClellan left the Company of Engineers in 1851 and spent the next four years participating in a variety of expeditions and surveys that broadened his engineering background. His first expedition, an exploration to find the source of the Red River, was commanded by Captain Randolph B. Marcy. Marcy, forty years of age when the expedition began and well known in the army for his explorations of the American west, had seen many years of frontier service in the Fifth Infantry. McClellan got along well with the veteran soldier, and they developed a close relationship that would last for many years. After the Red River expedition McClellan conducted a survey of rivers and harbors in Texas, a job he did not especially care for, but it put him in charge of something for the first time in his career. With the notable exception of Marcy, McClellan displayed a remarkable ability to find fault with his superiors. During his various expeditions, however, McClellan did not neglect his constant study of military history. He took a particular interest in Jomini's analysis of Napoleon's campaigns, reading books on the subject whenever he could get them. One letter home included his thanks for the "Jomini I have wanted badly." His interest in Jomini was less as a theorist than as a practical soldier. Where others saw Jomini's ideas as a rigid approach to war, McClellan "sought to emulate his flexibility and skill in devising strategies to fit specific military conditions."[25]

A transcontinental railroad survey from Minnesota to the Puget Sound followed his work in Texas, but he was starting to tire of peacetime duty. But Secretary of War Jefferson Davis offered McClellan a new challenge and sent him to the Dominican Republic to survey an anchorage for the U.S. navy. His satisfactory work for Davis bore fruit and kept him on active service for the moment. The always ambitious McClellan had been seeking promotion since the end of the Mexican War. In March 1855 his efforts were rewarded when Jefferson Davis appointed him a captain in the newly created First Cavalry. Before he could take up his new duties, however, he was selected as one of three officers to go to Europe to study the latest military developments and observe the Crimean War. McClellan, the youngest of the group, spent a year traveling widely in Europe, visiting battlefields and collecting material.

McClellan's report on the Crimean War, published by Congress in 1857, was well received, and the U.S. army adopted the cavalry manual he wrote based on Russian regulations. He had been favorably impressed by the training and administration of professional armies in Europe, the value of field fortifications, and the necessity for adequate logistics support. His engineering background and his experience with Scott in Mexico where maneuver was preferred over frontal assaults may have caused him to focus on the usefulness of defensive works in the Crimean. But he obviously understood the difficulties of overwhelming an entrenched force by a frontal attack and noted that when defended by good troops, temporary fortifications could be of greater importance than popularly supposed. Since the Mexican War, technological changes in weaponry had shifted the advantage to the defense. In the Mexican War the smoothbore musket with its effective range of one hundred meters had been the primary infantry weapon, but in the Crimean War the infantry had used substantial numbers of rifled muskets that could reach out to five hundred meters. This allowed the defenders to take an attacking force under fire at a longer range, inflicting a greater number of casualties during the assault. While most authorities still extolled the offensive, McClellan was developing an appreciation for the increased power of the defense. This appreciation would earn him the thanks of his troops who did not have to endure frontal assaults, but it also caused him to be very wary of attacking any defenses head-on.[26]

McClellan came away from his European tour believing that the proper conduct of war depended on how well the commanding generals understood the object of their operations and how fast they then moved to attain them. In his comprehensive analysis of the Crimean War he was critical of the allied generals, French and English, for not keeping the objective of their campaign constantly in view and pressing "rapidly and unceasingly towards it." His proposed cavalry regulations emphasized that no properly prepared general "need hesitate more than a few minutes when he finds himself in the presence of the enemy."[27]

Shortly after completing his report McClellan resigned from the army to take up civilian pursuits and became the chief engineer of the Illinois Central Railroad. By 1858 he was vice president of the company. In 1860 he married Mary Ellen Marcy, daughter of Captain Marcy, McClellan's commander in the Red River expedition of 1851, and one of the few men he had found acceptable as a commander. He had courted Mary Ellen for many years, finally outlasting the competition from fellow officers, notably Lieutenant A. P. Hill, also a future Civil War general. Among the many prominent wedding guests at the ceremony on May 22 in New York City was General Winfield Scott.

In the wake of Lincoln's call for militia, McClellan became a much-touted candidate for high command. Even while pursuing a successful civilian career in railroading, he had kept up with his military interests, and knowledgeable Americans widely considered him one of the nation's most highly qualified men for senior command. His report on European armies was rushed into print "at the urgent request of the publishers" in 1861. It included a publisher's preface that referred to the report as "his [McClellan's] own military history written, unconsciously, in advance."[28]

In April, three states, New York, Ohio, and Pennsylvania, all sought his services to prepare their growing militia forces for war. He expressed a desire to serve his native state of Pennsylvania, but when he did not receive a call as soon as he expected, he set out by train from Cincinnati personally to visit the governor in Harrisburg. Along the way, however, he stopped in Columbus to discuss the military situation in the Ohio Valley with Ohio's governor, William Dennison. Impressed with McClellan, Dennison offered him command of the state militia on the spot, an offer McClellan immediately accepted. McClellan's expected call from Pennsylvania finally came in the form of a telegram offering him command of the state's militia. But, because it had been misrouted, it did not reach him until the day after he had accepted Dennison's offer in Ohio.

At their first meeting, Jacob D. Cox, a lawyer and politician with no previous military experience who had just that day been appointed a brigadier general in the Ohio Volunteers and would play a critical role in the first campaign, was favorably impressed with McClellan's modest appearance and considerable self-confidence. Cox recalled that McClellan's report on the Crimean War, "one of the few important memoirs our old army had produced," was enough to give him "a just reputation for comprehensive understanding of military organization, and the promise of ability to conduct the operations of an army."[29]

Commissioned major general of the Ohio Volunteers on April 23,

McClellan assumed command of all the state's militia forces on the same day that Lee accepted command of the Virginia militia in Richmond. The next day McClellan and Cox began the work of transforming the rapidly assembling Ohio militia forces into a competent fighting force. Training began at Camp Dennison, laid out just east of Cincinnati by William S. Rosecrans, an 1842 West Point graduate. A native of Ohio, Rosecrans, an engineer, had resigned from the army in 1854 to pursue a business career that took him to Ohio and western Virginia. His ventures were not especially profitable, and he left his position as head of an unsuccessful kerosene refinery in Cincinnati to accept a colonel's commission in the Ohio Volunteers on April 23.

Four days after taking command in Ohio, McClellan prepared a strategic plan "intended to relieve the pressure upon Washington, & tending to bring the war to a speedy close" and sent it to Scott in Washington. The plan proposed garrisoning key points in the Ohio Valley and sending a force of 80,000 men up the Kanawha Valley of western Virginia to Richmond. An alternative proposed sending the 80,000-man force straight to Nashville. In any case, McClellan thought it clear that the forces available to him "should not remain quietly on the defensive."[30]

It was the first effort by any Union general to develop a strategy for defeating the Confederacy, but Scott rejected it as impractical. Scott's comments on the plan included a prescient note that a "march upon Richmond from the Ohio would probably insure the revolt of Western Virginia." Scott may have considered McClellan's proposal hastily conceived and logistically flawed, but it probably prompted him to do some strategic planning of his own. In his notes that critique McClellan's plan Scott essentially outlined what would soon become his cordon, or Anaconda, strategy to surround the Southern states. McClellan's plans exhibited a desire to move toward the objective immediately with all possible speed, and it provided Scott the impetus for developing the Union's Civil War strategy.[31]

The plan may also have had a more direct effect on Federal strategic thinking. McClellan had proposed that the "region North of the Ohio, and between the Mississippi and the Alleghenies, forms one grand strategic field in which all operations must be under the control of one hand, whether acting offensively or on the defensive." On May 3, the day after Scott reviewed McClellan's strategic views, he outlined what came to be called the Anaconda Plan and created the Department of the Ohio with McClellan in overall command. The new department included the states of Ohio, Indiana, and Illinois, the area described in McClellan's proposed strategic plan. The department was shortly expanded to include western Virginia, and the unity of command thus attained in the theater of operations would contribute directly and positively to the first offensive Federal operations of the war.[32]

Lincoln forbade any incursion into the Old Dominion until after the May 23 referendum confirmed Virginia's secession from the Union. McClellan worked hard to organize his forces and kept a watchful eye on events in nearby Virginia. He was aware of the pro-Unionist activity in western Virginia, and he was determined to take advantage of it if and when he was able to launch his forces across the Ohio River. By the end of April the Ohio state legislature had authorized nine more regiments of volunteers than the number requested for Federal service. These additional regiments remained in state service under McClellan's command and provided him with the potential for offensive operations should the opportunity arise.[33]

Urged on by Dennison, the political situation in western Virginia provided a tempting target for McClellan's strategic planning. In contrast to the strategic problems facing Lee, McClellan had a relatively simple task. Lee had to plan for defending Virginia from attacks that could come from four different directions, one of which was through the western counties. McClellan could concentrate on planning to conduct a single invasion launched from a secure base in Ohio. From Lee's perspective, any Federal movement through

the western mountains of Virginia was only one of the threats he
had to consider, but the geography of the area provided McClellan
with more than one route through the mountains.

There were two possible invasion routes through western Virginia: the northern route along the Staunton-Parkersburg Turnpike,
and the southern route along the James River and Kanawha Turnpike. McClellan had already proposed a strong force to move along
the southern axis of advance, but in order to protect the railroad
lines his initial advance into Virginia followed the northern route.
He did not neglect the southern route, and as Ohio continued to
raise more regiments, he soon had adequate forces to launch a second advance into the Kanawha Valley. His desire to have the entire
Ohio Valley under a unified command would prove invaluable,
because it gave the theater commander the capability to coordinate
the movements of forces along two different axes of advance. He
also had the advantage of interior lines that allowed him to move
forces rapidly over long distances by taking advantage of steamboats on the Ohio and Great Kanawha Rivers and the railroads.
The road network between the east-west turnpikes offered opportunities to transfer forces between the two axes of advance, but by
using the rivers and railroads, troops could move faster and arrive
in better condition even though the distances might be greater.

For the first few weeks of their commands Lee and McClellan
were fully engaged in organizing their respective forces while
awaiting the outcome of the political events that would shape the
opening of the war. But as the armies began to take form and war
loomed inevitable, they each turned to matters of strategy. In the
first campaign McClellan's plans for invading western Virginia
would directly challenge Lee's defensive preparations in that part
of the Old Dominion. In his initial planning McClellan was already
thinking at the strategic level in proposing a command structure
that would put all Federal forces in the theater of operations under
a single commander. Lee, however, was still thinking tactically as

he parceled out militia commands to a variety of officers with no plan for unity of command or even clear channels for coordination of their efforts. Without a coherent command structure, the inherent strength of the defense in western Virginia was weakened at the outset of the campaign.

The outcome of the campaign directly affected the reputations of both men. One did well and received rapid promotion, the other fared poorly and was moved out of command. But, as is frequently the case, the results of the first campaign do not necessarily reflect the outcome of the war, and the reputations Lee and McClellan made in the first campaign in western Virginia did not endure the four years of war. It may be that one man's failure caused him to learn from his mistakes, while the success of the other led him to overlook his weaknesses.

CHAPTER FOUR

A Railroad Man at War

WHEN THE VIRGINIA Convention passed the secession ordinance on April 17, it put Governor Letcher in a bit of a quandary. The convention's actions would not become binding until the May 23 referendum confirmed secession, but in the meantime Letcher had to assume that it would pass and prepare the state for war. By refusing Lincoln's request for troops, he had already set Virginia's course. Confident of the results of the referendum, Letcher began talks with the Confederate government, the result of which was a military alliance that would place Virginia's militia at the disposal of President Jefferson Davis. The Virginia Convention quickly ratified Letcher's military agreement and the Constitution of the Confederate States on April 25. Two days later, clearly anticipating that the May 23 vote would confirm its actions, the convention sent an invitation to Davis to make Richmond the capital of the Confederacy. He immediately accepted the offer.

In the western counties the convention's activities spawned meetings that both supported and opposed the proposed secession ordinance. In Clarksburg, on April 22, 1,200 people unanimously approved the resolutions, prepared by Carlile, which not only opposed secession from the Union, but proposed a convention of delegates from the northwestern counties to meet on May 13 in Wheeling to determine the future course of their area. The resolutions, published by the *Western Virginia Guard* and widely distributed, gave impetus to the Unionist movement in the west. In response to them, Joseph Johnson, a former governor of the state, presided over an April 26 gathering of "Southern Rights Men" in Clarksburg to denounce the proposed dismemberment of the state and to urge the formation of local militia companies that would support Virginia's course. While Letcher prepared to cooperate with the Confederate government, pro-Unionist activists in the western counties were making overtures to the Federal government. On April 25 George W. Caldwell, another western politician, wrote to Lincoln soliciting his approval and Federal assistance for the antisecession forces organizing in Virginia, and several westerners met with Lincoln on May 1 to discuss the situation.[1]

With Richmond now the Confederate, as well as the state capital, the need to prepare for a Federal invasion increased. Since Lincoln had given the secessionists until May 5 to "disperse and return peaceably to their respective abodes," conventional wisdom in Virginia anticipated, or at least hoped, that the Federal invasion would not begin before that date. Virginia law provided for an organized militia of four divisions, each commanded by a major general. These high-ranking officers were " 'prominent citizens' or elderly men of political influence," but the militia staff had never functioned effectively. There were many men in the volunteers, but they had never been organized into regiments, and in 1861 they had no officers above the rank of captain.[2]

Lee, now responsible for defending his native state, set about to organize the forces at his disposal. Under the circumstances his plans had to be formulated and executed almost simultaneously, and he did not have the benefit of an organized staff to assist him. One of the first officers to join Lee in Virginia, however, was Robert S. Garnett, who had been the adjutant when Lee was superintendent of West Point. Garnett became Lee's adjutant general, drafting many of the orders and correspondence required to get the state organized for war.

Lee's primary concern was to defend the territory of the Old Dominion. Despite what he may have recalled from his service with Scott in Mexico and the pressures put on him to do something in the wake of secession enthusiasm, he simply did not have the resources to undertake an offensive, nor was that the policy of the Virginia or Confederate governments. His initial estimate was that 51,000 troops would be needed to defend the state, and the convention decided that a term of one year would be required of all volunteers. Lee set the company as the basic unit for recruiting purposes, although those companies would later be organized into regiments.

On May 3, the same day Lincoln signed a second proclamation for an additional 42,000 volunteers for Federal forces, Letcher authorized Lee, the commanding general of Virginia's military forces, to muster volunteers into the service of the state. Lee's first call for volunteers went out on May 3, and subsequent calls went out on May 6, 7, and 9, each to different parts of the state. For the most part, enlistments came rapidly, although there were initial reports of dissatisfaction from the western counties.[3]

Raising troops, however, was simply the first step in developing an army. Weapons and equipment had to be provided before it could be an effective fighting force. Virginia had established a Department of Ordnance earlier in the year, appropriated $80,000 to purchase arms and ammunition, and authorized counties and cities to borrow money to equip the militia. But the rush to war was so frantic that the new department could not keep up with the rapidly growing army. Stored at Richmond and Lexington were some 60,000 small arms, the vast majority of which were flintlock muskets, inferior to the percussion muskets the Federals could expect to receive. There was hope that a considerable number of small arms damaged in the fire at Harpers Ferry might be salvaged and repaired for use, and perhaps some additional arms might be procured from excesses in other Southern states. It was not much to arm the force that would be necessary to initiate the defense of a state that faced possible invasion on four fronts.[4]

On May 1, Letcher wired Leroy Pope Walker, the Confederate secretary of war, that arrangements had been made to call out fifty thousand volunteers from the Old Dominion who would be "rendezvoused at Norfolk, Richmond, Fredericksburg, Alexandria, Harpers Ferry, Grafton, Kanawha, Parkersburg, and Moundsville." Letcher expected to raise adequate forces in western Virginia to defend the area. Troops at Parkersburg and Grafton would provide security for the turnpikes and railroads through the mountains in the north, while troops in Moundsville would hold the panhandle that thrust like a sword between the Northern states of Ohio and Pennsylvania. The forces at Kanawha could protect the turnpike along the Kanawha River, which provided a line of communications that could be used by Federal forces to advance into the Valley of Virginia.[5]

Even before Lee issued the first call for volunteers, a number of steps had been taken to encourage the recruiting efforts in western Virginia. In late April Letcher sent Lieutenant Colonel John McCausland to the Kanawha Valley to raise a force of ten companies of infantry and one of artillery. On April 29 Lee ordered Major Alonzo Loring of Wheeling to raise troops to protect the terminus of the Baltimore and Ohio Railroad. The next day Major Francis M. Boykin, Jr., "commanding Virginia volunteers, Weston, Virginia," received instructions to protect the railroad. Loring was directed to "put himself in communication" with Boykin so they could coordinate their efforts. On May 4 Colonel George A. Porterfield was dispatched from Harpers Ferry, where he was serving as a staff officer, to Grafton in order to raise a regiment and establish a training camp to protect that vital railroad junction. He was not to interfere with the peaceful use of the railroad, but was to cooperate with the management as much as possible.[6]

But pro-Union forces were also forming in the area. On April 15 a meeting in Wheeling resulted in the enrollment of thirty men for a Union guard, and by the 23rd there were five companies organized in the city. The Rough and Ready Guards, commanded by Captain A. H. Britt, was the first company to volunteer its services to the U.S. government. It was followed shortly by Captain E. W. Stephens and his Iron Guards. When Major Oakes, a U.S. army officer, arrived in Wheeling on May 9 to muster companies into Federal service, the two guards companies became the first to sign up. They eventually became Companies A and B of the First Regiment Virginia Volunteers.[7]

In Ohio, McClellan had the enthusiastic support of Dennison in defending Ohio from possible invasion from Virginia. The governor was prepared to take the offensive to "defend Ohio beyond rather than on her border" and offered pro-Unionists in the western counties the support of Ohio troops in their efforts. In early May he urged the War Department to add western Virginia to the Department of the Ohio. Soon after that request was granted, on May 13 Dennison encouraged McClellan to move into Virginia.[8]

Further west, in Indiana, preparations for war moved as rapidly as in Ohio. Governor Oliver P. Morton, like Dennison a founding member of the Republican party in 1856, offered Lincoln ten thousand men to defend the Union. Within days of the president's April 15 request for troops, Indiana was mustering regiments into Federal service. But in spite of Morton's enthusiasm, Indiana, like many other states, was initially ill prepared to deal with a large influx of volunteers. When the first Indiana troops arrived at Camp Morton, a training site established on the state fairgrounds near Indianapolis, they were quartered in horse stalls with no blankets. Upon learning of the problem, residents of the city in short order sent several wag-onloads of bedding for the men of the Sixth Indiana, the state's first regiment to be raised in the Civil War. Because Indiana had sent five regiments to the Mexican War, the state thought it proper that the first regiment for this war be designated the sixth. For several weeks the new soldiers drilled with broomsticks wearing whatever civilian clothing they had on when they arrived in camp while the adjutant general struggled to supply the new army with arms and equipment.[9]

Meanwhile, back in Virginia, on May 10 Boykin reported pes-simistically from Grafton that under Carlile's enthusiastic leader-ship "nothing is left undone by the adherents of the old Union to discourage those who are disposed to enlist in the service of the State." His assessment was that the area "is verging on a state of actual revolution" and that he needed at least five hundred men and a battery of artillery to be sent from the east in order to suppress dis-turbances that pro-Unionists might instigate. In response, the next day Lee told Boykin that he "must persevere and call out compa-nies from well-affected counties and march them to Grafton." But Lee was beginning to see the potential problems that might arise in the western counties, which put him in something of a dilemma. While he wanted to believe that his officers in the northwest part of the state would be able to find sufficient forces to defend the area, he was also concerned that sending troops from eastern Virginia might further exacerbate the antisecessionist feelings there. He went on to explain to Boykin that he did not "think it prudent to order companies from other parts of the State to Grafton as it might irri-tate instead of conciliating the population in that region."[10]

During early May Union activists in the western counties sought support for the convention set to take place in Wheeling. Proseces-sion forces had made it difficult to select delegates. In Fairmont a plot was hatched to kidnap Pierpont and take him to Richmond as a prisoner of war. The plan fell apart when James Otis Watson, Pierpont's business partner, intervened and advised Pierpont to take a train to Wheeling. Pierpont found himself forced to leave town before the polls opened, and he was "in a bad humor" when he reached Wheeling. He went directly to see the central committee, and when he was asked why he was not home voting, Pierpont declared that "the time for voting is past; the time for fighting has arrived." They were brave words, but he and his supporters would need more than words if they were to have a chance of staying with the Union. On May 13, ten days before the statewide vote on secession, 436 delegates representing twenty-seven of the northwestern counties gathered at the First Wheeling Convention to determine the most effective means for resisting secession in western Virginia. The convention lasted three days. The delegates, as demonstrated by their attendance, agreed on the need for such resistance, and there was a widespread belief that formation of a new state was the only appropriate action. The only real differences arose between those who wanted immediate action and those who argued for a more moderate approach. Carlile favored immediate separation from Virginia, arguing that delay would only deteriorate the western position. He had considerable backing, especially from delegates from strongly pro-Union towns.[11]

Carlile's opponents, foremost of whom were Pierpont and his longtime friend Willey, argued that immediate separation from Virginia was premature because they needed time to win support from the western populace and required assurances from the Federal government that military assistance would be available should it be needed. Willey and Pierpont wanted to focus the convention's efforts on garnering a heavy vote against the May 23 referendum to demonstrate popular support against secession, after which there would be time to determine a future course of action. The delegates finally agreed on a compromise in which the supporters of delay

were generally successful. The convention called on the people of
the northwest to oppose the secession ordinance and decried the
military alliance Letcher had engineered between Virginia and the
Confederacy. The idea of a new state, however, remained a viable
option. The delegates agreed to meet again on June 11 if, as
expected, the May 23 referendum favored secession. Delegates to
that convention would be selected by voters on June 4. In anticipation of the expected results, the convention established a central
committee headed by Carlile that would "attend to all matters connected with the objects of this convention." The idea behind delaying conclusive action until June was to impress the Federal
government with the support residents of western Virginia could
muster against secession. It would demonstrate more conclusively
than proclamations or resolutions that there was enough popular
support to warrant Federal military intervention.[12]

The Wheeling Convention received mixed reviews, but largely
because of the compromise that watered down its resolutions, much
of the reaction was negative. Northern editorials viewed the convention with suspicion. In Richmond politicians were angry, and some
were willing to let the panhandle go its own way to get rid of the problem; secessionists in the Kanawha Valley suspected the convention
was held to lure a Federal invasion of the western part of the state.
From Wheeling, Carlile and the central committee provided direction to pro-Union county groups organized to campaign against
the secession ordinance. Virginia's alignment with the Confederacy
was already having an effect on the western counties. The trade
between Ohio and Pennsylvania that constituted much of the economic activity in northwestern Virginia was threatened by both sides.
On the one hand, Letcher stopped sending provisions to northern
markets, while, on the other, the Federal government threatened to
seize goods intended for the insurgents. When secessionist-minded
postmasters began burning pro-Union material, Federal authorities
stopped mail service in many areas.[13]

The Wheeling Convention and its results did not hold up military preparations in Richmond; nor did they particularly stimulate any greater concern for the situation in the western counties. When Porterfield, a graduate of the Virginia Military Institute and a veteran of the Mexican War, arrived in Grafton by train on May 14, he found that the situation there was less optimistic than he had been led to expect. When he stepped off the train, there was no one to meet him, and when he inquired about the status of troops in the area, a railroad employee informed him that the nearest ones were in Fetterman, some two miles away. The colonel was also advised that since there was "a power of folks around Grafton that's all stirred up against you folks," it would be prudent to rent a horse and head toward Fetterman. At Fetterman Porterfield found Captain William P. Thompson and his company, the Marion Guards, in control of the town. Thompson had acquired 175 muskets at his own expense and used them to arm the men he recruited. Porterfield also learned that the telegraph operator was a Confederate sympathizer willing to intercept Federal message traffic. The postmaster, also prosecession, informed Porterfield that the residents of Grafton were mostly Irish railroad workers who had little liking for the Confederates.[14]

Grafton was a key transportation hub in northwestern Virginia. It had recently grown up as a railroad town where the Northwestern Railroad from Parkersburg on the Ohio River joined the Baltimore and Ohio Railroad. The town was also near the intersection of the Beverly-Fairmont Pike and the Northwestern Turnpike. The Pike ran south from Grafton, through Philippi, to intersect the Staunton-Parkersburg Turnpike at Beverly. Holding Grafton, therefore, meant controlling the primary communication routes through northwestern Virginia.

When Porterfield sent his first report back to Garnett, Lee's adjutant in Richmond, he stated that there were not as many forces or officers present as he had been led to believe, and he requested to be "reinforced by a detachment of not less than 250 men and a few pieces of artillery" from Harpers Ferry as soon as possible. Two days later Porterfield reported that he had managed to gather together some forces, but that they were woefully short of arms. He reported companies forming in Pruntytown, Philippi, Clarksburg, Weston, and Fairmont. Of the companies being organized, only two were known to be armed, and one of those has only "old flint-lock muskets, in bad order, and no ammunition," while the other "has a better gun and some ammunition." Although he had ordered all of the companies in the area to assemble in Grafton, he had no illusions about their immediate capabilities, expecting them to be no "more effective than undisciplined militia" for some months. In spite of Porterfield's plea for volunteers to rally in defense of Virginia, their "common mother," as he phrased it, he met with little success, reporting to Richmond that the people of the region were "apparently on the verge of civil war."[15]

Porterfield was to some extent successful in his plea for assistance from Richmond. On May 19 Lee wrote to inform him that a thousand muskets and rifles for his use were on the way to Beverly. Several companies with arms were also on the way, ordered to travel from Staunton to Beverly "to gather strength as they pass along." Lee still believed that he could raise enough men to defend the area with minimal assistance from the east. He wrote Porterfield on May 24, the day after the referendum for secession passed, expressing regret at the lack of recruiting success in the area and professing his disbelief "that any citizen of the State will betray its interests, and hope all will unite in supporting the policy she may adopt." In addition to the forces awaiting Porterfield in Fetterman, there were two companies in Pruntytown, a highway town west of Grafton on the Northwestern Turnpike. Here, at a meeting with local merchants and attorneys, he learned that there were also a number of militia companies being recruited and organized in the surrounding area. Porterfield established his headquarters at Philippi, a town south of

Grafton on the Beverly-Fairmont Pike that was more hospitable toward the Confederate cause. There he began to muster his forces. By May 26 he had assembled about four hundred men.[16]

While Porterfield organized his Confederate forces, Captain George R. Latham assembled the Grafton Guards, a pro-Union company. With militia companies forming on both sides of the secession question in close proximity, the first casualty was not long coming. On the night of May 22 Private Thornsberry Bailey Brown and Lieutenant David Wilson, members of the Grafton Guards, were socializing in Pruntytown. As they returned to Grafton, they met three men from the Letcher Guards, Privates David W. S. Knight, William Reese, and E. Glenn, who were guarding the intersection where the Northwestern Turnpike crossed the Baltimore and Ohio Railroad. When the Letcher Guards called for the two men to halt, Brown pulled a pistol and shot Knight's right earlobe off. Knight responded with a shot of "buck and ball" that put three holes in Brown's chest and killed him. As Wilson departed for Grafton, Glenn raised his musket to fire, but as he did so, Reese deflected the barrel and the shot hit the fleeing lieutenant on the heel of his boot. When Wilson reported the incident to his company commander, Latham decided to defuse the situation and move his men out of town. On May 24 the Grafton Guards, taking care to march around Fetterman, went to Valley Falls and caught the train for Wheeling where they soon became Company B of the Second Regiment Virginia Infantry. When Porterfield learned that the Grafton Guards were leaving town, he took advantage of the situation and on May 25 occupied the town.[17]

While Unionists were at work making political preparations in the northwest, military preparations were also going forward in Richmond. Lee had been commissioned a brigadier general in the Confederate army with "control of the forces of the Confederate States in Virginia" since May 14. Of the four possible lines of Federal invasion, two were in reasonably good shape. Virginia's forces had been reinforced at Harpers Ferry to block a possible invasion from out of the Valley, and Lee had sent Colonel Thomas J. Jackson, a mathematics instructor at Virginia Military Institute before being commissioned into the militia, to ensure the defense was in order. Lee had turned the defense along the rivers between Norfolk and Richmond over to Colonel Andrew Talcott, a former chief of engineers in the U.S. army and at one time Lee's superior. Lee had confidence that both the officers in charge and the resources available on those two avenues were adequate to the task at hand.[18]

But with a growing Federal army in Washington, just one hundred miles from Richmond, Lee saw a need to concentrate additional troops at Manassas Junction where Letcher had established a small force before Lee assumed command. Manassas Junction was of great strategic importance because it was where the Manassas Gap Railroad branched from the Orange and Alexandria Railroad. The Manassas Gap Railroad ran west from Manassas Junction over the Blue Ridge to Strasburg, thus providing a rapid means of moving troops from the Valley and eastern Virginia, while the Orange and Alexandria Railroad, running south from the junction, could potentially move forces into the heart of Virginia. If the Federals gained control of the junction, they could move forces south toward Richmond. Not only was Manassas Junction critical to stopping an invasion from Washington that could threaten the Confederate capital, it would provide the capability in Federal hands for rapid rail movement west into the Valley. A Union force moving from Maryland into the Valley combined with forces moving across the Blue Ridge using the Manassas Gap Railroad would make Harpers Ferry an untenable position to defend.

With his attention divided four ways, Lee concentrated on those avenues that offered the greatest threat to Virginia and Richmond. Conventional military wisdom rated a Federal invasion from western Virginia lowest of the four potential routes into the Old Dominion. It was the longest and most difficult route to Richmond, and, besides, in April the most visible threat was from the Federal forces assembling in Washington. Lee, therefore, made his defensive plans accordingly. But three factors combined to prove that assessment wrong. First, the political situation in the western counties, especially those in close proximity to Ohio and Pennsylvania, was unsettled at best, making it difficult to raise the loyal Virginia forces necessary to defend the region. Even with adequate forces, defending an area with a potentially hostile civilian population presents difficulties to seasoned troops, much less the newly raised, barely trained forces available in 1861. Second, Confederate military command in the west was fragmented, making an already difficult military situation worse. The officers Lee sent to various counties in the northwest were given small commands with instructions only to cooperate with one another. In addition, President Davis, early in May and without consulting Lee, commissioned the former Secretary of War John B. Floyd a brigadier general in the Confederate army and authorized him to raise a brigade of "mountain rifle-men with their own tried weapons" to conduct independent operations in the Kanawha Valley. No one was in charge of the overall defense of the western counties. Third, McClellan, supported and encouraged by the governors of Indiana and Ohio, was as busy as Lee, making his own plans for offensive action.[19]

For the most part, in spite of the increasing tension, people remained calm and kept their own counsel as election day approached. On May 23, not surprisingly, the state voted overwhelmingly for secession. Although voting in the western counties overall was about ten to one against secession, the voting pattern indicated that most of the pro-Union sentiment was concentrated in those counties that bordered Ohio and Pennsylvania. Other counties in western Virginia ratified the secession ordinance to a greater or lesser degree. In the southwestern region nine counties provided enthusiastic support for the Confederacy. The Kanawha Valley was particularly supportive of the Old Dominion's actions. All in all, throughout the western counties there was about a 60-40 split between Union and Confederate supporters. In spite of the efforts and rhetoric of the pro-Unionists, it was by no means a foregone conclusion that they would prevail in their desire for a separate state. The civilian population was divided on the issue, and Confederate military strength was growing in the area.[20]

The day after the election Porterfield was joined by Lieutenant Colonel J. M. Heck and five locally recruited militia companies, four of infantry and one of cavalry. On May 25 Porterfield wrote Richmond, pleading for more officers and weapons. To emphasize his plight he instructed Heck personally to carry the message to Richmond and stress the need for more troops. Heck left Fetterman shortly after midnight on the 26th and managed to report to Lee on the evening of the 28th where he met with some success. Lee promised that more muskets and powder would be sent west, and he authorized Heck to raise a regiment of infantry on his way back to Porterfield.[21]

Lincoln had been careful not to violate Virginia territory before the May 23 referendum, but once the vote was in, he wasted no time and sent eight regiments across the Potomac at Washington to seize bridgeheads in northern Virginia in anticipation of further offensive action and to keep Confederate forces at a distance. On May 24 Federal troops, the Eleventh New York, an infantry regiment commanded by Colonel E. Elmer Ellsworth, entered Virginia and occupied Alexandria. Ellsworth, a good friend of Lincoln, had accompanied the president-elect to Washington before returning to New York to raise his regiment, the "Ellsworth Fire Zouaves," from the New York City fire department. The regiment became the Eleventh New York when it was mustered into Federal service. Few shots were fired as the Union took its first small step to defend its capital, but one of them hit and killed Ellsworth. His body lay in state in the White House, and he became the North's first martyr of the Civil War. The Union now held two small bits of Virginia, Fort Monroe, east of Richmond, and Alexandria to its north. The next Federal move against the Old Dominion would come out of the west.

Since taking command of the Ohio militia, McClellan had been hard at work. Supported by an enthusiastic governor who was prepared to accept all the regiments that wanted to enlist, McClellan demonstrated his organizational capabilities. Ohio's share of the Federal call for troops was thirteen regiments, but in just over a week of assuming command, McClellan reported that the state had twenty-two regiments in training. Dennison placed the extra nine regiments under McClellan's command and persuaded the legislature to appropriate $3 million to provide for their arms and equipment.[22]

In Wheeling, Oakes had also been busy. On May 23 he mustered the last company of the First Virginia Infantry into Federal service. Colonel Benjamin Franklin Kelley, a former citizen of Wheeling who had moved to Philadelphia, left his position with the Baltimore and Ohio Railroad to become the regiment's colonel. Although he did not personally raise the regiment, he took responsibility for its training, and the new soldiers spent the month of May quartered at the fairgrounds near Wheeling. As with their fellows in Indiana who also drilled in a fairground, local citizens provided blankets for the men.[23]

Although the huge influx of men reporting to enlist in the Ohio militia initially caused considerable confusion, by the middle of May there was a remarkably good system of administration in place. When the president's second call for troops on May 3 required regiments to enlist for three years rather than three months, the new regiments had to be reenlisted. Not surprisingly, there were troops who wanted to go home rather than enlist for three years, a considerably longer commitment for what many considered a great adventure. These men became what Cox termed "mischief makers, seeking to keep the whole company from reenlisting" for three years. But by and large regiments had little difficulty making the transition. The Third Ohio, originally raised in

April as a three-month regiment, professed themselves "ready to do anything to escape the dull monotony," so they "listened to some patriotic speeches, indulged in a few hurrahs, and became a three-year regiment."[24]

As the raw recruits began to look something like soldiers, Captain Gordon Granger, a Mexican War veteran twice breveted for gallantry, who had arrived to muster the troops into Federal service, was moved to exclaim, "My God, that such men should be food for powder." In the spring of 1861 the eager recruits had yet to face battle, but the combat veteran of the Mexican War sensed what lay ahead. Granger believed the war was going to be a long one, and his opinions at Camp Dennison, where McClellan was training his forces, cast a sober note among the soldiers and officers, most of whom believed that one short campaign would take care of the rebels across the Ohio River.[25]

McClellan well understood the strategic problems facing Ohio across the river on the state's southern borders. In April Virginia took the first step toward secession, and as the situation in Kentucky unfolded, it appeared likely that that state might also leave the Union. Should that happen, Ohio could face hostile forces all along its southern border. There was widespread concern in the state for the safety of Cincinnati, lying just across the Ohio River from Kentucky. Early in May McClellan "took steps to concentrate the greater part of the Ohio troops at Camp Dennison, on the Little Miami Railroad, seventeen miles from Cincinnati," a location that presented "peculiar facilities for movement in any direction."[26]

Although McClellan's strategic plan for invading Virginia through the Kanawha Valley had been rejected by Scott, he still retained the old general's confidence in early May. On May 3 McClellan received command of the Department of the Ohio, a vast area that included the states of Ohio, Indiana, and Illinois, and on May 14 he was appointed a major general in the regular army. Although McClellan would regularly complain that he "received neither instructions nor authority" in his capacity as a department commander, it did not slow his efforts to prepare his forces for war. Dennison's incentive for raising large forces in Ohio was the threat of invasion from neighboring Virginia, one of the largest and most powerful Southern states, but McClellan sought an offensive opportunity to employ those forces.[27]

In consonance with Lincoln's desire not to make any moves into Virginia until May 23, McClellan, aware of the situation in western Virginia, bided his time and avoided the appearance of aggression, although he did station troops along the Ohio River on the Virginia border. Then, in order to keep tabs on events across the Ohio in western Virginia, McClellan sent First Lieutenant Orlando M. Poe, a U.S. army engineer, to collect information and organize an intelligence network. Poe, an 1856 graduate of West Point, had been surveying lakes before he became a member of McClellan's staff in Ohio. On May 4 Poe set out on his reconnaissance from Guyandotte, a town on the Ohio River in southwestern Virginia, and worked his way north to Wheeling. On May 13 he was in Cincinnati to report to McClellan.[28]

McClellan had already brought Allan Pinkerton, a railroad detective, into service as the head of intelligence gathering. On April 24 the newly appointed general had cryptically summoned the detective by stating that he needed "to make arrangements with you of an important nature." In his message McClellan cautioned Pinkerton to "let no one know that you come to see me, and keep as quiet as possible."[29]

On May 10, in response to Dennison's request, western Virginia and western Pennsylvania were added to the Department of the Ohio, giving McClellan an official interest in what was happening on the east side of the Ohio River. Poe reported that from the Kentucky line to Parkersburg the people were disaffected, but that north of Parkersburg they remained loyal to the Union. Along the way Poe enlisted the services of a number of residents as spies. This network provided information on secession activity along the Kanawha Valley and advised McClellan that moving Ohio troops into the area could arouse state loyalties toward Virginia.[30]

The day after the referendum passed, Scott sent a telegram to McClellan informing him that Confederate troops were occupying Grafton and asking if he could "counteract the influence of that action." Porterfield had been authorized to destroy railroad bridges should a Federal advance threaten Grafton. On May 25, convinced that there was movement in his direction, Porterfield ordered Colonel William J. Willey, half-brother of the popular politician, to burn the bridges. When McClellan learned from his intelligence sources that Willey had indeed burned the Baltimore and Ohio Railroad bridges at Farmington and Mannington, he ordered Federal forces into western Virginia on May 26. In doing so, he demonstrated his understanding of the delicate political situation in western Virginia. His troops were not on the way to destroy an enemy army by force of arms, they were "to restore peace & confidence, to protect the majesty of the law, & to rescue our brethren from the grasp of armed traitors." He told his soldiers they would provide protection so "the loyal men of Western Virginia" could organize and protect themselves.[31]

Porterfield was doing the best he could with the forces at his disposal to carry out Lee's wishes of defending the railroad. After occupying Grafton he requested reinforcements from General Joseph E. Johnston at Harpers Ferry, but no troops could be spared there. The separate companies Porterfield had gathered together had not been formed into regiments, and the men received little training or drill as they waited for the war to come to them. In Philippi, one man assessed the recruits as being "covered with mass ignorance." When Porterfield, with the aid of the pro-Confederate telegraph operator at Fetterson, learned of McClellan's plans to advance, he decided to consolidate his forces at Philippi. On the way out of Grafton he accepted the Upshur Grays, commanded by eighteen-year-old John

C. Higginbotham, into state service. The Grays were unarmed, but the young Higginbotham expressed great pride in the new white tents his company brought with them. At Philippi Porterfield was able to provide the new arrivals smoothbore muskets, but with no cartridge boxes or cap pouches available, they had to carry what little ammunition was available in their pockets.[32]

At the same time McClellan issued the general orders to the invading forces, he issued a proclamation, "to the Union Men of Western Virginia." The proclamation explained that the "General Govt" had waited for the results of the secession referendum before moving into Virginia so as not to influence the outcome. But now that the citizens had shown "that the great mass of people of Western Virginia are true & loyal," it was time to "proclaim to the world that the faith & loyalty so long boasted by the Old Dominion are still preserved in Western Virginia."[33]

McClellan, as an experienced railroad man, perhaps understood better than other contemporary general officers the emerging symbiotic relationship between the railroad and the telegraph. The nation's railroads had been operating on thousands of miles of track for twenty years before the telegraph became a functional method of coordination. But as rail traffic increased, it became more of a problem to operate trains in two different directions on the same single line. The Erie Railroad first used the telegraph to coordinate running trains on a single track in 1851, and by 1861 it had become commonplace to expect a telegraph at a railroad depot. The telegraph lines generally paralleled the railroad right of way not because it was the shortest route, but because it was generally the easiest path, especially in rugged areas such as western Virginia. Clearing forested lands to lay rails left room for the telegraph poles, the right of way was accessible, and passing trains could identify breaks in the line.[34]

Anticipating the value of the telegraph, Dennison had contacted Anson Stager, the general superintendent of the Western Union

Telegraph Company in Cleveland, and asked him to manage the telegraph lines in southern Ohio, especially those along Ohio's border with Virginia. In May, McClellan appointed Stager "superintendent for military purposes of all the telegraphic lines within the Department of the Ohio," and directed that "his instructions will be strictly obeyed." On May 27, the same day Stager was appointed superintendent of the telegraph lines that ran alongside the railroad between Grafton and Cincinnati, W. G. Fuller was made assistant and dispatched to Parkersburg along with Colonel Frederick West Lander of McClellan's staff to construct telegraph lines in support of the Federal advance into Virginia.[35]

By advancing along the Baltimore and Ohio right of way McClellan's forces could secure both the railroad and the telegraph lines, so the main drive was toward Grafton. The First Regiment Virginia Infantry, with Kelley in command, left Wheeling and led the Federal advance into the western counties. On May 30 McClellan wrote to Lincoln to apprise him of the situation in Kentucky and western Virginia. He informed the president that he had dispatched Federal forces into Virginia in response to the bridge burning along the Baltimore and Ohio Railroad, and then went on to write that he was preparing to take three or four regiments and go in person to "seize the valley of the Great Kanawha" in an endeavor to capture the "some 1,200 secessionists encamped there." He planned to occupy the towns of Grafton in northwestern Virginia and Gauley Bridge in the Kanawha Valley to "hold the passes thro' the mountains between Eastern & Western Va," in the hope of securing "Western Virginia to the Union."[36]

McClellan's letter outlined his campaign plan for western Virginia. His goal in western Virginia was to secure the region for the Union. To do that he had to create a climate that would provide pro-Union political forces in the area the opportunity to gain control of the population. By moving to occupy Grafton and Gauley Bridge, McClellan would hold the two key transportation centers in western

Virginia. Grafton was the junction for the railroads that connected Wheeling and Parkersburg with the east, and it was located on the Northwestern Turnpike near Pruntytown, where a good secondary road ran south to join the Staunton-Parkersburg Turnpike at Beverly. In the Kanawha Valley, the town of Gauley Bridge was located on the James River and Kanawha Turnpike where the New and Gauley Rivers joined to become the Kanawha River. From Gauley Bridge an important secondary road ran north to Weston, connecting the James River and Kanawha Turnpike with the Staunton-Parkersburg Turnpike. Control of these two transportation hubs meant control of western Virginia.

In May McClellan was preparing to conduct a campaign with forces moving on two axes of advance, a departure from the Napoleonic concept of concentrating forces. The rugged nature of the area, however, offered the opportunity to gain control of the two key centers of transportation that would establish the military conditions necessary for attaining the political goal of securing the region for the Union. McClellan clearly understood the political implications of the Federal advance into Virginia. This was evidenced by the proclamation to his soldiers and the population of the region as the Federal invasion got under way. He was using the military forces of the Union to attain a strategic objective that supported political goals.

CHAPTER FIVE

Philippi

C OLONEL BENJAMIN F. Kelley led the First Regiment
Virginia Infantry out of Wheeling as the advance element
of the Federal invasion of western Virginia. On May 27 the
regiment boarded train cars on the Baltimore and Ohio Railroad
for their trip south. At the age of fifty-four, Kelley, sporting long
wavy hair and a full beard, had no experience of war. He had frequently served as drillmaster for various semimilitary companies in
Wheeling, but this was the first time "Old Ben" had led troops into
battle. He was popular with his men and confident that he could
carry out McClellan's instructions to capture the Confederate forces
holding Grafton, the strategic transportation hub located on the
Northwestern Turnpike at the intersection of the Baltimore and
Ohio and Northwestern Railroads.[1]

In addition to Kelley's loyal Virginians, there were several Ohio infantry regiments that McClellan had telegraphed, ordering them into Virginia. The Sixteenth Ohio, commanded by Colonel James Irvine, encamped since May 23 at Bellaire, Ohio, just across the Ohio River from Wheeling, crossed the river and joined Kelley on the 28th. In addition to the forces moving out of the panhandle along the Baltimore and Ohio Railroad, the Fourteenth Ohio with Colonel James B. Steedman in command received orders to occupy Parkersburg, Virginia, on the Ohio River, and then move east by train along the Northwestern Railroad to Clarksburg, checking bridges and tunnels along the way.[2]

While the Ohio regiments were moving into the theater of operations, McClellan was in Indianapolis on May 29 with Governor Morton to review the Indiana troops who had been training at the fairgrounds before he ordered them to Virginia. The Ninth Indiana, under the command of Colonel Robert Huston Milroy, an 1843 graduate of Captain Partridge's Academy in Norwich, Vermont, was the first of the state's new regiments to march off to war, boarding trains on the morning of the 30th. As they moved across Ohio they received cheers at every stop. The next day the Sixth Indiana, commanded by Colonel Thomas Turpin Crittenden, an Alabama-born lawyer and nephew of the U.S. Senator from Kentucky who proposed the compromise that attempted to avert the Civil War, was on its way to Virginia. On the 31st, while marching through Cincinnati, Crittenden halted his regiment to present arms to Major Anderson of Fort Sumter fame who was visiting his brother Larz. Like the Ninth before it, the Sixth was well received as it crossed Ohio by train. The two regiments joined the Seventh Indiana under the command of Brigadier General Thomas A. Morris. By the end of May, McClellan had a considerable force on the way to Grafton, although he planned to remain in Ohio for the time being.[3]

While McClellan concentrated his forces and attention on preparing to move into western Virginia, Lee, back in Richmond, had his thoughts focused elsewhere. The eastern approach to Richmond demanded his attention. Reports of dissension between the army and navy at Norfolk caused Lee to depart Richmond on May 16, his first foray out of Richmond since his arrival in April, for a personal inspection of the defenses along that avenue of approach. Dissatisfied with the progress on the fortifications in Norfolk, Lee replaced the army general in charge. In mid-May the greatest threat to Virginia was the Federal army assembling in Washington, D.C. Lee therefore sent what officers and troops he had available to reinforce the position at Manassas Junction. On May 28 Lee again left Richmond for a quick inspection of the forces at Manassas Junction. On his way back to Richmond the next day, a crowd assembled at Orange Court House and demanded a speech from the general. Lee told the crowd he had more important matters on his mind than making speeches, and advised the assembly "to attend to their private affairs and avoid the excitement and rumors of crowds." The remarks did little to raise the public confidence in the commander of the Virginia militia. Upon his return to Richmond, Lee found that Davis had arrived, and with his arrival the government of the Confederate States of America had taken up residence in the city. With the inspection and arrival of Davis, Lee had little time to think about western Virginia, leaving Porterfield on his own.[4]

Porterfield, commanding what Confederate forces there were in northwestern Virginia, had been in Grafton since May 14, raising militia and attempting to destroy the railroad and its bridges. Indeed, it was the Confederate bridge-burnings along the Baltimore and Ohio Railroad between Mannington and Farmington that had finally prompted McClellan to order Federal forces into Virginia. Porterfield actually knew of the Federal advance before it began. The telegrapher at Fetterman intercepted McClellan's orders and passed them on to Porterfield, who decided to withdraw his meager army in the face of superior forces. He retired from Grafton and moved back down the Beverly-Fairmont Pike to Philippi on May 28, the day after Kelley began his advance. There he managed to gather another two hundred or so troops, but his forces still had little in the way of arms, ammunition, or equipment. By June 2 he had about six hundred infantry and one hundred seventy-five cavalry troops. They were mostly independent companies with rudimentary military training, inadequate equipment, and virtually no experienced officers.

Arriving at Grafton on May 30, Kelley made immediate plans to pursue Porterfield to Philippi. He intended to move south of Porterfield's position and block the macadam-surfaced Beverly-Fairmont Pike below Philippi where it crossed the river on a covered bridge. By moving at night he hoped to avoid detection, surprise the Confederates, and cut off their escape route to Beverly. In theory, the concept was sound, but a night march can be difficult even for trained and experienced infantry troops under the best of circumstances. In Kelley's case, his militia men had only a few weeks' drill under their belts, and they were about to be introduced to the fog and friction of war where even the simplest things often go wrong.

On June 1 Steedman and his Fourteenth Ohio reached Clarksburg, a town about twenty miles east of Grafton. Before commanding the regiment Steedman had been an Ohio legislator who had served in the Texas army, but thus far in his military career he had seen no combat. Shortly after the Ohioans arrived, Colonel Frederick W. Lander, an aide-de-camp to McClellan who had accompanied the regiment from Parkersburg, rode ahead to Grafton to confer with Kelley about pursuing the Confederates. Lander, a railroad surveyor, engineer, and explorer of some note, had been the motivating force that had pushed a reluctant Steedman to keep the regiment moving along the railroad. Steedman had taken to heart McClellan's admonition to use "due care" in his advance and stopped the train to investigate every one of the twenty-eight tunnels along the eighty-mile trip. Lander, frustrated by Steedman's caution, took the two six-pounder cannons of Barnett's Ohio Battery and moved ahead of the infantry. With the artillery moving in front of the regiment, Steedman became more daring and increased the rate of march. The infantry reached Clarksburg, just west of Grafton, shortly after Lander. Kelley, with Lander's agreement, planned to move on Philippi with two converging columns along each side of the Tygart's Valley River. They were prepared to move on the evening of June 1, but when Morris and his Indiana brigade arrived, the general assumed command. Although Morris was an 1834 graduate of West Point, he had served only two years of active service as a second lieutenant of artillery before he resigned to pursue a career in railroading and engineering. After a conference to discuss the situation, Morris approved the plan, but "deemed it advisable to postpone the attack until the succeeding night." He was concerned with spies in the area and wanted time to "give a false impression" of the actual scheme.[5]

While the officers planned, the troops waited and admired the Virginia countryside, new to most of them. E. R. Monfort, an Ohio soldier, admired the "crested mountains covered with rich forests of oak, chestnut, pine, beech" that softened "the harsh aspects of the rugged mountains." In the Ninth Indiana Ambrose Bierce, a young private, recalled after the war that it was "a strange country." Most of his regiment had not seen a mountain before arriving in Virginia, and Bierce thought the "region was a perpetual miracle" in which "space had taken on a new dimension." Bierce, a printer's apprentice before he enlisted in the Indiana militia, was but one of thousands of soldiers who wrote of their wartime experiences, but his works were among the best. His autobiographical newspaper articles and short stories vividly described the war as he saw and experienced it. He remained in the army until 1865, but the campaign in western Virginia gave him his first glimpse of war and he recalled a number of those memories years later. At this early date in the war, before the fighting, Bierce and others admired the scenery and made light of their lack of soldierly skills. The Sixth Indiana thought it "quite laughable to see how awkward" they were as they went

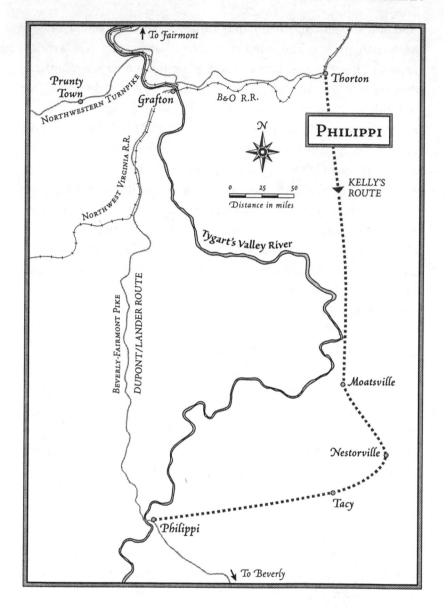

about trying to put up their tents for the first time, and "not yet understanding the ditching process, [they] got flooded" when it rained during the night. As the campaign went on, the dense foliage, rugged mountains, and pouring rain would become less entertaining for the troops.[6]

The final plan conformed with Kelley's initial concept of blocking the Beverly-Fairmont Pike south of Philippi, but with Morris's arrival more troops could be committed to the effort. Six regiments of infantry were to move in two separate columns along either side of the Tygart's Valley River at night. Kelley would head one of the columns while Colonel Ebenezer Dumont, commanding the Seventh Indiana, would lead the other one. The two columns would not be in contact with each other once they left Grafton, and they were to arrive in position around Philippi at four o'clock in the morning of June 3 for a coordinated attack on the Confederate positions. Morris, as overall commander of the operation, planned to remain in Grafton.

Kelley left Grafton by train on the Baltimore and Ohio Railroad the morning of June 2, heading east with 1,600 infantry troops. In addition to his own Virginia regiment, he had the Ninth Indiana under Colonel Robert H. Milroy and Irvine's Sixteenth Ohio. Their announced destination was Harpers Ferry, a ruse intended to fool Southern supporters in Grafton who might inform Porterfield. But they actually planned to move east only about six miles, to Thorton, where they would detrain and rest until nightfall. They were then to move south under cover of darkness, by way of rough and rarely used back roads along the east side of the Tygart's Valley River through the villages of Moatsville, Nestorville, and Tacy. Kelley was to position his forces east and south of Philippi in blocking positions to prevent the Confederates from eluding capture and retreating south to Beverly. Dumont, leading the other column, was a veteran of the Mexican War where he had been an officer in the Indiana state volunteers. He left Grafton with his regiment on the evening of

June 2. They moved west by train along the Northwestern Virginia
Railroad to join Crittenden's Sixth Indiana and Steedman's Fourteenth Ohio in the town of Webster. Lander went with Dumont to
scout ahead of the advance and to emplace the two cannons of
Ohio artillery. The three infantry regiments and the artillery totaled
about 1,450 troops. They were to proceed along the Beverly-Fairmont Pike on the west side of the Tygart's Valley River and arrive
north of Philippi at the same time Kelley moved into blocking positions on the south and east of the town.[7]

When both forces were in position, Kelley was to open the attack
by firing his pistol. The only control measure to coordinate the
actions of the two forces was the planned four o'clock arrival time,
a rather tenuous thread for an all-night march in an era when
watches were rare and imprecise at best. In any case, at Kelley's signal, Dumont's forces were to advance into town and force the Confederates south where they would be captured by Kelley. Along this
rugged terrain, the turnpike was the only route out of town. In case
Porterfield withdrew before the Federals arrived, Kelley was to take
overall command of the united force and conduct a vigorous pursuit, at least as far as Beverly.

Morris was well advised to be concerned about spies. In spite
of the Union efforts at deception, the Confederates received notice
of the movement before noon on June 2 from Mrs. George
W. Whitescarver, whose husband was a soldier at Philippi. The
Whitescarvers were from Pruntytown, a highway town that provided
food and lodging for travelers on the Northwestern Turnpike, and
which Porterfield had found very receptive to his earlier recruiting
efforts. When he moved his forces, including George Whitescarver,
out of nearby Grafton, Mrs. Whitescarver, wanting to be near her
husband, arranged to spend some time with Mr. and Mrs. Shaw of
Philippi. As rumors of a Federal advance reached the Confederate
forces, Mrs. Whitescarver returned to Pruntytown to see what she
might learn. With her access to the small town's information

grapevine, she soon knew the Federal plan and returned to Philippi to give it to Porterfield. Nor was Mrs. Whitescarver the only bearer of news. Later that Sunday afternoon two young women, Miss Abbie Kerr and Miss Mollie McCleod of Fairmont, arrived in Philippi with additional information confirming the next morning's planned attack. Armed with this intelligence, Porterfield determined that the only hope of avoiding capture was once again to withdraw his forces to the south.[8]

Porterfield met with the captains of his companies that evening at about nine o'clock, and they agreed that in the event of a Federal attack in the morning they would conduct an orderly retreat to Beverly. Porterfield instructed the company commanders that each would be responsible for his unit, leaving Philippi as best they could. They were all to assemble at the Big Rock, an easily recognizable landmark south of Philippi along the Beverly-Fairmont Pike. Once there, Porterfield planned to organize a more orderly withdrawal to Beverly. Unfortunately, there was some confusion among the company commanders as to when they were to begin the movement out of town. Some thought they would simply pack up and leave early in the morning, while others believed that withdrawal depended on the appearance of Federal troops. The company commanders issued their orders during the night, and even with no universal understanding about the withdrawal plans, the troops knew that nothing would happen until morning. They knew they were getting ready to leave, but at the time they went to bed they didn't know exactly when or on what signal.[9]

The night of June 2 was dark and rainy, making the Federal advance an exhausting, sodden affair. It was all the officers could do to keep the troops moving. The night was so dark that the troops kept their hands on the man in front to avoid getting lost. The constant rain slowed the advance and made footing treacherous. In the middle of the night, Charles Denger, Company I, Seventh Indiana, slipped on a wet log while crossing a small stream, accidentally discharged his gun, and shot himself in the leg. His comrades carried him to a nearby farmhouse and summoned a physician, but Denger bled to death before help arrived.[10]

Dumont was determined to carry out his part of the plan, and to keep track of the lead elements of his regiment, he directed Lieutenant Ricketts of Company B to lead the march south carrying a large, lighted, red lantern. Ricketts initially demurred, expressing concern that the red light would not only let the colonel know where the lead elements were, but the enemy as well. "I don't want a record as the first man killed," Ricketts argued. Dumont insisted, however, and Ricketts dutifully carried the lighted lantern until dawn without incident. As it turned out, the entire regiment could have carried red lanterns with little fear of enemy reaction.[11]

During the march Dumont moved constantly along the column giving pep talks to the tiring soldiers and shouting, "Close up, boys! Close up! If the enemy were to fire now they couldn't hit a one of you." He finally exhorted his green troops to double-time the last five miles of the march, and they arrived in position in an hour and a quarter, as scheduled. While Dumont positioned the infantry, Lander emplaced the two six-pounder cannons on the southern slope of Talbott Hill where they overlooked the town of Philippi and the Confederate encampment. As he peered into the predawn gloom, the only thing he could discern clearly was a neat row of white tents, so he selected them as the initial aiming point. The artillery was to open fire in support of the Federal attack at the sound of Kelley's pistol.[12]

For Kelley, foul weather was only one of the difficulties encountered during the night. Where Dumont had the relative luxury of a hard-surfaced road and a shorter route, Kelley's troops had to endure a circuitous route of little-used trails and roads that turned into mud soup under the feet of the struggling infantry. The roundabout march had been designed to fool the Confederates, but it fooled the Federals more. A local guide, Jacob Baker, managed to get himself, Kelley, and the small, wet army lost during the night by taking a wrong turn on a small side road, a mistake Kelley later alleged was made deliberately, although nothing ever came of the charge. They never did find the planned route. Four o'clock came and went with Kelley's infantry still marching soggily on the wrong road, but there was no way to inform Dumont or Lander of the delay. In the meantime, the Ohio cannoneers on Talbott Hill, anxious to begin their first battle, became ever more nervous in the growing light of dawn as they strained to hear pistol shots so they could open fire.[13]

Even with Kelley behind schedule, the Federals still had an excellent chance to bottle up the town and trap the sleeping Confederates. As the Federal troops slogged their way south, the Confederates had also been getting wet and feeling miserable. Although they did not know it, the rain actually favored the Federal attackers by confusing the defenders. Porterfield posted pickets, but he was of the opinion that there would be no attack in the event of rain. Having determined that "any army marching tonight must be made up of a set of damned fools!" the pickets took it upon themselves to come in out of the rain about midnight and, like the rest of Porterfield's command, go to bed to rest up before the morning movement. Had Ricketts, sloshing south ahead of his regiment, known of the confusion in the Confederate camp, he would have certainly been less nervous about carrying Dumont's red lantern.[14]

With no Confederate outposts to detect their approach, Kelley's delay should have presented no real problem for the Federal plan, but as frequently happens in war, the unexpected happened. Philippi, like Pruntytown, had been very receptive to Porterfield's presence, and many of its young men had volunteered for military service to protect the state of Virginia from the Federal invasion. The residents in and around the town, therefore, viewed Federal forces as the enemy. As dawn approached and Dumont's forces deployed into position, Mrs. Thomas Humphreys was awakened by Federal

soldiers moving around her house on the north side of Talbott Hill.
Looking out her bedroom window, she saw the enemy and knew
that Porterfield and her son Newton, who had recently joined the
Barbour Grays, a local infantry company, were in for an unpleasant
surprise. Taking immediate action, she put Oliver, Newton's twelve-
year-old brother, on a horse to sound the alarm. When Federal soldiers unhorsed young Oliver, Mrs. Humphreys retaliated with a
fusillade of firewood, kindling, and small stones. After a second
attempt to put Oliver on the horse failed, she retreated momen-
tarily to the house and, much to the dismay of the Federal soldiers,
shortly returned with a loaded pistol and opened fire. Lander, anxiously waiting just over the crest of Talbott Hill, heard Mrs.
Humphreys' pistol shots. Since he was unaware that Kelley was not
in position, he naturally assumed it was the signal to begin the attack
and ordered his nervous cannoneers to open fire on the most obvious aiming point in the town below, the fine, white tents that were
the pride of the Upshur Grays. The sound of the guns surprised both
Porterfield and Kelley, neither of whom was ready to start the fight.
It was also the first the Confederates knew of the Federal presence.
And as the smoke cleared and the sun came up, it became evident
that Kelley's forces were not south of town as planned. Their mis-
routing during the night put them north of town, across the river
from Dumont's forces, leaving the road south wide open.[15]

The surprised Confederates reacted to the unexpected artillery
fire by beginning their planned retreat immediately. The Ninth Indiana was supposed to have been in position to block the Confederate
retreat at the Big Rock, a prominent landmark on the Beverly-
Fairmont Pike south of Philippi. By coincidence the same rock had
also been designated a Confederate rallying point and would have
allowed the Federals a chance to capture the retreating troops. However, Milroy, colonel of the regiment, veteran of the Mexican War,
and a former judge, had also managed to get lost. The regiment
ended up a mile and a half from where it was supposed to be and

well out of position to block the road to Beverly. Like Kelley, Milroy blamed a local guide for the mistake, but, whatever the reason, the result left a clear avenue of escape for Porterfield and his forces. The Federals were learning that not everyone in Virginia was glad to see them, and that some might be willing to provide false information to what they viewed as invaders, not saviors.[16]

The Confederates took advantage of the Federal miscue, and once over their surprise, retreated in fine fashion. Newspapers later dubbed the affair the "Philippi Races" and observers on the scene described it as a shirt-tail retreat with Confederates skedaddling "pell-mell" and "helter-skelter" out of town. Correspondent Whitelaw Reid of the Cincinnati *Gazette*, an eye witness traveling with the Ohio militia, wrote of "cannon balls crashing into their huts and stirring out the rebels like a stick into a hornet's nest."[17]

It was confusing, as battle usually is. At one point during the melee, Porterfield, thinking he recognized one of his companies, the Hardy Blues (so named for the color of their uniforms; gray was not yet standard for Confederate uniforms), holding the east side of the covered bridge over the Tygart's Valley River, rode toward them until one of his officers pointed out that they were marching under the stars and stripes. At that juncture, Porterfield turned and rode slowly out of town to avoid attracting attention and being recognized. He and two of his officers were the last of the command to leave town. Porterfield tried to rally his forces at the Big Rock, but once they were on the road south nothing was going to stop them. Although the Confederate withdrawal had been anticipated, the crashing surprise of the Federal artillery caused the new troops to panic and leave behind a considerable amount of weapons, ammunition, commissary supplies, wagons, horses, medical stores, and camp equipment of all sorts that they could ill afford to lose. The Upshur Grays, who had packed the night before, was the only company to get out with its baggage relatively intact, except for its white tents. Their young commander, Higginbotham, concerned

about the rain and the welfare of his men, had arranged for them all
to spend the night at the home of Mr. and Mrs. Shaw, but they left
their wet, white tents set up, where they served nicely as Lander's
aiming point and went down in the first cannon volley.[18]

Virtually all of the Confederates made it to Huttonsville, forty-
five miles from Philippi, by June 4, but there were a few casualties
and prisoners. Lieutenant Colonel William J. Willey of the Virginia
militia, left behind with typhoid fever, was a harbinger of things to
come. Before the campaign was over, both sides would lose more
men to illness than to hostile fire. Another Confederate casualty,
Private James E. Hanger, eighteen years old, of the Churchville
Cavalry had been hit by a six-pound solid shot during the Federal
cannonade. He remembered that the ball hit the ground, rico-
cheted, and struck him in the leg, leaving him unable to join his fellows in the retreat. Surgeon James D. Robison of the Sixteenth
Ohio amputated Hanger's leg seven inches below the hip, and
Hanger thus became the first amputee of the Civil War. During his
initial recuperation at Cherry Hill farm near Philippi at the home of
Thomas Hite, Hanger fashioned a wooden leg to replace the one he
had lost. After a prisoner of war exchange in August 1861, Hanger
spent the rest of the war making artificial legs for other Confederate
amputees in Richmond, and after the war the Virginia state legislature commissioned him to make them for veterans. He patented the
"Hanger Limb," developed additional devices, and established J. E.
Hanger's, Inc. When he died in 1919, there were branches in
Philadelphia, St. Louis, Pittsburgh, Atlanta, Paris, and London.
Bierce, only a year older than Hanger, underplayed Hanger's experience, recalling after the war only that the Federal cannonade "shot
off a Confederate leg at Philippi." More than forty years later Bierce
dropped by to see the successful businessman, noting afterward that
Hanger was "still minus the leg; no new one had grown on."[19]

A second Confederate casualty, Captain Fauntleroy Daingerfield, commander of the Bath County Cavalry, was wounded in the

knee by a minie ball as he left Philippi. One of the cavalryman res-
cued Daingerfield and carried him on horseback to the Big Rock
rallying point. From there, he traveled to Beverly in the back of a
wagon. Doctor John T. Hoff amputated the mangled and useless leg
on the kitchen table of a private home using a saw borrowed from a
local carpenter.[20]

Five Union soldiers were wounded at Philippi, one of whom was
Kelley. He was shot in the right breast by William Sims, the Confederate assistant quartermaster. Sims was immediately captured by
a group of Union soldiers who wanted to kill him on the spot
because they thought "Old Ben" had been mortally wounded. After
Kelley had been carried into a nearby tavern, Bierce happened by
and saw his first casualty of the war. He recalled that Kelley's wound
was "spang through the breast, a hole you could put two fingers in."
In spite of the image created by Bierce's vivid description, Kelley
survived his injury to fight again.[21]

In the midst of the Union discussion about what to do with their
Confederate captive, Lander happened by and declared Sims a
prisoner of war, and sent his captors down the road after the retreating enemy. After seeing to Kelley and Sims, Lander continued his
pursuit of the retreating Confederates, in what has been described
as "the most hazardous ride ever seen by man," a bit of hyperbole
that gained him considerable attention in national newspapers
starving for war heroes at this early date. In spite of Lander's dramatic efforts, however, the Union advance had effectively been
halted. The confusion caused by the news of Kelley's apparent
death, and the weariness of the long night march finally setting in,
left the troops with little enthusiasm to continue the pursuit. They
had had their first taste of battle and had no wish to overindulge at
this early date in their military careers.[22]

Porterfield reported to Lee that "our troops at Philippi have been
attacked by a large force under McClellan and drew back to Beverly. We must have as large a number of troops as possible from

Richmond without a moment's delay or else abandon the North-west." But Lee had already received criticism of Porterfield's han-dling of the affair. Major M. G. Harmon, commanding Virginia forces in Staunton, charged in a letter to Lee (a copy of which he also sent to Porterfield) that Porterfield was "entirely unequal to the position" of commanding in the northwest.[23]

Porterfield demanded the opportunity to clear his name, and on June 20, at Lee's direction, a board of inquiry met at Beverly to con-sider the matter. After hearing witnesses and examining what records were available, the board reported on July 4 that the defeat came as a result of Porterfield's "failure to take proper defense mea-sures, failure to withdraw before a superior force because of weather conditions, and a misunderstanding of orders which resulted in pickets coming in, leaving the post exposed under attack." In its censure of Porterfield, however, the board did men-tion his "coolness, self-possession, and personal courage" during the retreat. But even before the board returned its findings, Lee had decided to respond to the setback by replacing Porterfield with the recently promoted Brigadier General Garnett, his adjutant general in Richmond.[24]

The affair at Philippi, sometimes billed as the first land battle of the Civil War, can hardly be called a battle. Neither side fired more than a few shots, and while they were indeed surprised, the Confed-erate retreat was not a spontaneous reaction to the Federal attack. Porterfield had directed his forces to be prepared to move early on June 3. While no signal to begin the evacuation had been established beforehand, when the Federal cannonade began, the Confederates all knew it was time to go, and off they went. The Federal plan demanded perfect timing and flawless execution from officers and troops, most of whom were facing the chaos of war for the first time. Kelley's instructions from McClellan had been to capture Porterfield and his forces, and that is how he designed his attack. In spite of its complexity and the pouring rains that would be characteristic of the entire campaign, the plan almost succeeded, but it did not accomplish its objective—virtually all the Confederate forces escaped to fight again. In a nation eager for good war news, however, Philippi was ballyhooed in Northern newspapers as a great success for McClellan, the "Boy General," in spite of the Federal failure to capture the Confederates.

Even though most of Porterfield's forces successfully eluded capture, the debacle prompted the dispatch of additional Confederate forces into western Virginia to bolster the faltering defense. The fact that Richmond had recently become the Confederate capital, and could therefore be vulnerable to a successful Federal invasion into Virginia, may have contributed to the rapid decision to reinforce the Confederate military forces in the western counties. From a military perspective, Philippi was inconclusive, but it did set the tone for the campaign. As they labored to attain the strategic objective of controlling the western counties, the newly raised volunteer forces on both sides continued to make fundamental tactical errors, although, since the forces engaged were generally small, their mistakes usually resulted in little loss of life. Relatively small battles with few casualties soon characterized the campaign in western Virginia. By the end of the year, losses as a result of nonbattle injuries and disease would far outnumber the men killed or wounded in actual fighting.

Porterfield's withdrawal from Grafton, the key transportation center in northwestern Virginia, offered McClellan the opportunity to move more forces from Ohio and Indiana into the theater of operations faster than the Confederates could respond. It also gave the Federals control of the railroads in northwestern Virginia. But the real winners after Philippi were the pro-Union civilians who favored secession from the rest of Virginia. They had received tangible evidence that the Federal government was prepared to provide military support for their efforts to remain loyal to the Constitution.

The Union success encouraged the western politicians and paved the way for the unimpeded election of delegates to the convention at Wheeling that would establish a new state government. Indeed, expressing their gratitude for the Federal assistance would be uppermost in the delegates' minds when they opened their convention in early June. With the ratification of the secession ordinance, and bolstered by the Federal success at Philippi, the plans made at the First Wheeling Convention in May went into effect. Delegates from more than thirty northwestern counties gathered in Wheeling on June 11 for what came to be known as the Second Wheeling Convention. Wheeling, the most prominent city in the northwest, far out of reach of the Richmond government, and the political center of pro-Unionist activity in Virginia, gave the convention a warm reception.

Convention delegates were of two classes: members of the Virginia General Assembly elected in the May 23 election who wanted to attend, and men selected to represent their counties to the convention. Methods of selecting representatives varied because the desire to remain with the Union was by no means universal in the western counties. The Richmond government opposed the Second Wheeling Convention, and many local officials in western Virginia, responding to that opposition, sought to repress it. Since public elections could not be held in some areas, a variety of means were used to select delegates. Some prospective delegates simply circulated petitions gathering the signatures of their supporters. In disputes between competing candidates, the person with the most signatures became the delegate. Union caucuses in some areas named delegates and provided letters of appointment. A credentials committee screened each delegate before allowing him to be seated.[25]

Of the delegates in attendance at the opening session on June 11, thirty-four were there because they had been elected to the legislature: twenty-nine to the house of delegates, and five to the senate. Not all the western counties were represented. In some areas fear of retaliation from strong pro-Confederate secessionist groups deterred anyone from attending. The requirement to take an oath of loyalty to the Union at the opening of the convention resulted in at least one expulsion when a delegate refused to swear his allegiance.[26]

Wheeling may have been hundreds of miles from Richmond, but Governor Letcher knew what the convention was doing. On June 14 he issued a proclamation directed to the population of northwestern Virginia. After pointing out that Virginia's secession from the Union had been approved by a majority vote and that it was "the duty of good citizens to yield to the will of the State," he concluded by warning that the "heart that will not beat in unison with Virginia now is a traitor's heart; the arm that will not strike home in her cause now is palsied by a coward's fear."[27]

The Second Wheeling Convention began by debating whether its purpose was to form a new state government loyal to the Union to counter the secessionist government in Richmond or to break away from the Old Dominion altogether. Led by Carlile, the delegates agreed to form a new state government, although one of the convention's first orders of business was to pass a resolution thanking the Federal government for the "prompt manner in which they have responded to our call for protection." The main business of the convention soon became to organize the government of Federal Virginia, since the delegates believed the actions taken in Richmond against the Union were illegal. If Letcher had harbored any real hopes of dissuading the Wheeling Convention from its work with his proclamation, he was disappointed. On June 17 the delegates in Wheeling responded by approving a Declaration of the People of Virginia that proclaimed that the Virginia Convention that had met in Richmond in February had abused the powers entrusted to it and exercised other powers that "will inevitably subject [the people of Virginia] to a military despotism." The declaration went on to state that the acts of the earlier Virginia Convention that tended "to separate this Commonwealth from the United States, or to levy and carry on war against them, are without authority and void." It concluded by declaring vacant the offices of any state officials who adhered to the Virginia Convention's actions, thereby clearing the way to form a new state government in Wheeling. The vote on the declaration was fifty-six for and none opposed. Carlile took the opportunity to add symbolism to the event by reminding the delegates that there had been fifty-six signers to the Declaration of Independence. His remarks brought "great applause and feeling" to the moment.[28]

On June 19 the convention enacted an ordinance that declared all state offices vacant and established a Reorganized Government of Virginia at Wheeling that remained loyal to the Union. The new state government included a governor, lieutenant governor, attorney general, and a five-member advisory committee to serve for six months or until elections could be held to elect their successors. Delegates who had been elected to the legislature and would swear their loyalty to the United States became the new legislature. The next day delegates unanimously elected Pierpont governor and selected an appropriate complement of state officials. Daniel Polsely became lieutenant governor and James S. Wheat, attorney general. Pierpont took charge of the Reorganized Government immediately and began the formidable task of assuming control of the machinery of state government. With Pierpont and the new state government organized and operating, the Second Wheeling Convention adjourned on June 25, after agreeing to reconvene on August 6.[29]

Governor Pierpont immediately set to work to make the Reorganized Government a reality. Since most of the sheriffs, county attorneys, and judges supported the Richmond government and secession, Pierpont needed troops to maintain order and protect life and property. His first action was to inform Lincoln by telegram of the actions taken in Wheeling and introduce himself as the governor of Virginia. The next day Pierpont sent a letter to confirm the telegram and request Federal assistance to suppress the rebellion and protect loyal citizens of Virginia. Four days after Pierpont sent his letter, the Federal response from the secretary of war, Simon Cameron, arrived addressed to the "Governor of the Commonwealth of Virginia." The letter recognized the new government, promised military support in the near future, and gave the loyal governor authority to raise troops and commission officers.[30]

Pierpont next turned to money. The first funds made available to the Reorganized Government were from Pierpont himself. He borrowed $10,000 from Wheeling banks on his personal note. Shortly thereafter he was able to obtain $44,857.13 from the Federal government under the provisions of the Distribution Act of 1841 that had allocated part of the proceeds from the sale of public lands in the western United States to be apportioned among the states. The act was repealed after one year, but Federal funds had been made available to the states in 1841. Virginia officials at the time, fearing acceptance of the money might compromise their strong feelings of states' rights, refused the money, so, upon Pierpont's request, it was made available to the Wheeling government. Upon learning that Letcher planned to withdraw $27,000 in state funds that were on deposit in the Exchange Bank of Weston in Lewis County for building a state hospital there, Pierpont dispatched John List to bring the money to Wheeling. When List requested military assistance to protect him from pro-Confederate secessionists, McClellan sent the Seventh Ohio, commanded by Colonel Erastus B. Tyler, a former fur trader who reportedly knew "every hog-path in Lewis County," to accompany the mission. The money was seized on June 30 and shortly thereafter was deposited in the Northwestern Bank of Virginia in Wheeling. As a result of his success at Weston, List was commissioned by Pierpont to visit other banks and sheriffs to appropriate any other state money in their possession, thereby providing additional revenue for the new government.[31]

Pierpont appointed James S. Wheat as temporary adjutant general to create a state military department that could raise forces and commission officers. Before the end of June, Pierpont was able to report to Secretary of War Cameron that the three regiments the president requested from Virginia had been formed, although the Second and Third remained without arms and equipment.[32]

The legislature of the new government met on July 2, and that body elected Carlile and Willey to fill Virginia's seats in the U.S. Senate. In the meantime, the Thirty-seventh Congress convened in special session with no members from Virginia present. On July 11 the seats were declared vacant, and Carlile and Willey were seated with a minimum of difficulty. In the House of Representatives five western men presented themselves as representatives of the Old Dominion, and they too were seated. The Reorganized Government had now been recognized by both the president and Congress as the lawful government of Virginia. Lincoln further recognized the Wheeling government in his Fourth of July message to Congress with the words: "These loyal citizens, this government is bound to recognize, and protect, as being Virginia."[33]

On July 22 the legislature of the Reorganized Government considered a bill to declare the western counties a new state. After much debate the legislature refused to adopt the bill, but it did pass a series of resolutions to consider separation from the eastern part of the state at a more opportune time. It also determined that the question should be referred to a convention rather than be considered by the legislature. The legislature called for a constitutional convention to meet on November 26 in Wheeling to take up the matter of forming a new state, tentatively to be called Kanawha.

Although the Wheeling state government got off to a good start, providing a rally point for pro-Union Virginians in the region, it never really controlled more than twenty or twenty-five counties in the northwest. The new government did not receive support from everyone in the western counties. Twenty-one western men remained in the Richmond legislature and others served in the Confederate congress. Allen T. Caperton, a lawyer and planter from Monroe County in the southern portion of western Virginia, became a Confederate senator, and five others, including Charles Wells Russell of Wheeling, held seats in the house of representatives in Richmond. Even in those counties that did respond to the Wheeling government, maintaining law and order was always problematic, frequently requiring the use of Federal troops to prevent disruptions during the elections.

Although the events of June in the northwest were a setback for Letcher and dimmed the hopes of keeping Virginia intact for the Confederacy, the issue had by no means been settled. Military reinforcements for the Confederate forces were on the way west even as the new Wheeling government began doing business. McClellan's forces may have won the first battle of the campaign, but the residents had not universally accepted the Federal occupation, and Lee was not ready to give up that easily.

CHAPTER SIX

Lee's Divided Command

T HE MILITARY DEBACLE at Philippi prompted action in Richmond. In early June, with the news of the Federal advance into the western counties and the upcoming convention in Wheeling, it was becoming more apparent that the people of western Virginia were not going to rise to the defense of the Old Dominion as Lee had anticipated in his mobilization planning for the state. Clearly, reinforcements and strong leadership would be needed if Virginia had any hope of holding on to its western counties.

When Porterfield was censured for his failure to take proper defensive measures at Philippi, Lee turned to his adjutant, Robert S. Garnett, to take command of the forces there. Garnett's mission in western Virginia was to prevent a further Federal advance along the Staunton-Parkersburg Turnpike and to take action against the Baltimore and Ohio Railroad. On June 6 Garnett received a commission as brigadier general in the Confederate army. An 1841 graduate of West Point and veteran of the Mexican War where he was twice breveted for gallantry, Garnett was considered one of the finest officers in the U.S. army at the time of his resignation to join Virginia's militia. Garnett had been the adjutant at West Point when Lee was the superintendent there, so they were well acquainted and used to working together. It is a measure of Lee's concern with the situation in the northwest that he sent Garnett, widely considered one of Virginia's best officers, to the west. Garnett, however, was not very optimistic about his new command, telling a friend just before he left Richmond that he felt he was being sent to his death.[1]

Meanwhile, Jefferson Davis, as president of the Confederacy, had commissioned Henry Wise a brigadier general in the Confederate army without consulting Lee, commander of Virginia's military forces, and given him authority to raise a legion of men. Davis sent Wise to the Kanawha Valley to take control of the defense there. With Floyd, Wise's one-time political rival, already raising a brigade in the southern end of the Valley of Virginia, Davis had unwittingly put in place elements that would create a spectacular personal feud between the two men. Floyd and Wise were both capable of the strong leadership required in the western counties. Unfortunately, neither was particularly interested in following anyone else's orders. As long as each had an independent command, it was possible that they could bolster the sagging defenses. But this division of authority further fragmented the Confederate command structure in western Virginia.

Davis's appointments of Floyd and Wise as brigadier generals apart, Lee had for some time been having difficulties with divided command authority, and the situation did not improve when Letcher transferred control of the military forces of Virginia to the Confederate army on May 8. The transfer of state forces to Confederate authority should have made it possible to bring all the defending forces in western Virginia under a single command, but it never

happened. Two days after the transfer, as the Confederate government settled into Richmond, Lee had been given command of Confederate forces operating in the Old Dominion, but on May 15,
again without consulting Lee, the War Department in Richmond
instructed Joseph E. Johnston, a brigadier general in the Confederate army, to take command of the forces at Harpers Ferry, replacing
Colonel Thomas J. Jackson who had been busy organizing the militia recruits there. A Virginia native, Johnston, the quartermaster
general in the U.S. army since 1860, had been the highest-ranking
officer to resign, and many thought him to be a more capable officer than Lee. As regiments from other Southern states arrived in
Virginia, the Confederate War Department assigned some of them
to Lee's control, but some were assigned to other Confederate commanders in Virginia without consulting him.[2]

With the transfer of state forces to the Confederate government,
Lee no longer had any troops to command. After completing his
report on the mobilization of Virginia military forces on June 15, he
became an advisor to President Davis in Richmond, acting as a sort
of assistant secretary of war. Both Davis and Lee followed events in
the west. Lee had been authorized to continue correspondence with
Garnett and receive reports of his activities, while Davis communicated with Wise. It was not the best way to ensure unity of effort by
the scattered Confederate forces in western Virginia.[3]

With the Federal army in Washington, D.C., occupying the attention of the military planners in Richmond, the lack of a unified Confederate command structure in western Virginia went largely
unnoticed. An invasion force traveling east through mountains had
only two avenues from Ohio to the Valley of Virginia: the railroad
and turnpikes in the northwest and the Kanawha Valley in the
south. Garnett had been sent to deal with McClellan's advance in
the northwest, and in June there was no Federal presence in the
Kanawha Valley to threaten Wise's activities. For the moment Davis
and Lee were comfortable with having two commanders in western

Virginia, both of whom reported directly to Richmond. Neither
Davis nor Lee anticipated that McClellan was planning a coordinated attack along both avenues under a single commander. Nor
did they forsee a situation in which the Confederate commanders in
the theater would not fully cooperate with one another against a
Federal threat.

After his retreat from Philippi, Porterfield, acting on his own,
moved his forces east and established his headquarters at Huttonsville, on the Staunton-Parkersburg Turnpike. Heck, in the meantime, had been raising the regiment Lee had authorized, and he also
assembled his recruits at Huttonsville. When Garnett arrived there
on June 14, he found the forces, twenty-three companies of infantry,
"in a miserable condition as to arms, clothing, equipment, instruc-
tion, and discipline." He organized twenty of the companies into two
infantry regiments of ten companies each. Porterfield, designated
colonel of the Twenty-fifth Virginia, did not ever serve in that capacity, leaving Heck, the regiment's lieutenant colonel, actually in command. The Thirty-first Virginia was commanded by Lieutenant
Colonel William L. Jackson, a resident of Parkersburg, former lieutenant governor of Virginia, and second cousin to Colonel Thomas
J. Jackson. The remaining companies became the Ninth Battalion
commanded by Lieutenant Colonel George A. Hansbourgh.[4]

After organizing his forces, Garnett planned to block the Federal
advance by establishing defensive positions on passes through the
Laurel Mountain range on the western edge of the Alleghenies. The
first position was on Laurel Hill where the Beverly-Fairmont Pike, a
north-south road that ran between the Northwestern and Staunton-
Parkersburg Turnpikes, crosses the mountain range. The second
position was at the western foot of Rich Mountain on the Staunton-
Parkersburg Turnpike itself. Although these two positions effectively blocked the turnpike, they were nine miles apart and did not
lend themselves to mutual support.

Garnett remained at Laurel Hill with most of his troops. The rest he deployed to Rich Mountain under Heck's command. The Rich Mountain force included the Twenty-fifth Virginia and the Churchville Cavalry company. The artillery consisted of three six-pounder cannons from the Danville Artillery and a section of the Eighth Star Artillery, so named because Virginia was the eighth state to secede from the Union. Unfortunately, the Eighth Star Artillery had no cannons of its own. It did bring four pieces of artillery into the Valley, but the unit was ordered to give them to a battery in Lynchburg. In the meantime the Eighth Star men drilled on the Danville guns in the hope of someday acquiring cannons of their own. Heck and his forces arrived at Rich Mountain and began to fortify the position, named Camp Garnett, on June 16.[5]

While Garnett organized his forces and prepared the defensive positions at Laurel Hill, McClellan departed by train from his head-quarters in Cincinnati on June 20 to take personal command of the campaign in western Virginia. The day he left for Virginia, McClellan telegraphed General Morris, commander of the Federal forces holding Grafton and Philippi, advising him that additional forces were on the way and cautioning him to "be prudent but do not give one inch that you can avoid." McClellan also told Morris that he had requested that a column of Pennsylvania troops move on Romney by way of Cumberland, Maryland, "to cut off retreat of the rebels."[6]

With his request for a supporting column from another department, McClellan demonstrated a grasp of warfare that went beyond the Napoleonic concept of seeking the big battle by concentrating forces. He saw the possibilities of having several different military departments provide mutual support to defeat an enemy by maneuver rather than sheer force. As commander of a military department, McClellan also had the capability to maneuver Federal forces on more than one axis of advance. On the Confederate side, however, the fragmented command structure in western Virginia mitigated against that possibility. Both Lee and McClellan sought to emulate Scott's performance in Mexico and avoid frontal assaults by using maneuver, but McClellan's unity of command in the theater of operations gave him a significant advantage over Lee, who had no single commander who was responsible for all of the Confederate forces operating in western Virginia.

McClellan reached Parkersburg on June 21. Along the way the ever-confident McClellan wrote his young wife of just over a year that he had been cheered at every station where crowds had assembled to get a look at the "Young General," as he styled himself. Mary Ellen Marcy McClellan, in her sixth month of pregnancy, remained in Cincinnati with her sister and mother who had joined her there when her father, Randolph Marcy, became McClellan's chief of staff. During the campaign McClellan, conscious of her condition, wrote to Mary Ellen frequently to assure her that he was safe and sound.[7]

At Parkersburg, Fuller, McClellan's assistant superintendent of military telegraphs, had been at work preparing for a novel experiment in military history—constructing a field telegraph to support an army as it advanced. Disparaging remarks by some regular army officers had not discouraged him, and both Fuller and his superior, Stager, were hopeful of demonstrating the capabilities of a field telegraph for military use in western Virginia. McClellan, however, already a believer, was prepared to take advantage of continuous communications with the War Department in Washington as well as other parts of his large command.[8]

In a telegram to the War Department sent from Parkersburg on June 22, McClellan reported his intent to move east that day toward Clarksburg and review the forces he had assembled for the advance. Although he intended to "be cautious in [his] movements," McClellan was confident that he had adequate force to fight the enemy wherever he might find them. Accompanied by his staff and escort of troops, he arrived in Grafton the next day at two o'clock in the morning. There, he issued a proclamation to the residents of western Virginia that the Federal forces were "enemies to none but armed rebels, and those voluntarily giving them aid." The feelings about volunteer troops that he had developed in Mexico had apparently not improved, witness his writing to Mary Ellen of the difficulties in getting "these Mohawks [a derisive term for volunteers in the Mexican War] in working trim."[9]

McClellan stayed at Grafton for about a week. His forces in western Virginia by then totaled about twenty thousand men. While at Grafton, McClellan wrote to Samuel P. Chase, the secretary of the treasury and former governor of Ohio who had expressed an interest in the welfare of the Ohio regiments, outlining his plans to move his main force from Clarksburg to Buckhannon and then to Beverly. Even as he worked out the tactics of advance against the Confederate positions, McClellan did not forget the strategic military objective of the campaign in western Virginia. He was confident, he wrote to Chase, that he would be able to sweep the enemy "into & across the mountains," after which he would "sweep the Kanawha & overrun the country with small columns & assure the Union men."[10]

When McClellan reached Buckhannon on July 2 he decided to take action against Wise's advance into the Kanawha Valley and sent orders to Cox, back in Cincinnati, to organize a brigade and move into Virginia. Once across the Ohio River, McClellan wanted Cox to "remain on the defensive & endeavor to keep the rebels near Charleston until I [McClellan] can cut off their retreat by movement from Beverly." In ordering Cox to move into the Kanawha Valley, McClellan was exercising unity of command and taking advantage of strategic mobility. He was in direct command of the forces advancing on Garnett, but Cox also reported to him while he prepared to move into the Kanawha Valley. Because McClellan commanded all of the Federal troops in the theater of operations, he could maneuver his forces more efficiently than the Confederate forces that were scattered about western Virginia under a variety of commanders. Since he also had the telegraph, which allowed him to coordinate operations on two axes of advance into western Virginia, he could conclude his telegram to Cox with the instructions to "[c]ommunicate frequently. A telegraph line follows me out." By July 5 the Federal field telegraph was in operation in Buckhannon. Now that he was in the field, McClellan had a personal bodyguard of troops, Company A of the Second Virginia Infantry. The company had been organized in April in Pittsburgh, but when it was not accepted by Pennsylvania, the unit had moved to Wheeling where it was mustered into service on May 21. It accompanied Kelley's regiment to Grafton where it remained until detached as McClellan's bodyguard.[11]

With McClellan already advancing toward his positions, on July 5 Garnett wrote Lee that he did not think the enemy would advance further into Virginia. Lee, however, now fully aware of the Federal threat from Ohio and the potential loss of the western counties, sent a message to Garnett on July 11 warning that he did "not think it probable that the enemy will confine himself to that portion of the northwest country which he now holds, but, if he can drive you back, will endeavor to penetrate as far as Staunton." Lee, in Richmond, recognized that a Federal advance all the way to Staunton would open the Shenandoah Valley to Union occupation from the west, and he sent a message informing Garnett of that concern. But it was too late. By the time Garnett had dispatched his erroneous estimate of the situation, McClellan and the Federals were already moving toward him in force.[12]

Both Ohio and Indiana continued to send regiments into the Old Dominion, and McClellan reported the disposition of his considerable forces already in western Virginia to the War Department on July 5. Morris and his Indiana brigade remained at Philippi with instructions from McClellan to keep the Confederates at Laurel Hill amused and to be prepared to advance against the defensive positions. McClellan organized the regiments with him into two brigades, one commanded by Rosecrans, the other by Brigadier General Newton Schleich, an Ohio politician commissioned at the same time as Cox. McClellan was somewhat less than enthusiastic about his immediate subordinates, commenting in a candid letter to his wife on July 3 that "I have not a Brig Genl worth his salt–Morris is a timid old woman–Rosecranz [sic] a silly fussy goose–Schleich knows nothing."[13]

In addition to the forces arrayed in front of Garnett at Laurel Hill, McClellan had left Brigadier General Charles W. Hill, a Vermont native who had been active in the Ohio militia before the war, in Grafton to defend the railroad lines and the Cheat River. To do this Hill had three Ohio regiments. There were eleven companies along the Cheat River to cover the Federal left flank; a regiment at Grafton; eight companies at Clarksburg along with some local recruits; six companies at Parkersburg with two Indiana regiments on the way to that location; and two more Indiana regiments on the way to Bellaire just across the Ohio River from Wheeling. There were also six companies of Ohio militia in Wirt County Court House, just south of Parkersburg where, McClellan reported, "Union men have suffered much." Near Ravenswood, a town on the Ohio River, Federal troops had recently made contact with a Confederate force commanded by Captain O. J. Wise, son of General Wise who was by now conducting operations in the Kanawha Valley. This made Cox's impending move more important. A strong push north along the Ohio River by Confederate forces from the Kanawha Valley would threaten the Federal line of communications back to Ohio.[14]

In spite of his reservations about his brigadiers, McClellan was confident of success as he prepared his forces for battle. Troop morale was high and improving daily. The local populace acclaimed them wherever they went. As McClellan prepared his plans, the lessons from Scott's use of maneuver in Mexico and his own observations at Sebastopol–that even temporary defensive positions can be very difficult to assault–influenced him. His goal in the upcoming battle was to attain success by "manoeuvering rather than by fighting." McClellan sought to avoid sending "these men of mine into the teeth of artillery & intrenchments" by repeating Scott's "manoeuvre of Cerro Gordo."[15]

McClellan knew of the Confederate defensive positions at Laurel Hill between Philippi and Beverly. By moving south from Clarksburg he would reach the Staunton-Parkersburg Turnpike at Weston where he could then move east to Buckhannon, putting him south of Laurel Hill with the main force of about eight thousand men, while Morris's brigade remained at Philippi with about four thousand troops. The remainder of the forces were dispersed along the Northwestern and Baltimore and Ohio Railroads to prevent Confederate interference with the lines. McClellan's plan was for Morris to advance on Laurel Hill while he attacked the positions at Rich Mountain. Whether by chance or design, McClellan was preparing to attack the weaker Confederate defensive position with the bulk of his forces.

McClellan celebrated the Fourth of July in Buckhannon with a review of the Third and Fourth Ohio. The Third Ohio remembered the day of the review as "excessively warm, and the men, buttoned up in their dress coats, were much wearied when the parade was over." In the Fourth Ohio, the review had a more positive effect. Those troops were reportedly inspired "with confidence that their commander knew how to handle his troops, be they few or many." Conducting a review to inspire his troops was something McClellan had proved he could do, but he had yet to maneuver his forces in battle.[16]

McClellan planned to begin the move against Rich Mountain on July 6, but in consonance with his penchant for detailed preparations and concern for defensive positions he intended to move slowly. He expressed concern to his wife that he needed to be very cautious because "everything requires success in my first operation." A good part of his cautious preparations entailed building up a stock of supplies before he continued his campaign into western Virginia. While he did not specify just what "everything" entailed, it was probably a combination of his ambition to be recognized for his military accomplishments, his concern for the lives of his men, and the need to impress the pro-Union supporters in western Virginia with a Federal victory. Whatever the reason, on July 7 he was still in Buckhannon where Fuller had established a telegraph station on July 5. The delay might have been longer, but Captains Saxton and McFeeley, McClellan's chief quartermaster and chief commissary, both acknowledged that without the telegraph, McClellan could not have moved as soon as he did. They credited the telegraph because it gave them the capability to order needed supplies quickly and receive acknowledgment that they were on the way. Even at this early stage of the war, Federal forces were reluctant to move until there was an adequate supply base for their planned operations. Bolstered by the support for his field telegraph, Fuller prepared to follow the Federal advance to Rich Mountain.[17]

While McClellan prepared to advance, Garnett increased his forces. During June three regiments–the Twenty-third Virginia Infantry, commanded by Colonel William Booth Taliaferro, an aristocratic officer who had served in the Mexican War and had commanded the Virginia militia forces at Harpers Ferry during John Brown's raid; the Thirty-seventh Virginia Infantry, commanded by Colonel Samuel Vance Fulkerson, a lawyer and judge who had served in a Tennessee regiment in the Mexican War; and the First Georgia Infantry, under the command of Colonel J. N. Ramsey–all arrived to bolster the Confederate defenses on Laurel Hill. These forces were new to war, and for many battle would come as a rude awakening to the grim realities of war rather than the grand adventure they had anticipated when they enlisted.[18]

The men of the Twenty-third Virginia had had a pleasant trip west. They had traveled by train to Staunton in sunny weather and had been cheered along the way by crowds who had gathered to see them. Although the march from Staunton found "fifty or sixty men falling from the ranks every day from sheer exhaustion," one of the new soldiers later recalled that he had been "filled with admiration and wonder at the grandeur and sublimity of the scenery." Like the Ohio and Indiana soldiers on the other side of the hill, the Virginians of the Twenty-third were new to the area. Before long, the weather and the mountains would take on a rather different appearance to them.[19]

Among the companies that had been organized into the Thirty-seventh Virginia was the Glade Spring Rifle Company, "brought into existence at a great rally of the people" on April 16 at Abingdon, Virginia, where they had gathered as a result of the firing on Fort Sumter. The ninety men of the company soon "became proficient in company drill and attracted much attention among the ladies." By May 25, when the Glade Spring Rifles were mustered into the Confederate army, the company had acquired two flags, made and presented by local women. The first was from a Miss Doran and the other from Mrs. Sallie Floyd, wife of Brigadier General John B. Floyd, who had recently been appointed by President Davis to raise a brigade for service in western Virginia. According to the second lieutenant of the company, P. S. Hagy, as the company moved to Richmond to become part of the Thirty-seventh Virginia, "many of the boys appeared to consider [the trip] as a holiday excursion and kept up a jollification all the way except in their hours of sleep."[20]

In his first detailed situation report to Lee on June 25 Garnett stated that most of the people in the area were opposed to secession and that he was finding it almost impossible to gather any accurate information about the number and location of Federal forces facing him. He also reported the disposition of his forces, writing that he regarded "these two passes as the gates to the northwestern country, and, had they been occupied by the enemy, my command would have been effectually paralyzed or shut up in the Cheat River Valley." He went on to outline plans for threatening the Baltimore and Ohio Railroad by moving a force to Evansville, a town on the

Northwestern Turnpike about halfway between Grafton and the railroad bridge across the Cheat River, in the hope of luring away the Federal forces defending those locations. In the event there was no Federal reaction to that move, Garnett planned to destroy the rail lines at Independence, some five miles from Evansville, and attack the Federals at the Cheat River bridge. But to do all that he needed significant assistance from local western Virginians, and since there was little of that available to him, he concentrated on preparing defensive positions.[21]

On July 1, with about 4,600 men in his command, Garnett asked for further reinforcements, believing he could not recruit nearly enough local forces effectively to defend the passes. He also expressed the opinion that if Wise and his legion, which by this time had advanced well into the Kanawha Valley, were to move toward Parkersburg in force, it would threaten the Federal rear and might relieve some of the pressure from McClellan. Lee already had more troops on the way to Garnett, and he communicated the idea of cooperation to Wise. By the time Wise responded with all the reasons why he could not, and should not, comply with Garnett's suggestion, it was too late to do anything to help the Confederates defending Rich Mountain. The lack of a single overall Confederate commander located in western Virginia to facilitate communications among forces operating in the theater continued to make it difficult, if not impossible, to coordinate the defense there, even in the face of a significant Federal threat.[22]

Meanwhile, at Camp Garnett, located at the base of the Rich Mountain site, troops built fortifications on both sides of the turnpike and cleared trees and brush for a distance of 150 yards in front of their positions in anticipation of a frontal attack by the advancing Federal forces. The four artillery pieces were spread along the defensive line, one at each end, with the other two in the center. Local Confederate sympathizers assured the defenders that there was no way to flank the position. In June Major Nat Tyler with eight companies of the Twentieth Virginia arrived at Camp Garnett. The regiment had been organized by Lieutenant Colonel John Pegram, a former U.S. army officer who arrived a few days after Tyler with the other companies. When Pegram arrived, he immediately claimed command of Camp Garnett because he held a commission in the regular Confederate army, while Heck held his rank only in the Virginia militia. Pegram had been a lieutenant in the Second Dragoons, spent two years in Europe, and had fine social graces, but he possessed no more experience of war than Heck and knew nothing of the wild mountain country surrounding Rich Mountain. While Pegram did assume command of the position, his attitude did not endear him to the volunteer officers there.[23]

Arriving with Pegram was Jedediah Hotchkiss, a native of Connecticut. In 1846, while on a tour of western Virginia, he accepted a position as a tutor in Mossy Creek where he eventually established his own academy. In 1859 he and his brother opened the Loch Willow Academy near Churchville, Virginia. The school did quite well until Virginia seceded from the Union, at which time a number of students volunteered for military service. Hotchkiss closed the academy. His hobby was mapmaking, and he had come west with the troops to offer his services to Garnett. With his natural instinct for terrain, he quickly adapted to the rugged hill country and produced several maps of the Confederate positions at Rich Mountain.[24]

On July 6 McClellan sent Morris instructions to move his forces down the Beverly-Fairmont Pike to Belington and prepare to pursue a Confederate retreat from Laurel Hill in anticipation of the success of the Federal move against Rich Mountain. While McClellan was making meticulous preparations to ensure all went according to his plans, Schleich became impatient and sent out a reconnoitering force toward Rich Mountain. The opening skirmish of the battle took place when a detail of about fifty men from the Third Ohio exchanged fire with pickets of the Twenty-fifth Virginia who were guarding the bridge at Roaring Creek at the foot of Rich Mountain.

The brief flurry of activity left one Ohio soldier, Private Samuel Johns, dead, and five others wounded. The defenders held their positions, suffering only three wounded.[25]

When news of the skirmish reached McClellan, he was furious. The unauthorized reconnaissance cost Schleich his job, and he was soon on his way back to Ohio. On July 10 McClellan sent McCook, now leading a brigade of two regiments, the Fourth Ohio and his own Ninth Ohio, reinforced with a battery of artillery and a company of cavalry, to conduct a reconnaissance in force. The Confederate pickets, Higginbotham's Upshur Grays, now Company A in the Twenty-fifth Virginia, wisely fell back after a few shots at the larger Federal force. As they fell back, they met Tyler coming forward with two companies of the Twentieth Virginia, but they were no match for the two Ohio regiments. In the ensuing retreat two Confederates were captured by the Federals. Higginbotham reported of the incident that he got his "pants and boot-legs riddled with bullets, but without serious injury 'in fact no meat hurt.' " The Confederate withdrawal left the Ohio regiments in possession of the crossing at Roaring Creek, about two miles from Camp Garnett on Rich Mountain. During the skirmish Lieutenant Poe, the engineer who had earlier gathered intelligence in western Virginia for McClellan prior to the invasion, found a low ridge that offered a potential site for artillery that might provide flanking fire into the Confederate position if a road could be cleared to get the guns there, but he was unable to locate a route by which the defenses might be turned by maneuver as McClellan had hoped. The two prisoners added to McClellan's anxiety and reinforced his propensity to overestimate the defenders by claiming that there were eight thousand to nine thousand troops backed by artillery behind the defensive works when, in reality, the number was closer to thirteen hundred. From McClellan's perspective, the prospects for another Cerro Gordo did not look good.[26]

While McCook and his Ohioans were busy at Roaring Creek,

Morris, complying with McClellan's instructions, had moved his brigade toward the positions on Laurel Hill with the veterans of the Battle of Philippi, the Seventh and Ninth Indiana and the Fourteenth Ohio, leading the way. Garnett's defenses on Laurel Hill consisted of "earthworks along a low ridge of a hill . . . constructed of stone, felled trees, and abatis." Early on the morning of July 7 pickets from the Twenty-third Virginia saw the approaching Federals, fired a few shots, and headed for Laurel Hill to alert the defenders. Garnett sent Ramsey and his First Georgia to support the pickets who had already moved a half mile to the rear. Ramsey immediately ordered a charge, and the Georgians pushed the Ninth Indiana and Fourteenth Ohio back. The Federals set up their own positions, and the two sides settled in to engage in periodic skirmishes that occupied them for the next few days.[27]

Back at Camp Garnett, Pegram was watching the Federal activities from his position on Rich Mountain. Unlike McClellan, he underestimated the forces facing him and considered attacking the Federals with his 1,300 or so troops. Garnett discouraged his enthusiastic subordinate from doing anything rash. While Pegram had to give up his thoughts for an attack, the Federals were planning for an assault on Rich Mountain on July 11. Neither McClellan, advocate of maneuver, nor Rosecrans, whose brigade was slated to make the attack, was particularly happy with the idea of a frontal assault, but that appeared to be the only choice until a local teenager appeared in the Federal encampment the day before the planned attack with an alternative. The young man, David B. Hart, lived with his family on a small farm just two miles behind and above the Confederate positions near the spot where the turnpike crossed the summit of Rich Mountain. He claimed to know of a path that would take the attacking troops around the left flank of the defensive line. Questioned by Rosecrans about the route, Hart assured the general that the path would provide for the passage of a considerable force and even offered his services as a guide. Rosecrans, excited by the prospect of avoiding a costly frontal assault, went to McClellan at about 10 P.M. on July 10 with a proposal for a move around the Confederate left flank.[28]

McClellan was not quite as enthusiastic as Rosecrans about young Hart's proposal. He listened to Rosecrans's arguments and studied a sketch of the proposed flanking movement. Marcy, McClellan's chief of staff and father-in-law, however, was satisfied that the plan would work, and Rosecrans argued that he could lead his brigade around the flank and be in position to attack by 10 A.M. the next morning. By midnight McClellan gave his reluctant approval, but he stipulated that he had to receive hourly reports on the progress of the flanking march. The revised plan called for McClellan to lead an attack on the front of the Confederate positions when Rosecrans reached the top of the mountain and was ready to strike from the flank. With little time to spare, Rosecrans returned to his brigade to give the necessary orders; McClellan wanted them on the move at 4 A.M.[29]

During the night regimental commanders prepared their troops for battle. In the Third Ohio, Colonel Andrews ordered his troops out of their tents shortly after midnight so he could address them. In an effort to impress them with the seriousness of the impending attack, Andrews informed his soldiers that they had been selected to lead the assault against a larger force in a heavily fortified position reinforced with cannon. "Marching to attack such an enemy so intrenched and so armed is marching to a butcher shop rather than to a battle," he declared solemnly. After that speech, with thoughts of mothers, wives, and sweethearts they might never see again, the soldiers of the Third did not get much sleep, but by dawn they were again excited about the prospect of their first battle. But when the sun came up, they found themselves detailed to guard the baggage trains while other regiments marched to the assault line.[30]

Rosecrans's troops were awakened at 3 A.M. and given a day's rations. He had four infantry regiments and a company of cavalry in

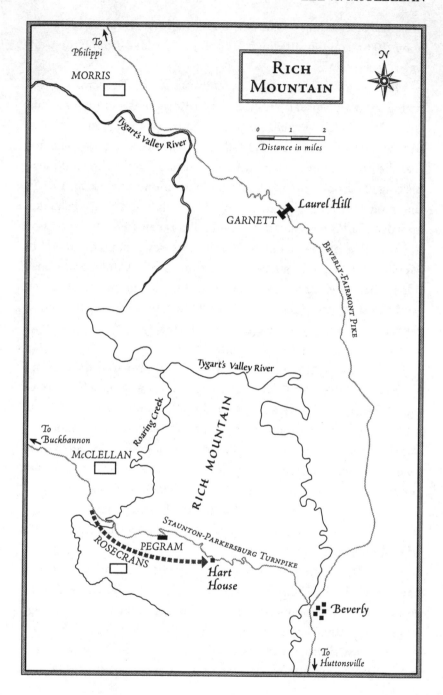

his brigade totaling almost two thousand men. The Eighth Indiana was first in the order of march, followed by the Tenth and Thirteenth Indiana and the Nineteenth Ohio. Burdsall's Cavalry brought up the rear, charged with the mission of providing the messengers that were to keep McClellan informed of Rosecrans's progress and position during the march. In spite of the order to prepare quietly, bugles sounding assembly and lights in the camp of the Nineteenth Ohio alerted the Confederates at Camp Garnett that something was going on. With the bugles quickly silenced and the lights quenched, the brigade moved out with young Hart and Lander of McClellan's staff leading the way through the dense woods and laurel thickets.[31]

At 6 A.M., with the brigade well on its way up the mountain, it began to rain. Lander, veteran of the rain-soaked night march at Philippi in June, pushed on through the downpour without stopping. But, as at Philippi, the march did not occur precisely as planned. Clawing their way through thick vegetation, heavy with rainwater, the troops took almost seven hours longer than the anticipated three hours to complete the march. The delay worried McClellan, who was not receiving the hourly reports he wanted, so he decided to call the whole thing off. He dispatched a messenger from the First Ohio Cavalry, Sergeant David A. Wolcott, to recall Rosecrans. Things did not go well for Wolcott. On his way out of the Federal position, he was stopped by pickets from the Third Ohio, who had been left to guard the Federal camp from a possible Confederate attack. They tried to tell him that he was on the wrong road, that he was not heading in the same direction that Rosecrans and his brigade had gone some hours earlier. When Wolcott insisted he was on orders from McClellan himself, the pickets relented, and the messenger headed up the turnpike, straight toward the Confederate position. Shortly after passing the pickets, Wolcott was shot from his horse and taken prisoner.[32]

Pegram had been expecting an attack. As he made his final preparations for the inevitable Federal assault, he learned of the possibility of a flanking attack from McClellan's message that Wolcott was carrying to Rosecrans. Garnett had earlier alerted Pegram that there was an overgrown roadway that connected with a little used footpath that wound its way to Roaring Creek on the right flank of the position, so that is where he expected the Federal attack. That belief was reinforced when Wolcott was captured on the right. Pegram sent Captain Julius A. De Lagnel, an artilleryman who had served fourteen years in the U.S. army, with one of his guns, a six-pounder commanded by Lieutenant Charles Statham, and five understrength infantry companies with a total of about three hundred men from the Twentieth and Twenty-fifth Virginia back toward the top of the pass over Rich Mountain where the Hart house, home of the young man guiding Rosecrans, was located. In the meantime, the irrepressible Higginbotham had twice sent word to Pegram that his soldiers had been hearing the sounds of chopping off to the left, but the young captain was told "to mind his own business." In planning for the impending assault, Pegram also knew that Colonel William C. Scott and his Forty-fourth Virginia Infantry had stopped for the night in Beverly on their way to reinforce Garnett at Laurel Hill. The regiment had orders from Garnett to hasten their march to Laurel Hill on July 11, but no sooner had they started north than Pegram sent an urgent message telling Scott to move west of Beverly and put his regiment in a position on the Staunton-Parkersburg Turnpike at the intersection of Merritt Road, a potential route into the rear of the Confederate positions. Pegram also assured Scott that he would let Garnett know that the orders to proceed to Laurel Hill had been changed. Scott, who "supposed the enemy were already in their march," turned his regiment around and headed back to Beverly in accordance with Pegram's wishes.[33]

Rosecrans, struggling along with Lander and Hart in the rain and unaware of McClellan's decision to discontinue the attack, was running hours behind schedule. When he finally reached the summit about noon, he called a halt for his weary troops while he and

Lander took a look around. They found they were still some distance from the Hart farm, and while their presence had not yet been detected by the Confederate defenders who were looking for an attack on their right, neither were the Federal attackers aware that there were troops waiting around the two-story Hart house. De Lagnel and a number of companies from the Twentieth and Twenty-fifth Virginia were preparing defensive positions in anticipation of an attack from their right flank using logs they found lying around the Hart property. Rosecrans began to move across the small valley toward the house between 2 and 3 P.M., with the Tenth Indiana, commanded by Colonel Joseph John Reynolds, an 1843 graduate of West Point, leading the way. Company A, deployed ahead of the advancing regiment as skirmishers, shortly came under fire from the Confederate pickets. The brief exchange came as a surprise to both sides. The Federals, thinking they had been led into a trap by the young Hart, halted the attack. The Confederate pickets quickly returned to their lines to report that the attack was coming from the left rather than the right as they had been led to expect.[34]

Both sides took advantage of the lull to adjust to the situation. Sheltered by woods, the Federals formed a line of battle with the Tenth Indiana in the center, the Thirteenth Indiana on the right, and the Nineteenth Ohio on the left. The Confederates reacted to the Federal attack by moving their positions to meet the assault that was about to come from their left. As the Federal line emerged from the underbrush, it came under immediate fire from the Virginians' muskets and Statham's six-pounder firing spherical shot. The fire forced a short halt by the Federals. Encouraged, the Confederates thought they had won and expressed their relief with loud shouts. At about the same time, there were reports of a large body of infantry advancing from Beverly, but it soon retreated back down the hill, playing no role in the battle. De Lagnel immediately dispatched a messenger to Pegram to let him know the Federal attack had come and been repelled. But a battle is not over until both sides

agree, and Rosecrans was not ready to concede. He ordered the
Eighth Indiana to march in column through the line of battle and
attack the cannon. Their first time under fire and the normal chaos
of battle combined to confuse the Indianans, and they became part
of the line rather than passing through it. Their enthusiasm, however, infected the entire brigade and resulted in a charge that dispersed the defenders and overwhelmed the Confederate position.[35]

Down in Camp Garnett, Pegram on the morning of July 11 faced
a dilemma. He was confronted by the possibility of attack from both
front and rear. After he learned of the Federal flank attack by Rosecrans, there had been a brief action in front of the Confederate position. The Third Ohio had finally been ordered into action, and
Major J. Warren Keifer, in charge of the Federal picket line along
Roaring Creek, had led a small force of the eager Ohioans forward
but had been driven off by cannon fire. Pegram, hearing the sounds
of the firefight near the Hart house to his rear at about the same
time as the Ohio engagement, rushed toward the sound of the guns
behind him only to discover that his troops there were on the brink
of collapse. Pegram returned to Camp Garnett with the idea of organizing a counterattack to drive Rosecrans off the high ground. He
started back toward the Hart house with six companies of infantry
and a cannon, but before the relief force could reach a position to
aid in the defense, it had to retreat. After briefly consulting with the
other officers, who did not have a lot of faith in him after his earlier
altercation with Heck, Pegram decided that an attack on Rosecrans's forces would be useless. He therefore ordered Tyler to take
the five companies of the Twentieth and one company from the
Twenty-fifth Virginia and lead the small force out of the area and
either join Garnett at Laurel Hill or Scott and the Forty-fourth Virginia, waiting on the turnpike. At 6:30 P.M., after sending Tyler and
his charges on their way, Pegram set out to return to Camp Garnett.
It took him five hours to negotiate the two miles or so back to the
camp because, believing that the area would be swarming with

Federals, he stayed off the turnpike and avoided the roads, taking whatever trail he could find. Drenching rain and a fall from his horse did not improve his spirits. While Pegram struggled through the dark, Tyler successfully led his small force to Beverly where they joined Scott the next morning.[36]

While Rosecrans was fighting, McClellan was fretting. He had moved the Fourth and Ninth Ohio forward in anticipation of attacking Camp Garnett in coordination with Rosecrans's flank attack, and he had also assigned the Fourth Ohio the job of clearing the way for the artillery to be positioned on the ridge that Poe had located earlier. But by midafternoon the guns were not in place to support the attack, nor was he receiving the hourly reports he wanted from Rosecrans. When the sounds of gunfire began, three hours later than expected, he hesitated to initiate the assault against Camp Garnett. When McClellan and his staff galloped forward to investigate the gunfire, they stopped in the midst of the Third Ohio, "and a thousand faces turned to hear the order to attack; but no order was given." Instead, the general sat on his horse, "indecision stamped on every line of his countenance." In the heat of the moment, McClellan seemed to forget his own admonition in his cavalry regulations that "no general need hesitate more than a few minutes when he finds himself in the presence of the enemy." Unsure of the meaning of the gunfire in the distance and believing the worst when he heard the cheering from the Confederate position in front of him that resulted from De Lagnel's premature news of repelling Rosecrans, McClellan finally decided to withdraw his forces to Roaring Creek. McClellan, certain that Rosecrans had been defeated, planned to attack the next day. He hoped to have artillery support for the frontal assault from the ridge Poe had found. By dusk the road to the artillery position was finished, but only one gun had been emplaced. McClellan left the Ninth Ohio to guard the artillery, pulled in the picket line, and returned to Roaring Creek for the night.[37]

After clearing the defenders from the field around the Hart house, Rosecrans occupied the top of Rich Mountain and prepared for a counterattack. The Federals were now holding positions astride the Staunton-Parkersburg Turnpike, cutting off Camp Garnett from Beverly. Any Confederate movement along the turnpike would have to come through the farm, and Rosecrans expected there would be an attempt to clear the road since there were still Confederate forces on both sides of his newly won position. He had learned from a prisoner that the Forty-fourth Virginia held the road to Beverly and that there were more troops still in Camp Garnett, so Rosecrans prepared to defend another attack from either end of the short length of road he held.[38]

While Rosecrans consolidated his position, Pegram was wearily wending his way back to Camp Garnett. Reaching the position just before midnight, Pegram found a tired, wet, disheartened force. Heck, in the absence of Pegram, or any clear idea of the situation facing him, had taken command of the position and held a short meeting with the officers there. They had decided they would continue the defense, but on Pegram's return, the officers reconvened and all agreed that in light of the situation they should join forces with Garnett on Laurel Hill as soon as possible. Pegram, exhausted by his efforts that day, looked to Heck to lead the men out with Hotchkiss's assistance. He planned to stay with Doctor Archibald Taylor of the Hardy Blues to attend to the sick and wounded who would stay in Camp Garnett and wait for the Federal occupation of the position. At about 1 A.M. on July 12 the column began to make its way toward Laurel Hill. Captain Robert Doak Lilley, the Augusta-Lee Rifles, and Company C of the Twenty-Fifth Virginia were in front while Hotchkiss, the guide, took the lead. Facing torrents of rain, the march was miserable and confusing for the tired, hungry men. Moving troops at night in wet weather is not an easy thing to do as the Federals already had found out at Philippi and again during their recent movement around the Confederate flank at Rich Mountain. With new troops it becomes almost impossible. The Confederate withdrawal from Camp Garnett ran into trouble almost immediately.[39]

As the last of the six hundred troops started out of Camp Garnett, Pegram had second thoughts about staying behind and decided to join the bedraggled column. He sent his orderly forward to halt the column while he moved to join Heck and Hotchkiss and take charge of the withdrawal. But the courier did not get all the way forward, and the order to halt did not reach Hotchkiss at the head of the column. When the mapmaker reached the crest of the mountain about daylight, he was surprised to find only about fifty men of the Augusta-Lee Rifles still behind them. Deciding that the best thing to do was to move along, Hotchkiss and Lilley led the small column along the same road that Tyler had successfully used earlier, and they reached Beverly about 11 A.M. After a brief stop to gather a few supplies, the party continued to move south, arriving at Huttonsville in midafternoon. Upon reaching the head of the stopped column, Pegram discovered the error, but there was nothing to be done at that point. He took command from Heck and proceeded to lead the force aimlessly through the wet night. At dawn the column was in sight of Beverly, but mistaking Hotchkiss's small group in the distance for Federals, Pegram decided not to head for town and stayed in the mountains. That night Pegram, "exhausted and very weak," according to Heck, decided to surrender. After consulting with his officers about surrendering, only two, Heck and J. B. Moorman, opposed the idea. About midnight Pegram wrote a note from his headquarters at "Mr. Kettle's House" offering McClellan the surrender of the exhausted troops under his command as prisoners of war. McClellan accepted the offer, and 553 officers and men laid down their arms on July 13 at Beverly. Pegram served a short captivity, and after a prisoner exchange returned to the Confederate army where he rose to the rank of brigadier general before being killed in action in February 1865.[40]

While Pegram had been preparing for the withdrawal from Camp Garnett, Rosecrans had organized his defenses and sent pickets out to be sure they were not surprised during the night. About 3 A.M. the pickets captured a prisoner who informed them that Camp Garnett had been abandoned. Rosecrans organized his forces to move west along the turnpike and investigate. Taking no chances, he sent Company C of Reynold's Tenth Indiana and Burdsall's Cavalry down the road while the Nineteenth Ohio covered the south side and the Thirteenth the north. They moved cautiously down the turnpike and reached Camp Garnett at 6 A.M., finding it under a white flag with "about a hundred and seventy men, with all their artillery, transportation, camp and garrison equipage, and quartermaster's stores."[41]

Garnett, waiting in his position at Laurel Hill, received little news of the events on Rich Mountain during the course of the day. To his front Morris, in accordance with his instructions from McClellan, was amusing the Confederate positions with periodic artillery fire. But from all outward appearances Garnett remained relatively unconcerned with events during the day. He knew of the threat to Pegram's forces and communicated by messenger with Scott and the Forty-fourth Virginia near Beverly, reminding them to be prepared to assist Pegram if necessary. Garnett also instructed Scott to keep him informed of any enemy movements in the area.[42]

Scott had a more exciting, if more futile, day than Garnett. Hearing the sounds of gunfire from the top of Rich Mountain, he sent a civilian volunteer from Beverly, John M. Hughes, who had been a delegate to the Virginia Convention, to find out how Pegram wanted the Forty-fourth Virginia to assist him. Unfortunately, De Lagnel's pickets shot and killed Hughes, mistaking him for a Federal in the excitement of battle. When Hughes did not return, Scott moved his regiment a bit further up the eastern side of the mountain where it had been seen by the Confederates at the Hart house. As Scott advanced toward the fighting, Lieutenant A. Cochrane of the

Churchville Cavalry met him and reported that De Lagnel needed help. But before long, the firing stopped and was replaced with the cheers of the victorious Federals. Private Richard J. Lipford, standing nearby, volunteered to ride forward and investigate. Scott provided the private a horse, and he headed up the hill, but he was quickly captured by the waiting Federals. After another brief conference with Cochrane, Scott once again turned the Forty-fourth around and headed toward Beverly, where he provisioned the regiment, intending to join Garnett at Laurel Hill. But before he could issue the order, Lieutenant Colonel James L. Hubbard, the regiment's second ranking officer, started toward Huttonsville, not Laurel Hill. Scott stopped the regiment about two miles south of Beverly and again countermarched his troops back to the town. Upon his arrival in Beverly, the news of Garnett's withdrawal was waiting, giving Scott no alternative but to order the regiment to retrace its steps once more. The Forty-fourth finally left Beverly about midnight, headed south toward Huttonsville with "a train one, two, three miles in length," by Scott's rather imprecise estimate.[43]

Garnett learned of the defeat at Rich Mountain sometime during the evening of July 11. He quickly realized that the situation rendered the position on Laurel Hill untenable and began preparations for his forces to march south. He ordered the tents left in place and managed to get his forces under way without being detected by Morris. Initially, Garnett planned to move to Beverly before the Federals blocked access to the Staunton-Parkersburg Turnpike. But before he reached the town, he received the erroneous information that it had been occupied, so he turned north, planning to move around the northern end of the mountain to Staunton.[44]

While Garnett moved north with the forces from Laurel Hill, Scott and the Forty-fourth Virginia were on their way south to Huttonsville, Hotchkiss and Lilley's company were on their way across Rich Mountain to Beverly, and Tyler, with the companies of the Twentieth and Twenty-fifth Virginia, were with Scott. On July 12, Scott, Tyler, and Lilley all made it to Huttonsville, and from there they continued their retreat along the Staunton-Parkersburg Turnpike to Monterey, a town located on the eastern side of the pass over Cheat Mountain, leaving that critical route open to the Federal advance.[45]

While the Confederates were fleeing in all directions, McClellan was slow in taking up the pursuit. His forces at Roaring Creek had been up most of the night, not knowing what fate had befallen Rosecrans's brigade on Rich Mountain. Torrential rains chilled the troops as they anxiously awaited the dawn. As his artillery was finally moving into position, McClellan learned that Rosecrans held Camp Garnett, leaving the turnpike to Beverly open to the Federal forces. But McClellan did not push the advantage Rosecrans had gained, and it was noon before any Federal forces moved into Beverly. McClellan sent McCook's brigade through Beverly along the turnpike, and they occupied the pass over Cheat Mountain on July 14. From Beverly McClellan sent a message to Morris informing him of the success at Rich Mountain and telling him not to attack until he received further orders.[46]

McClellan continued to benefit enormously from the field telegraph. When the telegraph lines reached Rich Mountain on July 12, a Confederate prisoner took note and remarked to a comrade, "My God, Jim, no wonder they whipped us; they have got the telegraph with them." Fuller soon had an office set up in Beverly, and by the 15th there was a station in Huttonsville and the line extended to the pass on Cheat Mountain. Telegraph operator J. L. Cherry reported for duty in the Beverly office on July 15. Upon learning that Cherry's avocation was printing, McClellan procured a portable printing press and began mass producing messages and proclamations intended for public consumption.[47]

The Federal victory at Rich Mountain had opened the Staunton-Parkersburg Turnpike as far as Cheat Mountain, and it forced Garnett to evacuate the Confederate position at Laurel Hill. With Beverly in Federal hands, that position could be turned from the rear. Garnett, therefore, was in an untenable position with the forces under Morris to his front and McClellan threatening him from the rear.

While McClellan and Rosecrans had been at work at Rich Mountain, Morris had been occupying Garnett's attention in front of Laurel Hill as instructed. But exchanging the occasional shot with Confederate pickets soon became too routine for some of his Indiana troops. On the evening of July 11 a few soldiers from the Ninth Indiana decided to try something bolder for a change of pace. With no specific orders Private Bierce and some of his comrades "ran forward into the woods and attacked the Confederate works." Although they believed they had done "well enough, considering the hopeless folly of the movement," they "came out of the woods faster than [they] went in." The brief adventure cost Corporal Boothroyd of Company A his life and made Bierce a hero when he carried the mortally wounded Boothroyd from the battlefield while under gunfire. Although his feat was reported by a correspondent from the Indianapolis *Journal* who witnessed the affair, Bierce was reluctant to accept the accolade of hero, perhaps because he had not been seriously wounded while Boothroyd had died.[48]

On the morning of July 12, Morris discovered that Garnett had evacuated the defenses at Laurel Hill. He ordered a pursuit, but it was not until midafternoon that Federal troops occupied the abandoned defensive works. The pursuit was led by Captain Henry Washington Benham, McClellan's chief engineer. Although Benham was only a captain, he was an experienced officer. He had graduated from West Point in 1837 and spent the first ten years of his military career supervising the repair of various U.S. army forts. In the Mexican War he was wounded and breveted captain for gallantry in action at the battle of Buena Vista. He was promoted to captain in the engineers in 1848. In 1855, perhaps understanding where his strengths lay, Benham declined a promotion to major in the Ninth Infantry, preferring to stay in the engineers. He continued to work on various engineering projects until 1861 and had joined McClellan as chief engineer of the Department of the Ohio on May 14. On the evening of July 12 Benham led the Federal pursuit of the retreating Confederates, following a trail of cast-off equipment, slipping and falling in the mud left by the heavy rains that continued to plague the campaign. After a short stop for the night, Benham continued on the 13th, and about noon, Federal troops sighted Garnett's baggage trains slowly crossing the Cheat River at Kaler's Ford. As Benham prepared to attack with the Fourteenth Ohio and the Seventh and Ninth Indiana, the Federals lost the element of surprise when the "thoughtless firing of a musket . . . set the train rapidly in motion, and long lines of infantry were formed in order of battle to protect it."[49]

The long lines of infantry that deployed to protect the Confederate trains were troops of the First Georgia. Garnett ordered the regiment to establish a defensive line to delay the Federal attack until the wagons could make good their escape. Garnett quickly organized his rear guard to hold in successive positions with Taliaferro's Twenty-third Virginia alternating with the First Georgia, since the baggage train had to cross and then recross the winding Tygart's Valley River, first Kaler's, and then Corrick's Ford, some three and a half miles from Kaler's. At Corrick's Ford progress slowed again as some of the heavily loaded wagons stalled in the swiftly flowing water, swollen by the recent rains. The Twenty-third Virginia with three pieces of artillery occupied a strong defensive position overlooking the ford, and as the Fourteenth Ohio reached the crossing, Taliaferro's men fired a volley that opened the Battle of Corrick's Ford. For about thirty minutes the two sides exchanged fire. Benham brought up the two guns of Barnett's First Ohio Artillery traveling with the advance guard to respond to the Confederate artillery emplaced with the Twenty-third Virginia. Neither side caused much damage with artillery due to the large differences in elevation between the two batteries. Under the fire of both sides Dumont maneuvered his Seventh Indiana into position to turn the flank of Taliaferro's position. With ammunition running low and the Federals approaching his flank, Taliaferro withdrew, leaving about forty wagons to be taken by Morris's troops.[50]

Garnett, riding to the sound of the guns, met Taliaferro as he was withdrawing and asked for ten good riflemen to post behind a pile of driftwood where they could fire on the advancing Federals. Taliaferro initially provided an entire company, but since the selected position would only accommodate ten sharpshooters, Garnett selected the men he wanted and sent the remainder back to their regiment. After posting the marksmen, Garnett sat on his horse watching the cautious movement of the Federals through the thick underbrush. When the firing began, Garnett turned in his saddle and was struck by a bullet in his back, knocking him from his horse mortally wounded. A staff officer, Sam M. Gaines, tried to pull the dying general back on his own horse, but was forced from the field by the fire of the advancing Federal troops. Garnett's death brought him the dubious distinction of being the first general officer of the Civil War on either side to be killed in battle. Dumont, who had known Garnett during their service in the Mexican War, led his Indianans only about a mile beyond the ford before they halted in exhaustion. Garnett's death and the capture of the supply wagons halted fighting and brought the battle at Corrick's Ford to an end.[51]

What was left of Garnett's command took advantage of the Federal halt and kept moving north. Morris arrived at Corrick's Ford in the afternoon and waited until the next day before he continued the pursuit as far as St. George. Federal troops had carried Garnett's body to the nearby William Corrick farmhouse where it was packed in salt and placed in Garnett's own ambulance wagon, one of the many that had fallen into Federal hands in the retreat. Morris, a classmate of Garnett at West Point, saw it as his sad duty to take care of the fallen general's body. The remains and Garnett's personal items received an escort back to the railroad at Grafton, and ultimately returned to his wife's family for burial at Brooklyn, New York. On July 15 with the Confederates already more than fifteen miles ahead of him, Morris called the whole thing off and retired to the camp at Belington.[52]

The Southern troops initially fled in haste after Garnett's death, but Colonel Ramsey of the First Georgia assumed command of the retreat and managed to bring some order to the chaos. He led an all-night march along the Horseshoe Run Road to Red House, Maryland, and passed through there at five o'clock in the morning of July 14. Late that evening Mr. Parsons, a local Confederate sympathizer, offered his services as a guide to the First Georgia. After some skepticism on the part of the Georgians, they agreed to follow Parsons to his home where he promised them something to eat. By the time the weary troops reached the Parson place on the 16th, they had been without food for four days, and they fell upon the small amount of bread available in such a frenzy that most of it was trampled into the ground before it could be eaten. Fortunately for the hungry Confederates, Parsons was able to give them fifteen cows, which they butchered, cooked, and ate on the spot, giving them strength to stay ahead of the pursuing Federals.[53]

In an effort to head off the Confederate retreat from Laurel Hill, McClellan sent a telegram to General Hill in Grafton, in command of the Federal forces protecting the Baltimore and Ohio Railroad, changing the priorities for his forces. Not aware of Garnett's death when he sent the message, McClellan instructed Hill to "never mind the bridges if you can catch Garnett." Hill managed to gather five thousand men for the effort, but inadequate knowledge of the rugged terrain and poor cooperation from railroad employees hampered his efforts. Colonel Irvine, with the Sixteenth Ohio, was supposed to block the Northwestern Turnpike where it intersected with Horseshoe Run Road, but he established the position several miles too far west, and it was not until Hill reached the position that Irvine learned of the error. By that time, however, Ramsey had already led his tired troops across the Turnpike. Hill's forces missed their best chance at the Confederates when they finally got to Red House on July 14 two hours after the Southerners had cleared the town. For the next three days Hill pursued the retreating Southerners with little success. He got as far as Greenland in Hardy County before McClellan used his field telegraph to call off the chase on July 16, complaining that Hill should have attacked on the 14th. Given his hesitant performance before, during, and after the battle at Rich Mountain, McClellan really was in no position to critique delays in attacking or pursuing.[54]

During the pursuit, the gallant troops of the Glade Spring Rifle Company were learning about the more difficult side of soldiering. The "little traveled, rocky, hilly, and mountainous" road they followed during the retreat "was so different from the smooth turnpike over which [their] foot movements heretofore had been that telling effect both on the men and on the horses was soon felt." With sickness prevalent and most of the baggage gone, as the regiment neared Red House, "the doors of Northern prisons seemed to be standing wide open for [them]." The color bearer for the company, concerned about the two sets of colors given the company before they left home, decided to save at least one from capture. He therefore buried the set given them by Mrs. Sallie Floyd in the hope of recovering it after release from the Northern prison that seemed certain for them all during that miserable march. As it turned out, the Glade Spring Rifle Company avoided the Federals and eventually made its weary way to Monterey in Highland County, leaving Sallie Floyd's hand-sewn colors forever buried somewhere in the mountains.[55]

By July 20, what was left of the Confederate forces in northwestern Virginia managed to straggle into Monterey, where Brigadier General Henry Rootes Jackson had assumed command after Garnett's death. Jackson was a forty-two-year-old native of Georgia and a graduate of Yale who had been a U.S. district attorney and superior court judge before the war. He resigned a Confederate judgeship to accept his commission as a brigadier general. While Jackson organized the demoralized Confederates in Monterey, Wise had his hands full with McClellan's second invasion force that was beginning to move into western Virginia. On the Federal side, McClellan established his headquarters in Huttonsville and turned his thoughts to Cox and the Kanawha Valley.

CHAPTER SEVEN

"Something Between a Victory and a Defeat"

BOTH LEE AND McClellan recognized the strategic value of the Kanawha Valley in their early planning. McClellan had proposed using the valley to march into Virginia in the strategic plan he presented to Scott in April. Lee, anticipating that Virginia could defend its western counties with local militia, had dispatched recruiting officers to the Kanawha Valley in early May.

By the time McClellan established his headquarters in Huttonsville, the Federal column under Cox in the Kanawha Valley had already made substantial progress toward clearing the area of Confederate forces. Unlike the northwestern part of the state, the residents of the Kanawha Valley maintained close ties to the Valley of Virginia, from which many of their ancestors had come to settle in the mountainous area. The James River and Kanawha Turnpike provided an economic link with the rest of the state. People in this part of Virginia held mixed feelings about the war. The situation in three towns reflected the confused loyalties as Cox began his movement into the Kanawha Valley. At Guyandotte, the western terminus of the James River and Kanawha Turnpike on the Ohio River, the town flew the Confederate flag; just up the river at Point Pleasant where the Kanawha River emptied into the Ohio River, the Stars and Stripes was prominently displayed; but at Charleston neither flag flew because the town was so divided in its sympathies that neither secessionist nor pro-Union factions would permit the other side to raise its preferred colors.[1]

The day after he assumed command in Ohio, in his first effort at strategic planning, McClellan had proposed the Valley as an avenue of approach for a Federal invasion into the heart of Virginia. Lee also saw the Valley as a possible invasion route and, less than a week after taking command in Virginia, sent Lieutenant Colonel John McCausland to the Valley to muster ten volunteer companies and direct defensive operations there. McCausland, a twenty-four-year-old graduate of the Virginia Military Institute, was teaching there when Lee sent him on his mission west. On May 3, shortly after McCausland received his instructions, Christopher Quarles Tompkins, a graduate of West Point who had been a captain of artillery when he left the U.S. army in 1847, received a colonel's commission along with instructions to assume command of the militia forces in the Kanawha Valley. Tompkins was well known in the Valley. He owned a farm near Gauley Bridge that was reputed to be the most beautiful residence west of the Alleghenies, with a large library and fine paintings on the walls. When Tompkins headed off to war, his wife and four children remained on the farm. Initially, Tompkins and McCausland worked well together, something that did not always happen among Confederate commanders during the campaign in western Virginia. But their different personalities eventually began to erode the relationship. Tompkins was an experienced, pragmatic soldier, while McCausland was more hotheaded and prone to spur-of-the-moment judgments. About twelve miles west of Charleston near the Coal River, Tompkins established a training area on a farm belonging to William and Beverly Tompkins who were not related to the colonel. It was christened Camp Tompkins in honor of both its founder and the property owners. McCausland established a separate camp down the Kanawha River from Charleston near Buffalo in Putnam County.[2]

There were a few local militia companies when McCausland and Tompkins began their recruiting efforts, some of which had been organized for quite some time. The Kanawha Riflemen, an infantry company originally organized in 1856, were the pride of the city of Charleston. The Riflemen were commanded by Captain George S. Patton, grandfather of the well-known World War II general. Captain Patton was an 1852 graduate of Virginia Military Institute, and he had organized the company along the lines of the Richmond Light Infantry Blues, an elite militia organization in the state capital that dated back to 1793. Nearby Putnam County boasted an infantry company called the Buffalo Guards, which had been organized since 1859. In the spring of 1861 companies were forming under local leadership all along the Kanawha Valley. Some, such as the Elk Point Tigers and the Logan County Wildcats, had bold names for what were essentially untrained groups of young men on an adventure. Their garb was anything but uniform. The Fayetteville Rifles and the Mountain Cove Guards proudly wore light blue flannel jackets and dark grey trousers that had been sewn by the ladies in the Methodist Church of Fayetteville, while the fifty-three men of the Fairview Rifle Guards of Wayne County all wore new red hunting shirts. By late May, companies began gathering in designated camps to begin their transformation from recruits to soldiers.[3]

Because there was greater sympathy for secession and less organized pro-Union activity in the Kanawha Valley than in the northwestern part of Virginia, McCausland and Tompkins initially enjoyed greater success in their efforts to organize the defensive forces than did Porterfield working further north. Unlike the situation in the northwest, there was little active Union recruiting in the area to compete directly with Tompkins and McCausland, and they managed to muster enough companies for more than two regiments of infantry. Initially designated the First and Second Kanawha Regiments, they became the Twenty-second and Thirty-sixth Virginia, respectively, when they were mustered into the Confederate army in July. Tompkins commanded the Twenty-second, McCausland the Thirty-sixth.[4]

But by the end of May, Tompkins reported to Garnett, Lee's adjutant general in Richmond, that "except for the few loyal companies now mustered into the service of the State, there are few of the people who sympathize with the secession policy." He consolidated the forces he had organized at Camp Tompkins and dispatched McCausland to Richmond to "explain in detail matters that cannot be discussed by letter" concerning the difficulty they were having in securing reliable troops. Tompkins's pessimistic reports to Richmond had mixed results. President Davis sent additional forces to the Kanawha Valley under command of that aggressive champion of secession and seasoned politician, Henry Wise. Commissioned a brigadier general on June 6, Wise received authority to raise what came to be known as Wise's Legion, a body of troops that included infantry, cavalry, and artillery. Wise had instructions either to expel any enemy forces from Virginia or stop their advance as close to the border as possible. He was also told to be prepared to join his forces with those of Brigadier General John B. Floyd, who was then raising a brigade and guarding the Virginia and Tennessee Railroad in the Valley of Virginia. Should they join forces, Floyd, who had been commissioned a brigadier general by Davis in May, would be in command.[5]

After resigning as the U.S. secretary of war in December 1861, when Buchanan refused to order Major Anderson to evacuate Fort Sumter, Floyd had returned to his home in Abingdon, a town in southwestern Virginia near the Tennessee border. Floyd's indiscretion in handling government bonds in the War Department had sullied his reputation with many Confederate leaders, and he and Davis were long-standing political enemies. But Floyd had remained a popular figure in southwestern Virginia, and he wanted to play a role in the coming war. In an effort to mend fences with Floyd, Davis asked him to raise a brigade of mountain men in the upper part of the Valley of Virginia to guard the Virginia and Tennessee Railroad, the only direct line of communication between those two states. Agreeing to the request, Floyd became a brigadier general in the Confederate army in May, some weeks before Wise.[6]

Neither Floyd nor Wise had any military training or experience, and Davis had not consulted Lee on their qualifications for senior military command. The appointment of these two strong-willed politicians exacerbated the already fragmented Confederate command structure in western Virginia. Both were former Virginia governors, and each, while holding that office, had courted the western counties for political support. Floyd had supported an extensive internal improvement program that benefitted the area, and Wise had handled his western patronage adroitly enough to gain support there. Davis was hopeful that the popularity of the two men would encourage support for the Confederate cause in western Virginia. Initially, that was the case. Their ability as experienced politicians to gain votes was an asset in their recruiting efforts, and within weeks of receiving their commissions the two generals had regiments organized and were busy training and equipping them. But Davis had failed to coordinate what he expected them to do with their forces and just how they would contribute to the defense of western Virginia. Consequently, Floyd and Wise each had different plans. Floyd planned to lead his brigade into the Kanawha Valley and sweep the Federals back to Ohio if they attempted an invasion; Wise sought to move into the Valley and raise a partisan force of western Virginians that would be able to defend the Valley from an invasion. In June, Wise prepared to move west to head off any Federal movement into the Kanawha Valley, while Floyd established his headquarters at Camp Jackson near Wytheville, a town located in the southern end of the Valley on the Virginia and Tennessee Railroad. When Floyd learned of Wise's mission he was furious, asking repeatedly, "Why does he come to *my country?* Why does he not stay in the east and defend *his country?*" The outburst did not bode well for their future cooperation, should it become necessary.[7]

Wise recruited not just men for his legion, but arms and equipment also. The legion was a Confederate army organization that included infantry, cavalry, and artillery under a single commander. It was designed for independent operations, and Wise took his independence seriously. An advertisement in the Richmond *Enquirer* advised potential volunteers that "arms of all kinds: rifles, double-barrel shotguns, sabers, and revolvers, private arms of every description will be used by the Legion," and went on to explain that long-range guns would not be needed because "Gov. Wise is not the man to stand at longrange [sic]." Wise was to defend and rally the people in the southern portion of western Virginia. Support for secession was stronger there than in the northwest, and Wise, as a former governor, could appeal to the power elite and local authorities of the area, most of whom remained true to the Richmond government. The counties bordering the Shenandoah Valley had shown strong support for secession in the May 23 referendum, while those counties along the Ohio River opposed the idea by a large margin. Therefore, the further west into the Kanawha Valley Wise moved, the less support he could expect from the residents of the area.[8]

Within ten days of being commissioned, Wise had troops on the way to western Virginia. The men he had recruited were largely from the area around Norfolk, Wise's old congressional district where he was well known. Although most of the legion could be described as partisan forces carrying whatever arms they could find,

Wise did secure the services of some established militia companies, one of which was the elite Richmond Light Infantry Blues, commanded by his son, Obediah Jennings Wise. On June 14, accompanied by his son's infantry company, Wise established a training camp at Lewisburg, the county seat of Greenbrier County, located on the James River and Kanawha Turnpike.[9]

By July 1 Wise had moved his legion to Gauley Bridge and was preparing to move east into the Kanawha Valley. He arrived in Charleston on July 6 with 2,800 troops in his legion. Upon his arrival in the region, the forces of Tompkins and McCausland came under Wise's command, although their regiments were not considered part of the legion. Moving west, Wise established his headquarters on Tyler Mountain, five miles west of Charleston, and dispatched forces along both sides of the Kanawha River as far west as the mouth of the Coal River to await the Federals. He also sent several companies of his legion as far north as Ravenswood, a town on the Ohio River about halfway between the Kanawha River and Parkersburg. Keeping track of events throughout the Federal theater of operations, McClellan reported to the War Department from Buckhannon that on July 5 "4 Cos at Ravenswood repulsed O. J. Wise night before last," although an attempt to capture the young Wise by Ohio militia was unsuccessful.[10]

In contrast with the fragmented Confederate command structure in western Virginia, Federal forces operating in the area all remained under McClellan's command, allowing him to react to the buildup of Confederate forces in the Kanawha Valley and the potential threat to the rear of his line of operations from Parkersburg. On July 2, McClellan, the Federal theater commander, ordered Cox into the Kanawha Valley. Cox, commissioned a brigadier general in the U.S. army on June 22, was at Camp Dennison reorganizing the regiments in his brigade for three years' enlistment, but as each regiment was mustered into Federal service, it received orders to follow McClellan into Virginia. By the time Cox received his orders to move into the Kanawha Valley, there was only one regiment left at Camp Dennison, the Eleventh Ohio, and it had only five companies.[11]

In his message to Cox, McClellan had instructed him to take command of three additional regiments to replace those that had already been sent into Virginia. The Kanawha Brigade initially consisted of the First and Second Kentucky and the Twelfth Ohio. To round out his command, McClellan told Cox to ask for a troop of cavalry and six guns from the governor of Ohio. The brigade was to move to Gallipolis where the Twenty-first Ohio would also come under Cox's command. Cox was directed to cross the Ohio River to Point Pleasant, a pro-Union Virginia town five miles north of Gallipolis, and move up the Kanawha Valley with four regiments, leaving one to occupy Point Pleasant. The purpose of the movement was to "keep the rebels near Charleston until [McClellan could] cut off their retreat by movement from Beverly."[12]

With his orders to Cox, McClellan showed that he clearly saw the entire western portion of Virginia as a single theater of operations, and the movements of his forces were intended to eliminate the Confederate presence in the area by maneuver, thereby securing it for the Union. McClellan was planning and conducting his campaign at the operational level and taking advantage of the strategic mobility of the railroads and rivers to move forces from Ohio to Virginia and keep them supplied. The telegraph would allow him to communicate quickly with Cox as Cox advanced into the Kanawha Valley. Cox's move was intended to support the movement of the northern column and establish a strong Union presence in the Kanawha Valley that would deter further Confederate sympathies. It would also open a line of communications with the Federal forces to the north when Cox reached and occupied Gauley Bridge, the key transportation hub in the southern portion of the theater of operations. When McClellan ordered Cox into the Kanawha Valley on July 2, Federal forces in the northwestern portion of Virginia controlled Grafton and Philippi. The Federal success had provided the impetus for the formation of the Reorganized Government of Virginia in Wheeling, where Pierpont was functioning as governor. McClellan was bringing more regiments and supplies from Indiana and Ohio in anticipation of continuing his move east along the Staunton-Parkersburg Turnpike. The Confederates had yet to mount a coherent defensive against McClellan's theater-wide offensive campaign. There was no single commander for the Confederate military forces in western Virginia, and at the policy level in Richmond, Davis and Lee were not coordinating their attempts to provide reinforcements. In early July, however, both Davis and Lee were more concerned with the potential threat to Richmond posed by the Federal forces assembling in Washington.

After receiving his orders, it took Cox a few days to get his new brigade organized. He was authorized to take the Eleventh Ohio, the only regiment left out of the brigade he had organized, along with him to the Kanawha Valley. The regiment's missing companies would be recruited and sent later on. The only artillery available, however, was a section of two bronze-rifled guns that had originally been cast as smoothbores, and the cavalry amounted to thirty recruits useful only as messengers. Nonetheless, by July 6 he had one regiment on its way to Gallipolis by steamboat with the second following close behind. Cox departed Camp Dennison on July 7 with the Eleventh Ohio, and three days later he had all three Ohio regiments united and about to enter the theater of operations at Point Pleasant. The two Kentucky regiments took a few days more to arrive. Because of Kentucky's neutrality, both had been organized outside the state at Camp Clay, located across the Ohio River from Newport. Colonel James V. Guthrie recruited and organized the First Kentucky, which was mustered into Federal service on June 4. Two Louisville companies formed the nucleus of the Second Kentucky, raised by Colonel W. E. Woodruff and mustered into Federal service on June 13. According to Cox, many of the men in the two regiments were unemployed steamboat crews and long-shoremen who posed a bit of problem since they "were mostly of a rough and reckless class, and gave a good deal of trouble by insub-ordination." On the other hand, he assessed them as courageous; "after they had been under discipline for a while, [they] became good fighting regiments."[13]

By the time Cox reached Gallipolis, McClellan had new instruc-tions for him. Cox was to go on the offensive in the Kanawha Val-ley. He received command of a territorial district that included western Virginia below Parkersburg and north of the Kanawha River. The district would be enlarged as Cox proceeded east to occupy Virginia's western counties. He was to advance up the Kanawha to Charleston and Gauley Bridge with the bulk of his forces, but McClellan also wanted him to secure the Ohio River. Cox therefore landed the Second Kentucky at Guyandotte, seventy miles below Point Pleasant with instructions to suppress insurgents there, and he sent the First Kentucky to Ravenswood where they were to move inland to Ripley and secure communications along the road between Parkersburg and Charleston. He was uneasy about dividing his force into three columns, but he wanted "to show some Union troops at various points on the border," and he planned for the Kentucky regiments to protect the flanks of his main force once he reached Red House, some thirty-two miles up the Kanawha River from Point Pleasant. The entire force would even-tually be reunited below Charleston, at which time Cox would have about three thousand men under his command.[14]

Wise had not been idle while Cox was organizing his Kanawha Brigade for combat. While he did have some initial success in rais-ing additional forces and encouraging secessionist tendencies in the area, Wise, like Tompkins and McCausland, soon met with local resistance to his recruiting efforts. Taking full advantage of the broad authority given him to confiscate supplies and firearms for the use of his legion, Wise further reduced his popularity with his high-handed methods. The flamboyant general was quick to complain about the lack of popular support, reporting back to the War Department in Richmond that "a spy is on every hill top, at every cabin, and from Charleston to Point Pleasant they swarm."[15]

The spies that Wise complained about were not just local pro-Union residents. Back in Ohio, Pinkerton, now heading McClellan's intelligence-gathering efforts, had sent one of his employees, Price Lewis, into western Virginia on June 27 seeking information. Lewis traveled on the steamer *Cricket* from Cincinnati to Guyandotte at the western terminus of the James River and Kanawha Turnpike. Posing as an English citizen, Lewis and his servant, played by Samuel Bridgeman, one of Pinkerton's favorite employees, began traveling east toward White Sulphur Springs. Near the mouth of the Coal River they were detained by Confederate pickets and taken to see Captain Patton, who was in command of the detachment of the Twenty-second Virginia patrolling the area. Lewis played the part of an indignant tourist wanting to see the natural beauty of the area before returning home. So impressed was Patton that he gave Lewis a pass to Charleston and invited him to supper, bragging about the local Confederate defenses while Bridgeman surreptitiously took notes. When Patton invited Lewis to inspect the positions, the spy declined, fearing he would appear too eager. In Charleston Lewis met the less impressionable Wise, who refused to issue a pass to Richmond, stranding Lewis and his servant for a time, but learning that traveling on the roads east did not require a pass, Lewis and Bridgeman left Charleston, went south to Kentucky, and from there to Cincinnati where they reported to Pinkerton.[16]

While Wise was organizing the Confederate forces in the western end of the Kanawha Valley, Floyd was preparing his brigade at Camp Jackson, near Wytheville, in the Valley of Virginia. Floyd had been joined in Wytheville by Henry Heth, an 1847 West Point graduate who was to assist the new general in organizing his forces.

After graduating last in his class, Heth had spent fourteen years in the army on frontier duty before he resigned his commission as an infantry captain to offer his services to his native state of Virginia. Heth's standing at West Point did not accurately reflect his capabilities as a soldier. When he volunteered for the Confederate army, Davis had penned a note to the secretary of war that Heth was "a first rate soldier of the cast of men most needed." In his first assignment as quartermaster general of Virginia forces, Heth so impressed Lee with his efficiency and self-assurance that Heth became the only Confederate officer Lee called by his first name. Physically, Heth cut an impressive figure. He was of medium height, wore a bushy mustache, and had deep-set contemplative eyes. And as Floyd would soon learn, Heth was very opinionated. In Wytheville, as militia companies arrived, Heth mustered them into service. When he had the ten companies necessary to form a regiment, Richmond designated it the Forty-fourth Virginia, promoted Heth to colonel, and gave him command of the new organization. All of the companies in the Forty-fourth were from the southern end of the Valley, a largely rural area. Heth, an eastern Virginian and disciplinarian, was not popular with his subordinates, nor did he hold them in particularly high regard. As he began the process of turning the farm-raised recruits into soldiers, he organized night schools for the officers to teach them tactics but abandoned the idea when he discovered many of the officers could not read the manuals.[17]

The Federal movements along the Ohio prompted the Confederate War Department to reinforce Wise. On July 10, the same day Cox arrived at Point Pleasant, Floyd received orders at his headquarters in Wytheville to move his brigade into the Kanawha Valley. On July 12 the Forty-fifth Virginia left Camp Jackson and boarded trains to Covington, western terminus of the Virginia Central Railroad, and from there they marched west along the James River and Kanawha Turnpike to Camp Bee, near Sweet Springs in Allegheny County. Meanwhile, at the other end of the turnpike, Wise's force of more than three thousand men had been organized into five regiments and were training to be soldiers. With the news that the Federals were advancing, the monotony of their long days of drill at last seemed over. With great excitement, scouts and picket lines went out along the roads and rivers in the area, and a company was dispatched to occupy the top of Coal Mountain, which provided an excellent view of the James River and Kanawha Turnpike.[18]

Meanwhile, for the Federal troops in the Kanawha Brigade, the advance was more relaxing than exciting, at least at first. Cox recorded that July 11, the first day of their trip on steamers up the Kanawha, "was the very romance of campaigning." Although they were steaming through an area filled with pro-Union sentiment on a lovely summer day, there were just enough rumors of enemy activity to make "the exhilaration of out-door life more joyous than any we had ever known." What Cox did not know as he enjoyed his cruise was that at the same time he and his brigade began their move up the Kanawha River, McClellan and Rosecrans were fighting at Rich Mountain. Cox had three regiments in his column. Two of them traveled on steamers while the other patrolled the banks as an advance guard. The brigade proceeded up the Kanawha River, progressing about ten miles each day with only an occasional flurry of activity when a Confederate patrol was sighted. The day after the brigade left Point Pleasant, the advance guard of the Eleventh Ohio was fired on. Lieutenant Sol Treverbaugh, in command of the detachment of Ohioans, returned fire and a brief, but lively, fight ensued. No one was killed or wounded. For their first time under fire, the Ohio men "stood it bravely and seemed to enjoy the affair, rather than otherwise."[19]

On the evening of July 16 Cox encamped at Pocotaligo, better known locally as Poca, on the north side of the Kanawha River, about three miles downstream from the point at which Scary Creek enters the river from the south. At this point in the advance Cox, for a number of reasons, was preparing to leave the steamers that had been transporting and supporting his regiments: for two days there had been an increase in the skirmishing with Wise's scouts; there was less pro-Union sentiment of local residents the further east the column moved; the Kanawha River was becoming narrower, making the unarmored transports susceptible to artillery fire from the shore; and they were nearing the James River and Kanawha Turnpike, which would make land movement easier. There were delays, however, at Poca. Withdrawing Confederates had burned the bridge across the Pocotaligo River. Cox had sent an urgent dispatch for wagons so they could continue the advance east without the steamers, but on July 16 the wagons had not yet reached the brigade. The Second Kentucky, which had been making its way along the turnpike from Guyandotte, was also to join the brigade at Poca before the advance resumed.[20]

In anticipation of stopping at Poca for a few days to rebuild the bridge and consolidate his forces, Cox, on the morning of July 17, had sent a detachment of the Twelfth Ohio, under Lieutenant Colonel Carr B. White, forward on the south side of the Kanawha along the Charleston Road. As they neared the mouth of Scary Creek, the Federals encountered Confederate pickets and came under fire from soldiers in an old log house. White returned to Poca and reported to Cox that there were about five hundred troops entrenched on the far side of Scary Creek, holding the bridge and blocking the way to Charleston. Cox prepared to attack and clear the road he would need for his wagons to continue the advance up the Kanawha Valley. About noon Colonel John W. Lowe of the Twelfth Ohio took his regiment along with two companies of the Twenty-first Ohio, two guns from Battery A, First Ohio Artillery, and a few cavalry troopers across the Kanawha by steamer and began to advance toward the Confederate position.[21]

In the meantime, the Confederates moved to reinforce the position at Scary Creek that had been established by Captain Andrew Barbee's Border Riflemen of the Twenty-second Virginia the evening before. Barbee and his men were well suited to the assigned task. They hailed from Putnam County and knew "every path and grapevine along the river." The pickets that had fired on the Federal's early morning reconnaissance reported the encounter to Barbee, and he in turn dispatched a courier to Camp Tompkins where Patton immediately ordered the drummers to beat the long roll and fall out the companies. By ten o'clock Patton was on the march with nine hundred men and two guns from Hales Artillery, then a company in the Twenty-second Virginia, to join Barbee at Scary Creek where the Confederate forces formed a line of battle on both sides of the bridge in anticipation of the Federal attack. One gun, under Lieutenant William A. Quarry, was set up on a small rise overlooking the position, and the other, commanded by Lieutenant Welch, was situated on the road covering the bridge across Scary Creek.[22]

About 2 P.M. on July 17 the Federal cavalry moving ahead of the infantry encountered Confederate pickets and drove them back to Scary Creek. The infantry on both sides then exchanged volleys. Neither side gained an advantage in the infantry fight, although the rifled artillery of the Federals scored a direct hit on Welch's gun, killing him. Late in the afternoon Lowe organized a flanking move that would cross the creek and attack the bridge. The fighting was hand-to-hand as troops of the Twelfth Ohio, led by Lieutenant Colonel Norton, reached the bridge. But at about 5 P.M. the Confederates were reinforced by Captains James M. Corns and Albert Jenkins who arrived with the mounted troops of the Fairview Guards supported by an artillery piece. Their arrival rallied the Confederate defenders. The Federal attack faltered, and when Norton fell, severely wounded, the Ohioans beat a hasty retreat back across the bridge. The Confederates failed to follow the Federal retreat, perhaps because in the closing moments of action Patton received a wound in the arm and had to be carried from the battlefield.[23]

Battles are chaotic events that do not always produce a clear decision. Their results are frequently in the eyes of the beholder. Wise reported Scary Creek as "a glorious repulse of the enemy, if not a decided victory," while McClellan more accurately described it as "something between a victory & a defeat." Wise's first reaction was to order McCausland and his Thirty-sixth Virginia to capitalize on Patton's success and attack the Federal position at Poca, but after studying the situation, McCausland determined his forces were inadequate to the task. On the other side of the Kanawha River, Cox initially received favorable reports of the Confederates being driven from Scary Creek, but by nightfall the Ohioans were back at Poca admitting that they had been repulsed. Cox expressed disappointment that they had not held on and asked for assistance, but described the setback as "common with new troops." In his view, "they passed from confidence to discouragement as soon as they were checked, and they retreated." Cox recorded the losses as ten killed and thirty-five wounded. When Captain Barbee of the Border Riflemen learned that one of the Federal dead, Captain Thomas G. Allen, commanding Company D, Twenty-first Ohio, had plans to marry a young lady in Dayton, he sent Allen's letters and belongings to her along with a letter praising his bravery.[24]

But the dead and wounded at Scary Creek were not the only Federal casualties of the day. Cox's pride and standing with McClellan suffered a blow when three of his officers wandered off and ended up being captured. The three, Colonel William E. Woodruff and Lieutenant Colonel George W. Neff of the Second Kentucky and Colonel Charles A. DeVilliers of the Eleventh Ohio, were riding along the north bank of the Kanawha when they encountered a black man who informed them the Confederates were in retreat. The three, as new to war as the men they led, persuaded their informant to row them across the river to offer their congratulations to the victors. Unfortunately for them, the man's information was out of date and by the time the three Federal officers arrived on the south bank, the Confederates controlled the field and the officers were soon on their way to Libby Prison in

Richmond. Cox had not authorized their ride, much less the trip across the river, and he blamed "the hare-brained DeVilliers" for the incident, but McClellan characteristically passed the plight of the three unfortunates on to Scott with a plea for "some General Officers who understand their profession" and ranted that he could not be sure of success unless he personally commanded "every picket" and led "every column."[25]

Losing DeVilliers turned out to benefit the men of the Eleventh Ohio. DeVilliers had passed himself off as well versed in things military, but after observing him for awhile, Cox noted that his knowledge was "only skin deep, and he had neither the education nor the character" for commanding a regiment. When command of the regiment passed to Lieutenant Colonel Frizell, he appointed staff officers and instituted systematic drill and guard duty. The result, in the regiment's view, was that soon "all was working smoothly and far more to the satisfaction of all concerned than had been the case since leaving Camp Dennison."[26]

McClellan instructed Cox to remain in position while the Federal forces that had been victorious at Rich Mountain could move to threaten Wise's rear. Cox himself concluded that "the wisest course would be to await the arrival of the wagons" and prepare to move against Wise's camp at Tyler Mountain. It was July 24 before Cox resumed the movement up the Kanawha Valley with the Eleventh Ohio leading the advance. The required wagons had arrived the day before, and the bridge across the rain-swollen Pocotaligo River had been repaired by a company of the Eleventh Ohio. Working under the direction of its commander, Captain Philander P. Lane, the men of the company quickly put "a good and substantial bridge across the stream."[27]

Wise, in the meantime, had ordered a withdrawal on July 19. He feared that he would be cut off by McClellan's forces moving south behind him. He planned to withdraw slowly from the Valley, burning bridges and delaying Cox. Unaware of the debacle at Rich

Mountain and Garnett's death, Wise wrote to the War Department suggesting that the forces of Garnett and Floyd should be directed to support him. The Confederate defenders in western Virginia could not keep up with events. They had neither the telegraph for rapid communications with Richmond nor a single theater commander to make timely decisions.[28]

The success Wise saw in Scary Creek was short lived. Concluding that his rear could be threatened and his forces trapped in the Kanawha between Cox and McClellan, he took advantage of the part of his orders that allowed him to move to Covington at his discretion. It was a good decision. Cox approached Wise's Tyler Mountain position just as the legion was on its way out. The Federal advance guard, the Eleventh Ohio, exchanged a few shots with Confederate pickets as they hastily departed the camp, leaving supper still heating on the fire. Cox occupied Charleston the next day, putting the navigable portion of the Kanawha River in Union hands.[29]

By the time Cox resumed his advance up the Kanawha Valley, events outside the theater of operations had significantly changed the situation in western Virginia. McClellan's triumph at Rich Mountain soon paled in the face of a much more dramatic Confederate success in eastern Virginia. Davis and Lee had been correct in fearing a Federal advance from Washington, and their efforts to provide forces to stop it had proved more successful than they could possibly have hoped for. The results of a major battle at Manassas Junction on July 21 stunned the Union and filled the Confederacy with hope, and its effects soon reached the mountains of western Virginia.

CHAPTER EIGHT

Davis Turns to Lee

S INCE APRIL NORTHERN troops had been arriving in
Washington, D.C., in response to Lincoln's call. On May 24,
the day after Virginia's referendum confirmed the Old
Dominion's secession from the Union, Federal troops had occupied
the heights on the south side of the Potomac River to provide a
buffer zone against a Confederate invasion from Virginia. The few
Southern troops stationed in northern Virginia had fallen back to
the vicinity of Centreville. For the next month the Union army in
and around Washington grew in size, but to Lincoln's mounting dismay, the troops were apparently doing little more than drilling.
With the first regiments enlisted for only three months, the president was anxious to get some use of the army he could see all
around him. The commander of the Federal forces in Washington
was Brigadier General Irwin McDowell, a well-connected Ohioan

who owed his appointment less to military ability than to his acquaintance with Secretary of the Treasury Salmon P. Chase. McDowell had graduated from West Point in 1838 and had served in the army since then. An artilleryman who spent most of his time in the adjutant general's department, he was not by nature an aggressive commander, much to Lincoln's chagrin.[1]

While Lincoln gathered his army in Washington, Confederate forces were moving north to defend Richmond. By early July Davis had three small armies in Virginia covering the three most likely avenues of approach to Richmond. Protecting the route up the peninsula was a force of about 5,000 under Brigadier J. B. Magruder; Brigadier General Joseph E. Johnston was in the Valley with 11,000 troops; and in front of Washington Brigadier General P. G. T. Beauregard commanded a force of 23,000 eager Confederates. Each of the three Southern armies faced a larger Federal force, but they had the advantage of being able rapidly to reinforce each other; and the Confederates had another significant advantage–Johnston and Beauregard were two of the most highly regarded generals in the Confederate army. Johnston, like Lee a native Virginian and West Point graduate, had served as quartermaster general of the U.S. army before he became the highest-ranking officer to resign and join the Confederacy. Beauregard, also a West Pointer who had earned the nickname "The Little Napoleon" for his unabashed admiration of the Corsican, was considered the hero of Fort Sumter where he had won the South's first victory in the opening round of the war.[2]

Beauregard and McDowell, classmates at West Point, faced different pressures as they prepared for battle against one another. Beauregard wanted to hold Manassas Junction, a critical railroad intersection where the Manassas Gap Railroad from the Valley met the Orange and Alexandria Railroad that joined Washington and Richmond. The Manassas Gap Railroad was the crucial link that would allow Beauregard and Johnston to exploit their advantage of their interior lines because forces could be moved rapidly between the two armies, and the Orange and Alexandria Railroad was the main supply line for both armies. In Washington there was increasing pressure on McDowell to begin offensive operations against the Confederate forces assembling in northern Virginia. The popular view, both North and South, was that the war would be settled in one climactic battle that should be fought as soon as possible. The news of McClellan's progress through western Virginia, bolstered by his dramatic pronouncements of victory and liberal use of Napoleonic rhetoric, increased the popular clamor for action by the Federal army in Washington. Knowing that the forces available to them were not ready for an offensive, both Scott and McDowell wanted to delay a battle until the troops were better prepared.[3]

But on June 3 Scott asked McDowell to prepare "an estimate of the number of and composition of a column to be pushed toward Manassas Junction." In late June McDowell finally produced a plan for action. He proposed to advance on Manassas with thirty thousand troops organized into three columns. Although warning that the new regiments would not be very steady in the line, the general believed they would perform satisfactorily in battle "if they are well led." Scott did not agree with McDowell's optimistic assessment, but Lincoln wanted action, soon. At a June 29 special meeting of the cabinet, Scott's objections were overruled, and McDowell received instructions to go ahead with his plan. The date set for the advance was July 8. Problems with logistics and organization, however, postponed the beginning of the offensive a number of times, and McDowell did not get under way until July 16.[4]

In the meantime, on July 14, McClellan had reported his success at Rich Mountain to the War Department with a flourish. "We have annihilated the enemy in Western Virginia," he telegraphed Washington the day after Garnett's death at Corrick's Ford, and he declared that "Our success is complete & secession is killed in this country." At the time of his report, although the Confederates in the theater had been bloodied, they were certainly not annihilated in western Virginia. McClellan had followed the victory on Rich Mountain with a movement forward along the Staunton-Parkersburg Turnpike to occupy Beverly and the pass over Cheat Mountain, east of Huttonsville. The failure of the retreating Confederate forces to stop and defend the pass allowed the Federals to occupy it unmolested. The Confederates continued their withdrawal all the way to Monterey, on the edge of the Valley of Virginia, where they could regroup in safety. The withdrawal also gave McClellan's forces access to a good north-south road that led from Huttonsville to Lewisburg on the James River and Kanawha Turnpike.[5]

McClellan followed his report to the War Department with a stirring message to his troops on July 16. In an order printed on the portable printing press he carried with his headquarters to such good advantage, he announced to the "Soldiers of the Army of the West!" that he was more than satisfied with their performance. He told his soldiers, as well as newspaper reporters hungry for information, that his army had "annihilated two armies, commanded by educated and experienced soldiers, and entrenched in mountain fastness fortified at their leisure." After reminding them of the hardships they had endured to gain their triumph, he cautioned that the fighting was not yet over and that he "may have still greater demands to make upon you, still greater sacrifices for you to offer."[6]

The rhetoric of annihilation sounded good to the troops, and it certainly played well in the Northern press. News of Rich Mountain brought an abundance of editorial praise and made McClellan a national hero. The *New York Herald* dubbed him "the Napoleon of the Present War," and the *Louisville Journal* saw McClellan's accomplishments as "military workmanship by a master hand." The Federal government was as fulsome in its praise. The president and cabinet were "charmed," and Scott sent him "the applause of all who are high in authority here." Mary Ellen, the young general's pregnant wife, sent a telegram asking him to "come home and receive my congratulations."[7]

The adulation was nice, but McClellan, in spite of the rhetoric, was concerned, for the Confederate forces remaining in western Virginia still posed a viable threat to his forces. Two days after publishing the victory message to his troops, he telegraphed Hill to give up trying to capture the Southern forces retreating from Laurel Hill, instructing him to "abandon the pursuit to avoid the possibility of disaster." The news of the setback at Scary Creek brought Cox a reprimand from McClellan, the Federal theater commander, and a plea to "at least save me the disgrace of a detachment of my Army being routed." With his glowing press coverage and national reputation growing fast, McClellan could hardly afford a rout or disaster.[8]

When word of the Rich Mountain disaster and Garnett's death reached Richmond, the dismay was all the greater because many of the Confederate forces involved had been organized and trained near the capital city. As in the North, the population in the South believed McClellan's rhetoric. But Lee, seeing his fears of a Federal move into the Valley of Virginia on the verge of realization, moved to repair the damage. He sent orders for Floyd to go into the Kanawha Valley and join forces with the retreating Wise to support the defensive effort, and he dispatched Brigadier General William Wing Loring to the theater to organize a proper defense, hold the mountain passes, protect the Virginia Central Railroad at Staunton, and prepare to conduct an offensive to regain the lost ground. Lee was ready to go west in person, but Davis wanted him close at hand in Richmond. The Federal triumph in western Virginia was not the only problem facing Lee and the Confederate president in mid-July.[9]

On the afternoon of July 16, the green Federal army began its ponderous move out of Arlington. Two days later, on the 18th, it reached Centreville, twenty-two miles from the start point and six miles from Manassas Junction, already well behind McDowell's schedule. The regiments had little or no march discipline, and the inexperienced troops, burdened with three days' rations in their haversacks and the stifling July heat, took advantage of the numerous stops along the way to pick berries. The slow progress eliminated any chance of surprising the Confederates. A brief engagement between McDowell's leading division and two Confederate brigades near Centreville on the 18th caused the cautious McDowell to pause for two more days, while he brought up supplies, organized his forces for the attack, and looked over the Confederate defensive positions behind Bull Run.[10]

The two days proved fatal. McDowell's plan had assumed that he would face only Beauregard's army at Manassas. To ensure that that would be the case, Scott had directed Pennsylvania Major General Robert Patterson, an old friend who had been his second in command in Mexico, to keep Johnston's army in the Valley of Virginia occupied while McDowell moved on Beauregard. Patterson, however, in his first independent command at sixty-nine years of age, was simply not up to the task. He had moved into the Valley on June 16 when Johnston had abandoned Harpers Ferry as indefensible, but a few days later, when Scott recalled Patterson's regular troops, the elderly general quickly withdrew back into Maryland. It was not until the end of June that the cautious Patterson, assured that reinforcements were on the way, could be induced to venture back into the Valley. By mid-July, with the Confederates withdrawing in front of him, Patterson had moved only as far as Charles Town, while Johnston had established his headquarters in Winchester. Scott notified Patterson of McDowell's impending attack on July 16 and cautioned that Johnston must not be allowed to reinforce Beauregard.[11]

Meanwhile, from his headquarters in Beverly, McClellan was planning to continue his campaign out of western Virginia into the Valley of Virginia. On July 17 he sent a telegram to Scott proposing a movement to Staunton if that would fit into the overall Federal strategy. Staunton was a transportation hub of some importance in the Valley. It was the eastern terminus of the Staunton-Parkersburg Turnpike where it intersected with the north-south road that ran the length of the Valley, and it was a stop on the Virginia Central Railroad that ran east to Richmond. Scott optimistically replied the next day that McClellan's proposed move to Staunton, combined with a victory by McDowell at Manassas Junction, could lead to operations with Patterson to clear the lower Valley of Virginia of Confederate forces. But the coming events at Manassas Junction would soon make the proposed Staunton move an idea whose time had passed.[12]

Scott's optimism of the 18th contrasted with Beauregard's view of the situation facing him at Manassas Junction. On July 17, after the exchange with Tyler made it clear that the anticipated Federal attack was well under way, he anxiously telegraphed Richmond that "the enemy has assailed my outposts in heavy force. I have fallen back on the line of Bull Run." He also asked for reinforcements. In response to Beauregard's message, Davis sent a telegram to Johnston in the Valley of Virginia telling him that "Beauregard is attacked; to strike the enemy a decisive blow, a junction of all your effective forces will be needed." The message left the decision of just how to assist Beauregard with Johnston. He held a quick meeting with his brigade commanders and then decided to move his forces to Manassas the next day. On the Federal side, Scott sent word to Patterson on July 17 that McDowell had driven the enemy back and cautioned him not to let Johnston "amuse and delay you with a small force in front." But even as Patterson assured Scott on the 18th that "the enemy has stolen no march upon me," Johnston was moving out of Winchester, headed east across the Blue Ridge through Ashby Gap to Piedmont Station on the Manassas Gap Railroad. Two days later Johnston and the advance elements of his army arrived in Manassas with the remainder due to arrive that night.[13]

On Saturday, July 20, McDowell finished his plans and issued attack orders for the next morning. During his two days at Centreville his army had been thronged with official and unofficial visitors from Washington who had come out to watch the Federal army in action. Confident of a Federal victory and a quick end to the war, the hosts arrived in carriages with their own supplies. For the troops and the civilian observers alike, the war was still a grand adventure, and they regarded the anticipated battle as lively entertainment. According to one observer, they mingled freely with the troops and gave "the scene the appearance of a monster military picnic."[14]

On the other side of Bull Run, Beauregard, his spirits bolstered by the appearance of Johnston, also decided to attack on Sunday morning. When Johnston arrived, he was the senior Confederate general on the battlefield. Beauregard, however, being more familiar with the ground, continued to arrange regiments up front while Johnston stayed in the rear directing the movements of units arriving at Manassas to critical parts of the battlefield.[15]

Both sides stepped off to battle in the early Sunday morning hours of July 21, each planning to attack the other's left flank. In the Federal capital the first reports were optimistic, and after attending church, Lincoln went for a carriage ride believing that all was well on the battle front. But the Federal situation worsened during the day as Johnston directed a stream of reinforcements into the battle. Lincoln returned at sundown to learn from a War Department telegram that the army was "in full retreat through Centreville. The day is lost." The president spent a sleepless night on a sofa in the cabinet room of the White House where a seemingly endless line of eyewitnesses offered him their accounts of the disaster. In the morning he could see for himself the exhausted soldiers stagger past the windows looking for a place to sleep. One hundred miles south, in Richmond, the Confederate president, a former soldier, could not stay away from the battle, so on Sunday morning he boarded a special train for the front. Remaining in Richmond where Davis had left him, Lee waited anxiously while rumors of defeat swept the city until the official dispatches began to arrive during the evening. At long last Davis sent a telegram proclaiming that the Confederate forces had "won a glorious though dear-bought victory."[16]

The results of the battle elated the South and dismayed the

North. Confederate generals were hailed as heroes; Federal generals were demoted. As a result of his inspirational presence on the battlefield, Beauregard became as popular in the Old Dominion as he was in his native Louisiana, or in South Carolina, where he was remembered for his defense of Charleston Harbor. In Virginia, Johnston replaced Lee as the state's favorite general. On the other side, McDowell, in spite of his warnings that the Federal army was not ready, bore the brunt of the blame for the disaster. In the Valley, Patterson, who did not realize until July 21 that Johnston had eluded him, also drew fire for his inability to keep track of the Confederate forces that had slipped away to win the battle at Manassas. Within days of the battle McDowell had been demoted from army commander to commanding a division, and Patterson was relieved of his command to disappear into obscurity in Pennsylvania.[17]

In the South there was widespread belief that the repulse of the Federal encroachment into Virginia meant the end of the war, but Lee knew better. The triumph at Manassas did not erase the lengthy series of military setbacks in western Virginia where the command structure remained fragmented among inexperienced generals; and the situation remained bleak, if not hopeless, from the Confederate point of view. The Northern reaction was a shocked realization that the war would not be over quickly. But in the gloom of defeat there shone a series of small, bright lights of military success strung through the mountains of western Virginia at Philippi, Rich Mountain, and Corrick's Ford. One man, McClellan, laid claim to all these victories.[18]

In July 1861 both Lee and McClellan could look back on their first few months in command with some degree of satisfaction. Both had built and fielded sizable armies that had demonstrated the ability to fight and win battles. At Manassas Junction fully one-fourth of the Confederate force consisted of Virginia troops recruited, organized, and trained as result of Lee's actions as commander of the Virginia militia. Lee had also been largely responsible for the strategy that led to concentrating Johnston and Beauregard in front of McDowell. But, because he had not been in command during the fighting, his preparations went unnoticed as the South praised their new heroes who had actually conducted the battle. McClellan, on the other hand, having raised and fielded the Ohio regiments that comprised the bulk of the Federal forces in western Virginia, also led them in the campaign. Like Lee, McClellan's preparations went largely unrecognized, but because he also conducted the campaign, he received full credit, and more, for the victories his troops had won.[19]

In both Richmond and Washington the status of the campaign in western Virginia influenced the presidential reactions to Manassas Junction that resulted in changes of assignments for both Lee and McClellan. For Lincoln, the priority was to rebuild a shattered, demoralized army as quickly as possible. He needed a general who had proved himself in the cauldron of battle, one who could organize an army, inspire men, and win battles. In July there was only one such man in the Federal army, McClellan. McClellan had already announced that the campaign in western Virginia was over, and whether or not that was the case, Lincoln needed him in Washington. Someone else could take over in the west. The change for McClellan came quickly after the debacle at Manassas Junction. The day after the battle he received a curt summons from the War Department: "Circumstances make your presence here necessary. Charge Rosecrans or some other general with your present department and come hither without delay." McClellan sent a semi-encouraging telegram to Cox informing him of the situation and giving instructions to continue up the Kanawha and "if possible drive Wise beyond the Gauley Bridge." He then turned the command over to Rosecrans and left western Virginia for Washington as instructed. Arriving in the capital on July 26, he met with Lincoln the next day and assumed command of McDowell's army.[20]

In Richmond, Davis faced a different challenge. Where Lincoln had a defeated army in his capital where its plight was obvious to all, Davis's immediate military problem was far from the center of power, out of view of most people. But, as his need for a proven general was as great as Lincoln's, he looked to the man who had just won the Confederacy's first great victory, Johnston. The day after Manassas, Davis offered him the opportunity to command the Confederate forces in western Virginia. It was a challenging assignment to say the least, but success there might not bring fame. Johnston preferred to maintain a higher visibility, and turned down the offer, explaining that he should stay where he was, since the Federal army in Washington would soon be stronger than ever. With Johnston's refusal, Davis turned to the man who had served the Old Dominion so well in the first few months of the war. After discussing the situation privately with Davis, Lee agreed to go west.[21]

Davis had come to rely on Lee by late July. The two men had known each other for many years. About the same age, Davis had been a year ahead of Lee at West Point, and both had served with distinction in the Mexican War, although they were in different theaters. When Davis was the U.S. Secretary of War, Lee was superintendent of the Military Academy, and they corresponded frequently. In June, when Virginia state troops came under the control of the Confederate army, Lee became a general without an army. He remained in Richmond as a staff officer to Davis. They worked closely together in late June and early July organizing the Confederate defenses in northern Virginia, and Lee's advice had been instrumental in the strategy that led to the Confederate triumph at Manassas Junction. Davis wrote after the war that he had asked Lee to go to western Virginia in the hope that Lee's "military skill and deserved influence over men" would reconcile the feuding commanders there. Lee himself offered no insight as to why Davis turned to him, although his long-time aide, Captain Walter H. Taylor, believed it was simply because Lee was "the most available" of the "men fit for this duty."[22]

Before he was summoned to Washington, McClellan had declared the campaign in western Virginia over and a great success. In war, however, there are at least two antagonists and both must agree on the conclusion of a campaign. The declaration of victory by one side means nothing if the other side does not acknowledge defeat, and that the Confederates did not do. On the contrary, bolstered by the triumph at Manassas Junction, they increased their efforts to defend western Virginia by reinforcing their forces in the theater and preparing to take the offensive to regain lost territory. As McClellan arrived in Washington to reap the benefits of his success in western Virginia, Lee was preparing to turn around the fortunes of the Confederates in that theater of operations.

Robert E. Lee–Organized the Virginia Militia for war and commanded the Confederate forces in western Virginia late in the campaign. He grew his white beard while he was in western Virginia. *(West Virginia State Archives)*

George Brinton and Mary Ellen McClellan–He commanded the Federal forces in western Virginia. His frequent letters to his wife reveal much of what was on his mind during the campaign. *(Massachusetts Commandery Military Order of the Loyal Legion and the U.S. Army Military History Institute)*

Left: Ambrose Gwinnett Bierce–Served with the Ninth Indiana. Memories of the campaign in western Virginia influenced his later literary career. *(Daniel W. Strauss)*

Bottom Left: Frederick West Lander–Aide de camp to McClellan who participated in the battles at Philippi and Rich Mountain. *(Massachusetts Commandery Military Order of the Loyal Legion and the U.S. Army Military History Institute)*

Bottom Right: Jacob Dolson Cox–Commanded the Federal forces in the Kanawha Valley during the campaign in western Virginia. *(Massachusetts Commandery Military Order of the Loyal Legion and the U.S. Army Military History Institute)*

Right: Robert Latimer McCook—One of Ohio's "Fighting McCooks," a family that provided seventeen soldiers and sailors to the Union. He commanded the Ninth Ohio and was a brigade commander in western Virginia. *(Massachusetts Commandery Military Order of the Loyal Legion and the U.S. Army Military History Institute)*

Bottom Left: Randolph B. Marcy— George B. McClellan's father-in-law and chief of staff in western Virginia. *(Massachusetts Commandery Military Order of the Loyal Legion and the U.S. Army Military History Institute)*

Bottom Right: Orando M. Poe— An Army engineer lieutenant who developed a Federal intelligence network in western Virginia and reconnoitered for an artillery site at Rich Mountain. *(Massachusetts Commandery Military Order of the Loyal Legion and the U.S. Army Military History Institute)*

Left: Christopher Quaries Tompkins–Longtime resident of the Kanawha Valley who commanded the Twenty-second Virginia. *(West Virginia State Archives, Boyd B. Stutler Collection)*

Bottom Left: Erastus B. Tyler–Commanded the Seventh Ohio, the regiment that Floyd surprised at breakfast at Cross Lanes *(Massachusetts Commandery Military Order of the Loyal Legion and the U.S. Army Military History Institute)*

Bottom Right: William Starke Rosecrans–Brigade commander at Rich Mountain who replaced McClellan as Federal theater commander in western Virginia in July 1861. *(Massachusetts Commandery Military Order of the Loyal Legion and the U.S. Army Military History Institute)*

Right: Benjamin Franklin Kelley–
Commanded the First Virginia, the
Federal regiment that led the attack at
Philippi. *(West Virginia State Archives,
Boyd B. Stutler Collection)*

Bottom Left: Henry Washington
Benham–Led the Federal pursuit at
Corrick's Ford in July 1861 as
a captain, but disappointed
Rosecrans as a brigade commander
at Cotton Hill in November.
*(Massachusetts Commandery Military
Order of the Loyal Legion and the U.S.
Army Military History Institute)*

Bottom Right: William Wing Loring–
Commander of the Confederate
around Cheat Mountain. His arm
was amputated after he was wounded
in the Mexican War. *(Eleanor S.
Brockenbrough Library, The Museum of the
Confederacy, Richmond, Virginia. From an
original ambrotype by Rees, Richmond,
Virginia, 1862)*

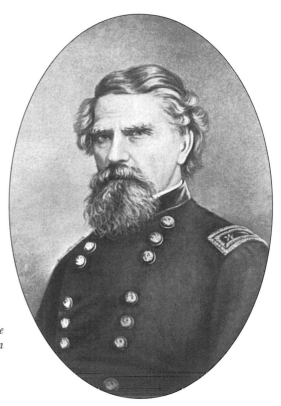

John Buchannon Floyd–
Former governor of
Virginia and political
rival of Henry Wise.
He commanded a
Confederate brigade in
the Kanawha Valley.
*(The Virginia Historical
Society, Richmond,
Virginia)*

Daniel Smith Donelson–
Confederate brigade commander
at Cheat Mountain. He selected
the site for Fort Donelson in his
native Tennessee. *(Eleanor S.
Brockenbrough Library, The Museum
of the Confederacy, Richmond,
Virginia)*

Henry Wise—Former governor of Virginia and political rival of John Floyd. He commanded a Confederate legion in the Kanawha Valley. *(The Virginia Historical Society, Richmond, Virginia)*

Albert Rust—Commanded the Third Arkansas. His disappointing performance as a brigade commander led to the Confederate failure at Cheat Mountain. *(Eleanor S. Brockenbrough Library, The Museum of the Confederacy, Richmond, Virginia)*

Henry Heth–Commander of the Forty-fifth Virginia, and provided advice on military matters to Floyd. *(The Virginia Historical Society, Richmond, Virginia)*

John McCausland–Recruited Confederate forces in the Kanawha Valley, and commanded the Thirty-sixth Virginia. *(West Virginia State Archives)*

John Pegram–Ill-fated commander of the Confederate forces at Rich Mountain. *(The Virginia Historical Society, Richmond, Virginia)*

CHAPTER NINE

Lee Goes to the Front

T HE CONFEDERATE VICTORY at Manassas Junction
changed the character of the campaign in western Virginia.
Garnett's death on July 13 necessitated a change in command for the Confederates in northwest Virginia, and McClellan's
recall to Washington nine days later left the Federals with a new theater commander. During July and August, with changes in senior
commanders for the Federal and Confederate forces in western Virginia, both sides underwent a period of reorganization and transition. As a result of the setback at Manassas Junction, the Federals
moved on the defensive to consolidate their positions in the mountains, while the Confederates, with increased confidence after their
recent victory, began to plan an offensive campaign to push the
Federals out of western Virginia.

As the senior Confederate officer in northwestern Virginia,

Brigadier General Henry Rootes Jackson, a Georgian judge, had assumed command of the Confederate forces upon Garnett's death. Jackson had been elected to the Confederate Congress, but his experience as the colonel of the First Georgia Volunteers in the Mexican War prompted him to enter military service, and he received a brigadier general's commission in the Confederate army in June. After the Confederate reverses at Rich Mountain and Corrick's Ford, Jackson had kept his head and rallied the remaining forces at Monterey and disposed them for defense as best he could, but he had no real desire to remain in command in western Virginia.[1]

Even before the Confederate victory at Manassas Junction, Lee had dispatched a new commander to take over from Jackson, Brigadier General Loring, a one-armed veteran of the Mexican War. A native of North Carolina, Loring joined the Florida Militia at the age of fourteen and earned the title "Boy Soldier" during the Seminole War. He received a direct commission as a captain in the Regiment of Mounted Riflemen in the regular army at the beginning of the Mexican War where he earned two brevets before being wounded in the arm during the fighting at Chapultepec. According to Doctor H. H. Steiner, when Loring learned the damaged arm had to be amputated, he "laid aside a cigar, sat quietly in a chair without opiates to relieve the pain, and allowed the arm to be cut off without a murmur or a groan." His men later buried the arm near where he was wounded "with the hand pointing toward the City of Mexico." Staying with the Mounted Riflemen after the Mexican War, Loring became colonel of the regiment in December 1856, where he remained until he resigned from the U.S. army on May 13, 1861. He received a brigadier general's commission in the Confederate army a week later. Loring departed Richmond the day after the battle at Manassas Junction with a small staff and assumed command of the Confederate forces in northwestern Virginia on July 24 at Monterey, where Jackson had gathered together what was left of

Garnett's army. While the Confederates had a tough, experienced commander in Loring, command of Southern forces in western Virginia still remained fragmented. Loring only commanded the troops holding the Staunton-Parkersburg Turnpike. Wise and Floyd continued to operate independently of Loring and each other.[2]

In addition to the demoralized veterans of Rich Mountain, Jackson controlled several other Confederate regiments that had recently arrived in the theater of operations. By the time Loring arrived in western Virginia, there were regiments from Tennessee, Arkansas, and North Carolina. At Monterey, Jackson briefed Loring on the situation facing him. From Monterey the Staunton-Parkersburg Turnpike led northwest to Huttonsville traversing two mountain passes. Because the first pass east of Huttonsville—Cheat Mountain at an elevation of more than 3,500 feet—had been strongly defended by Federal forces since shortly after the battle at Rich Mountain, Jackson had opted not to attack there. But the second of the two passes—Greenbrier over the Allegheny Mountains— although not as strong as the one at Cheat Mountain, was held by the Twelfth Georgia under Colonel Edward Johnson. Posted in supporting positions were the Third Arkansas and Fifty-second Virginia. Jackson had also taken steps to hold a second pass across the Allegheny Mountains through which a difficult, but usable, road ran from Millborough, located on the Virginia Central Railroad in the Valley, west to Huntersville on the Greenbrier River and then to Huttonsville. There he had posted the Twenty-first Virginia commanded by Colonel William Gilham and the Sixth North Carolina. Remaining with Jackson at Monterey were the Thirty-seventh and Forty-fourth Virginia and the First Georgia.

Loring remained at Monterey for a few days becoming familiar with the terrain. After satisfying himself that a direct attack on the Federal position on Cheat Mountain was out of the question, he decided to take direct command of the forces assembled at Huntersville. Leaving instructions for Jackson to move his three regiments west to the Greenbrier River and to prepare to cooperate with an advance against the Federal rear, Loring crossed the Allegheny Mountains to Huntersville. There he established his headquarters on July 30 and began preparations for a flank attack against the Federals on Cheat Mountain using the three Tennessee regiments and the Forty-eighth Virginia encamped there.[3]

Loring had a number of new regiments that had not seen battle in the young war. The Third Arkansas had been training in Virginia since early July. Its commander, Colonel Albert Rust, was a native of the Old Dominion whose family had moved to Arkansas when he was a boy. Rust, a tall, strong man, had been a U.S. congressman, but he resigned his seat in the House of Representatives when Arkansas seceded from the Union. He represented the state in the Confederate Congress at Montgomery, Alabama, but he was persuaded to return home and raise a regiment for service in Virginia. Arriving in Lynchburg in early July, the men of the Third Arkansas soon found themselves with sore feet from drilling under cadets of the Richmond Light Infantry. Receiving orders on July 15, the regiment moved by rail to Staunton where it stepped out on its first road march. With a "long, free swing gait, . . . they ate up the long hot miles." While they were en route to Monterey, they received bits and pieces of information about a big battle that was taking place somewhere in northern Virginia east of the Blue Ridge. When they finally settled into camp on the 24th, they learned that the Confederacy had won its first great victory at Manassas Junction. They were encouraged by the news, but their enthusiasm was soon dampened by a cold, steady rain that began on July 28 and continued for days.[4]

The First Tennessee reached western Virginia by a more roundabout route. Initially ordered to Manassas Junction to reinforce the Confederate army assembled there, its train arrived the night the battle ended. They were then sent to Staunton where they remained encamped for a few days before marching off to Huntersville. A veteran of Company H could not "remember of ever experiencing a harder or more fatiguing march. It seemed that mountain was piled upon mountain."[5]

On July 23, the day before Loring took over the Confederate command at Monterey, McClellan passed command of the Federal theater of operations to Brigadier General Rosecrans, the Ohio officer who had performed so well at Rich Mountain. McClellan left Rosecrans a memorandum detailing plans for going on the defensive in theater, and on the day McClellan departed for Washington the two generals rode together to Grafton. Along the way they discussed the difficulties of defending the western Virginia mountains with the Federal forces scattered and isolated throughout the theater. It was a smooth transfer of command that left Rosecrans in charge of the Department of the Ohio. There was a new Federal theater commander, but the campaign plan remained McClellan's. When Rosecrans assumed command, however, the strategic situation facing the Union had changed as a result of the Confederate victory at Manassas Junction, so he prepared to establish a chain of outposts along the Allegheny Mountains to defend the territory held by the Federals against a Confederate offensive. Rosecrans pictured "the ferocious triumph of the enemies of our government" and believed that he would soon feel its effects in western Virginia, as he set about to meet "the coming invasion of the rebels." After seeing McClellan off at Grafton, Rosecrans established the defenses to hold the routes in Federal hands. In the Kanawha, Cox was to go on the defensive, and J. J. Reynolds, former commander of the Tenth Indiana, was promoted to brigadier general and charged with holding the Staunton-Parkersburg Turnpike where it crossed Cheat Mountain pass.[6]

While McClellan and Rosecrans were coordinating their change of command, Cox, continuing his operations in the Kanawha Valley, finally received the wagons he wanted on July 23 and the next day resumed the advance up the valley using the James River and

Kanawha Turnpike. His advance guard had a brief skirmish with Wise's rear guard as the Confederates quickly withdrew from Camp Tyler, leaving supper on the table. On July 25 Cox entered Charleston unopposed. In an attempt to slow the Federals the departing Confederates cut the cables on the suspension bridge across the Elk River. Captain Lane and his company from the Eleventh Ohio, rapidly becoming experts on repairing destroyed bridges, were able to improvise a floating bridge from a number of coal barges in the vicinity. Cox spent the 25th developing a supply depot at Charleston and organizing a line of communications with Gallipolis on the Ohio River. That day the Twenty-second Virginia had a close call when Federal gunners fired on the steamer *Julia Maffitt*. When the boat, loaded with the regiment's men and supplies, took a hit, Phil Doddridge, pilot and member of the Kanawha Rifles, steered to the opposite shore and set it on fire. The troops on board managed to escape harm, but almost all of the regiment's supplies went down with the ship.[7]

Cox learned of the Federal defeat at Manassas Junction and the appointment of Rosecrans as the new theater commander before he left Charleston on July 26. He had received orders from McClellan, and again from Rosecrans, to remain on the defensive while the Federal forces in northwestern Virginia moved on Wise's rear. But Cox had been deeply embarrassed by the incident at Scary Creek and sought to redeem his reputation. When he learned that Wise was withdrawing, Cox decided to pursue the Confederates as fast as possible. While his decision meant disregarding the orders to stay on the defensive, the pursuit offered an opportunity to increase the amount of territory controlled by the Federals in the Kanawha Valley with little risk of casualties. Cox left Charleston with four regiments, the First and Second Kentucky and the Eleventh and Twelfth Ohio, on July 26 to continue the pursuit. His fifth regiment, the Twenty-first Ohio, a three-month regiment raised in excess of the national quota in the president's first call for troops in April, was left to garrison Charleston. The Twenty-first was nearing the end of its enlistment and the governor of Ohio wanted it back. Although regiments raised subsequent to the April call for troops enlisted for three years, in July and August the three-month regiments in Federal service were nearing the end of their enlistment in western Virginia. During the transition period in July and August there was a stream of Ohio and Indiana three-month regiments moving out of the theater, to be replaced by new three-year regiments. Thus, Rosecrans lost much of the combat experience that had been gained in the first few months of the campaign.[8]

Before leaving western Virginia, McClellan had attempted to keep some of the three-month units with him in service beyond their enlistment. He wrote on July 19 that he had called "upon the patriotism of [the] officers & men [Barnett's battery] for a short extension of their service" in anticipation of the move on Staunton. But despite his considerable personal popularity with the troops, he had no success with Barnett's troops or any of the other three-month units he appealed to. Two days later McClellan telegraphed Scott that he could no longer make the move to Staunton that he had suggested earlier because his "3 months men [were] homesick & discontented with their officers & determined to return at once."[9]

The Tenth Indiana, which had been part of Rosecrans's brigade during the fighting at Rich Mountain, remained in Beverly after the battle until July 24, when it received orders to return home to be mustered out of service in August. Upon the regiment's return to Indianapolis, its commander, Colonel Mahlon D. Manson, set about to reorganize it for three-year service. About eighty-five men reenlisted for the new regiment, and on September 18 it was mustered into Federal service and sent to Louisville. The men of the Sixth Indiana, the state's first Civil War regiment and veteran of the Philippi races, watched the Tenth pass by their camp on its way home. But the Sixth did follow them until they had filled the entrenchments and leveled the embankments of Garnett's defensive position at Laurel Hill. With thoughts of home and loved ones, the "boys cheated . . . as they put hundreds of rails in the bottoms of the ditches to fill up fast; and those earthworks, which in the ordinary way took General Garnett's men weeks to build, were leveled like molehills." Once home, Crittenden, like Manson, reorganized the regiment for three-year service and took it to Louisville in September.[10]

The loss of the three-month regiment did not halt Cox's move up the Kanawha Valley, but the advance was complicated by two incidents that exemplified the growing pains of an army conducting its first combat operations in hostile country. One day's march out of Charleston, camped "in a lovely nook between spurs of the hills," Cox was confronted by three of his subordinates after supper. They had determined that since Cox had little more military experience than themselves, he should consult them before making decisions. They informed him that they thought it was foolhardy to continue following the Confederates any further and that unless Cox could change their minds, they would not continue the pursuit. Cox considered their conduct mutinous but offered to forget the matter if they would apologize and promptly obey his orders in the future. They did, and although Cox considered the matter a part of his continuing military education, he reflected that the incident could have been avoided if the regiments he had trained for his brigade in Ohio had not been taken from him and replaced with ones he did not know.[11]

Later in the advance, Cox had the opportunity to further his education even more as a commander. In Charleston two newspaper correspondents had joined his brigade expecting to receive military rank and become a part of Cox's mess. According to Cox, when he provided them a tent and transportation but refused military rank and required their dispatches to be reviewed by one of his staff, they decided to take matters into their own hands and "write him down." They departed and wrote stories for their newspapers that reflected poorly on Cox's command. Since Cox was nearing the end of his Ohio appointment as a brigadier general and his commission in the

U.S. Volunteers had not yet been confirmed by the Senate, the stories caused him no little concern for the future of his army career.[12]

Reluctant subordinates and revenge-seeking correspondents turned out to be the biggest problems Cox had to face during the movement to Gauley Bridge. Wise's withdrawing force felled a few trees across the turnpike, and there were occasional skirmishes as the Confederate rear guard harassed the head of the Federal column, but by July 29 Cox had reached Gauley Bridge where his forces "captured some fifteen hundred stands of arms and a considerable store of munitions." Wise had departed two days earlier after burning the bridge across the Gauley River. By the time Cox arrived, the Confederates were well on their way to White Sulphur Springs to join forces with Floyd. Cox consolidated his forces around Gauley Bridge and sent a small detachment to follow Wise and "keep up his precipitate retreat." Both McClellan and Rosecrans sent Cox messages of congratulations for clearing the Kanawha Valley. In praising Cox, neither McClellan nor Rosecrans mentioned that Cox had disregarded their orders to defend rather than to pursue Wise. The success negated the bad publicity Cox had anticipated from the two offended gentlemen of the press. Their negative reports and the news of his clearing the Kanawha Valley of Confederates appeared in the newspapers at the same time. Cox received Senate confirmation as a brigadier general of the U.S. Volunteers shortly thereafter, allowing him to remain in command of the Kanawha Brigade.[13]

By the time Wise departed Gauley Bridge and Cox occupied it, Lee was on his way to western Virginia with instructions from Davis to coordinate the Confederate efforts in western Virginia. Unlike Loring, who had left Richmond with a staff of experienced officers to assist him in western Virginia, Lee traveled with only two aides, Colonel John A. Washington and Captain Walter H. Taylor. Both officers had been with Lee since May, helping him organize Virginia's military forces. Washington was the nephew of George

Washington and custodian of Mount Vernon, and Taylor was a militia officer with Virginia Military Institute training. Taylor would remain with Lee throughout the entire war; Washington would not be so fortunate. Lee's small party also included two family servants— Perry, who had worked in the dining room at Arlington, and Meredith, a cook from White House, a large Custis estate on the Pamunkey River that belonged to his eldest son, William Henry Fitzhugh Lee, known as "Rooney." Rooney Lee was already in western Virginia as Loring's cavalry commander when his father arrived at the one-armed general's headquarters near Huntersville.[14]

Lee's mission in western Virginia was somewhat ambiguous. He carried no written orders from Davis, who apparently wanted him to coordinate operations and suppress rivalries among the Confederate commanders. Davis had talked to Lee privately before Lee left Richmond, but there was no written record of what the two men discussed at that meeting. Lee had been given no direct authority over the commanders; he was simply to inspect and consult their campaign plans, apparently in the hope that his prestige and nominal command over all Confederate forces in Virginia would give enough credence to his opinions for them to be accepted. The Richmond *Enquirer* characterized Lee's mission as "one of inspection, and consultation on the plan of campaign." Davis had appointed two of the three brigadier generals, Floyd and Wise, for political reasons. The third was Loring, who himself had gained entrance to the U.S. army during the Mexican War where he, too, had been a politically appointed officer. Unlike Floyd and Wise, however, Loring had considerable military experience, and he had seen more combat than Lee. The three independent-minded commanders already in the theater of operations were not eager to surrender any of their authority. Unless Lee could induce them to cooperate with one another, planning and conducting the hoped-for Confederate offensive against the Federals would remain a divided effort, just as it had been during the ineffectual defense of western Virginia.[15]

On the evening of July 28, Lee and his party reached Staunton by rail and proceeded from there on horseback to Monterey, where Jackson still had his headquarters. At Monterey Lee saw for the first time the demoralization and sickness of the Confederate forces that had been part of Garnett's army. Leaving Monterey after a few days, Lee reached Loring's headquarters at Huntersville on August 6, unannounced and unwelcome. In command less than a week when Lee arrived, Loring made it clear that he was not pleased that the Confederate government had sent someone to supervise him. When faced with the confrontational Loring, the nonconfrontational Lee, whose style was to seek harmony and suggest options, tried to temper the situation by simply confirming that Loring was in command and then stepping out of the picture, something his role as a coordinator easily allowed him to do.[16]

In the wake of the Confederate success at Manassas Junction, Lee's arrival in western Virginia attracted little attention. The military leaders who attracted public attention in the South were the victors Beauregard and Johnston, while in the North, hopes for future military success centered on McClellan. Although not holding the unity of command that McClellan had enjoyed, Lee's mission in the western counties was to undo what McClellan had accomplished. Both Lee and McClellan had already demonstrated considerable skill in organizing relatively large military forces for war in a short period of time. But their accomplishments had not been met with the same recognition. McClellan had had the opportunity to demonstrate his ability to plan and conduct a successful campaign with the forces he raised and trained, while Lee had been forced to sit impatiently in Richmond as Beauregard and Johnston led the Virginia regiments he had organized and trained to victory at Manassas Junction. McClellan made sure that he received full credit for the Federal victories in western Virginia, while Lee's preparatory work of organizing and training the Virginia troops went largely unnoticed in the excitement of the Confederate victory

at Manassas Junction. Three months after becoming a general officer McClellan was a popular and heroic figure who was looked
upon as the savior of the Union, while Lee remained relatively
unknown and was overlooked as the Confederacy celebrated Beauregard and Johnston, the heroes of Manassas Junction. Although
Lee's instructions from Davis left him in an ambiguous position in
western Virginia, the new assignment offered him an opportunity to
gain success and recognition as a field commander.[17]

Meanwhile, the Reorganized Government of Virginia in Wheeling had been taking advantage of McClellan's successful military
campaign to extend its control over the counties in the northwest
that had been occupied by Federal forces. Since his inauguration as
governor in June, Pierpont had been actively recruiting regiments
for Federal service and guard companies to maintain order in several counties. Although the War Department had not sanctioned
such efforts, McClellan had encouraged Pierpont in this endeavor
in a July 20 letter in which he expressed disappointment with "the
extreme slowness with which recruiting goes on."[18]

On the same day Lee arrived in Huntersville, the adjourned session of the Second Wheeling Convention reconvened. In July the
legislature of the Reorganized Government had voted against autho-
rizing creation of a new state, indicating that such an undertaking
was more appropriate to the convention. When it reconvened, the
convention's primary item of interest was the formation of a new
state that would remain loyal to the Union, and the delegates created a special committee to deal with that issue. The idea, however,
was not universally popular in the western counties. The day after
the convention was called to order in Wheeling, Daniel Farnsworth
of Upshur County made a motion to adjourn, arguing that it was not
a good time to attempt a division of the state. After a parliamentary
debate the convention tabled the motion, making it clear that a
majority of the delegates favored creating a new state. The only
questions were when and how. The next day Carlile proposed a

series of resolutions that would create a new state consisting of thirty-three western counties and five Valley counties and provide for the drafting of a constitution that would be submitted to the voters on October 4. The convention narrowly rejected the resolutions, thirty-seven to thirty-five, but Carlile's proposal brought two critical issues to the fore—time and boundaries—that sparked the greatest controversy among the delegates.[19]

For almost two weeks the delegates argued heatedly over what the boundaries of the new state should be and when it should come into being. The special committee proposed including virtually all of the counties west of the Blue Ridge as well as the counties along the Potomac River near Washington, a significantly larger area than the Carlile recommendation. Opponents of dismembering Virginia took advantage of the proposal to advocate a popular vote in January 1862 in each of the counties proposed for the new state. They anticipated that since only the northwestern counties with a clear pro-Union majority would favor the idea, they would be outnumbered by those counties where Unionist minorities could be influenced by Confederate military forces. The convention rejected the large state idea, and the delegates heatedly debated how to find a compromise on a smaller area. Coming to the edge of disintegration, the delegates finally reached a compromise on August 20 that passed by a comfortable majority of fifty to twenty-eight.[20]

Under the compromise plan, the proposed state of Kanawha would consist of thirty-nine counties with provisions that specified seven more that could be included if a majority of the people in those counties approved. In addition, any counties contiguous to the new state could apply for admission if the residents so desired and the constitutional convention approved. The plan was to be referred to the voters living in the affected counties for approval. The referendum and election of constitutional convention delegates were set to take place concurrently on the fourth Thursday of October, the 24th. If a majority of the residents approved formation of a new state, the constitutional convention would meet in Wheeling on November 26. In the interim, the Reorganized Government would continue in full power.[21]

While the Second Wheeling Convention debated the future of Virginia in the northwest, two former governors of Virginia were engaged in a personal rivalry in the Kanawha Valley. Brigadier Generals Floyd and Wise had been political rivals for years, and that did not bode well for their military association. Floyd's commission in the Confederate army antedated Wise's by a few days, and he had instructions from the War Department to consolidate his brigade with Wise's forces in the Kanawha Valley at which time Floyd would assume overall command. Floyd and Wise met for the first time as generals at White Sulphur Springs in Greenbrier County on August 6. The meeting did not go well. Floyd arrived at White Sulphur Springs with Heth's Forty-fifth Virginia, intending to move his brigade west along the same route Wise had just used for his retreat. After his recent experience in the Kanawha Valley, Wise believed that the entire region was "wholly disaffected and traitorous." He thought Floyd's plan to regain the lost ground would be a mistake. Moreover, his troops were exhausted and their supplies all but gone after his precipitate withdrawal up the Kanawha in the face of the Federal advance. He wanted at least two weeks to refit his troops before embarking on further operations, and even then he favored drawing the enemy toward the Confederate position. Wise wanted the Federals to have to cope with the transportation difficulties presented by the Fayette Wilderness, an area that extended for forty miles east of Gauley Bridge, rather than inflict that problem on the Confederate forces. Floyd, however, was adamant in his desire to carry the fight to the Federals. The meeting ended with no resolution of the differences between the two men. Indeed, if anything, their animosity toward one another had increased.[22]

As the Federal and Confederate forces adjusted to their new commanders and plans, both had to endure an unprecedented period of rain and cold in the western mountains. Snow fell during the night of August 14. A Southern survivor later recorded with understandable exaggeration that it had "rained 32 days in August." Captain Taylor, Lee's aide, recorded that "it rained daily and in torrents; the condition of the roads was frightful; they were barely passable."[23]

In such miserable weather conditions even veteran armies with experienced leadership would have had difficulties. Lee and Rosecrans were both new to senior command, and their armies were largely filled with raw recruits who had yet to see combat. Rosecrans, however, had the advantage of a command structure that put him clearly in charge of the Federal forces in western Virginia, while Lee not only faced battle with Rosecrans but would have to contend with three very independently minded commanders as he tried to regain control of the theater of operations. Not only did Lee face challenges from the Confederate generals, but the Federal success in western Virginia had sapped the spirits of the Confederate troops there. The Confederate offensive would begin with rather less of the enthusiasm and optimism that had marked the beginning of the Federal invasion in May. Where the Federal troops had marched off to war in fine spring weather to what they considered a grand adventure, the Confederates faced rain and cold and Manassas Junction had shattered any thoughts of a short war. As the Confederate forces in western Virginia were preparing to take the offensive against a chastened Federal army, neither side approached the prospect of renewing the campaign with any real enthusiasm. Lee faced coordination problems among the Confederate forces, and Rosecrans worried about the safety of the Federal supply lines that extended from the Ohio River.

CHAPTER TEN

Lee's Warring Generals

LEE'S ARRIVAL AT Loring's headquarters may have caused feelings of jealousy in the old one-armed veteran, but Rosecrans, carrying "the gloom of . . . disaster," assessed Lee's presence in western Virginia as a sign of an "offensive campaign to recover possession of Western Virginia." Erroneously assuming that the various concentrations of Confederate forces in front of him were conducting operations in coordination with one another, Rosecrans interpreted their movements as confirmation that he was about to face a massive offensive. McClellan's two-pronged advance from Ohio had driven the Federals deep into western Virginia, resulting in a favorable atmosphere for pro-Union political activity there, and it provided the potential for a further movement into the Valley of Virginia. But the advance had also created long supply lines that stretched from the Ohio River to the

Alleghenies. In light of the potential Confederate offensive, those lines appeared vulnerable. With the Confederate forces under Jackson on the Greenbrier River menacing the Federal position at Cheat Mountain, Loring at Huntersville with another brigade, Wise in a position to advance toward Cox at Gauley Bridge, and Floyd on the way into the Kanawha Valley, Rosecrans thought of nothing but defense.[1]

When Rosecrans took over as theater commander in western Virginia, he had brought with him few of McClellan's qualifications for high command. He was a graduate of West Point where he finished fifth in the class of 1842, but he missed the Mexican War and his career in the army's Corps of Engineers was unremarkable. In 1851 he applied for a professorship at the Virginia Military Institute but lost the appointment to Thomas J. Jackson, later known as "Stonewall" for his brigade's performance at Manassas Junction. Shortly after a promotion to first lieutenant in 1853 he resigned from the U.S. army. Western Virginia was not unknown territory for him, however. He had been an engineer and superintendent of the Canal River Coal Company, a British-American firm with extensive holdings in the Kanawha Valley. While living in the Valley, Rosecrans made the acquaintance of Christopher Tompkins, at that time superintendent of the Paint Creek Coal and Iron and Manufacturing Company in Kanawha County. Leaving western Virginia, Rosecrans and two partners built a kerosene refinery in Cincinnati, but they were unable to produce the clear, colorless product that would not foul the lamp wick that customers wanted. While experimenting with a method to develop a marketable kerosene, Rosecrans received severe burns on his face that took eighteen months to heal. The resulting scars left his face with a permanent "smirk." In April 1861, driven by what he called a "strong sense of duty," Rosecrans volunteered for state military service and became a member of McClellan's staff as an engineer colonel in the Ohio Volunteers. Promoted to brigadier general, he led the flank attack at

Rich Mountain that led to victory and brought McClellan national recognition. Although McClellan did not acknowledge the critical role Rosecrans played at Rich Mountain, McClellan agreed when Scott suggested that the brigadier general be named theater commander, and before departing for Washington, he offered Rosecrans his ideas for defending western Virginia.[2]

Cox described Rosecrans as "tall but not heavy," with an "aquiline nose and bright eyes." Rosecrans's speech was apt to grow hurried, almost to stammering, when he was excited. Another observer put Rosecrans as "nearly six feet high, compact, with little waste flesh, nervous and active in all movements." Although not as charismatic as McClellan, Rosecrans worked well with his staff and inspired confidence in his soldiers.[3]

Under Rosecrans the Federal forces in western Virginia continued to enjoy the benefits of a single commander to coordinate their efforts, but defending the gains made in western Virginia was but one of Rosecrans's concerns as commander of the Department of the Ohio. Shortly after taking command, Rosecrans was in Clarksburg dealing with administrative and logistical matters related to the Federal occupation of western Virginia. He also had to deal directly with the governors of Indiana and Ohio, the states that provided most of the Federal troops in the theater. The three-month regiments from Ohio and Indiana would soon have to return home to be replaced by three-year organizations. To further complicate matters, Pierpont, governor of the Reorganized Government of Virginia in Wheeling, wanted Rosecrans to turn over any captured equipment to the new regiments being raised for Federal service.[4]

Fearing a Confederate offensive, Rosecrans considered withdrawing Cox's Kanawha Brigade to the northwest where the Federal forces could be consolidated to defend the most pro-Union part of western Virginia. Cox, however, saw the situation in a somewhat more favorable light. Wise had withdrawn from the Kanawha Valley, and by the end of July Cox was well on the way to making

Gauley Bridge, "the gate through which all important movements from eastern into southwestern Virginia must necessarily come," a defensible position. The small town of Gauley Bridge, located where the confluence of the New and Gauley Rivers created the Kanawha River, was a major intersection on the James River and Kanawha Turnpike. The Turnpike followed the north bank of the Kanawha River and crossed the Gauley River on a substantial wooden bridge that had given the town its name. In Cox's view it would also be an important link in any chain of defensive outposts established to protect the Ohio valley from an attempted Confederate movement out of the Valley of Virginia, because it was the most advanced logistically supportable position that could protect the Kanawha Valley from attack. The few buildings of Gauley Bridge rested on a sloping hillside along the west bank of the Gauley River. The Gauley Bridge and Weston Pike ran along the west bank of the Gauley River passing north through Carnifex Ferry, Summersville, and Sutton on its way to Weston, while the Giles, Fayette and Kanawha Pike crossed the Kanawha River at Montgomery's Ferry, just below Gauley Bridge, and ran south to Fayetteville and Beckley. By the time Cox occupied the town, Wise had burned the covered bridge as part of the delaying tactics during his hasty retreat from the Kanawha Valley, leaving only the stone piers standing in the water. A witness described the burning as giving "the appearance of a bridge of gold with frescoed work of the finest skill."[5]

The missing bridge posed a problem for Cox, but Captain Lane of the Eleventh Ohio had by now almost perfected the techniques of repairing bridges. Lane was able to reconstruct bridges almost as fast as the retreating Confederates could destroy them. Gauley Bridge, however, posed a formidable challenge to his skills. The span had been five hundred feet long across a three hundred-foot-wide river, and the supporting stone piers, set one hundred fifty feet apart, were all that remained when the Federals reached the crossing site. With the swiftly flowing Kanawha River in front of

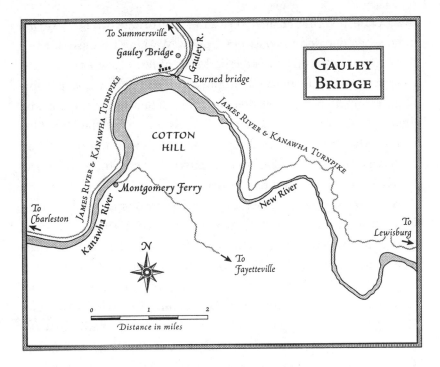

To Summersville

Gauley Bridge

Gauley R.

Burned bridge

JAMES RIVER & KANAWHA TURNPIKE

COTTON HILL

JAMES RIVER & KANAWHA TURNPIKE

Montgomery Ferry

Kanawha River

New River

To Charleston

To Lewisburg

To Fayetteville

N

0   1   2
Distance in miles

GAULEY BRIDGE

him, Lane determined that replacing the bridge would take too long, so he decided to construct a ferry. Working furiously for five days, Lane and his troops stretched a giant ferry hawser across the river using the stone piers for support and built a ferry boat capable of carrying "two hundred men or four loaded army wagons and their animals, or two guns and their caissons." With the ferry Cox could move troops across the river where they could provide an early warning of any Confederate move up the James River and Kanawha Turnpike toward the town.[6]

After occupying the town and moving troops across the river, Cox set about to establish a strong defensive position at Gauley Bridge to prevent the Confederates from moving back into the Kanawha Valley. He benefited from the assistance of a number of engineers. Colonel Whittlesey, a West Point graduate and chief engineer of Ohio's Governor Dennison, was with Cox, and although he was getting on in years, he provided wise advice. Rosecrans, inspired by word from McClellan in Washington that Lee and Johnston had joined forces to crush the Federals in western Virginia, sent engineer Lieutenant Wagner, a recent graduate of the Military Academy, to supervise fortifications for Cox. Captain Benham, veteran of the action at Corrick's Ford and an engineer with twenty-five years of experience, arrived shortly after Wagner, modified the lieutenant's defensive plans slightly, and returned to Rosecrans's headquarters after a few days to find a commission as a brigadier general awaiting him. For all the engineering skill allocated to the Kanawha Brigade, Cox was of the opinion that it required but little work to reinforce adequately the natural defenses around Gauley Bridge.[7]

In addition to deploying his forces in a defensive posture, Cox sent reconnaissance parties south along the Giles, Fayette and Kanawha Pikes to Fayette Court House, east along the James River and Kanawha Turnpike as far as Sewell Mountain, and north along the Gauley Bridge and Weston Turnpike to Summersville. Frizell, commanding the Eleventh Ohio, led a detachment of his regiment to Summersville to break up a Confederate recruiting station reported to be established there. Upon reaching the town, however, they found no station. But the colonel investigated the residents and administered an oath of loyalty to the United States to those whom he regarded as suspect in their loyalties. One woman, "although a violent secessionist, was very badly frightened at being in the power of the 'Yankees.' " Frizell, ascertaining that a loyalty oath would do no good, but feeling that something should be done, required the woman to get down on her knees and recite the Lord's Prayer.[8]

After receiving reports from all his scouting parties, Cox reported the results to Rosecrans on August 7, writing that the "retreat of Wise has every characteristic of a final movement out of the Valley." It was Cox's opinion that unless someone other than Wise led the offensive, the Confederates would not soon be moving back into the Kanawha Valley. For Cox, the destroyed bridges and abandoned stores and equipment were more than ample evidence that Wise "intended to take final leave of our region."[9]

Although Wise may not have planned to return to the Kanawha Valley, Floyd had other ideas. He wanted to regain the ground he felt Wise had abandoned unnecessarily. Their first meeting on August 6 had confirmed that simply donning uniforms had not ameliorated their previous political differences one whit, and the rivalry set the tone for their military operations. Wise convinced himself that in spite of his first ignominious experience as a commander, his failure to hold the Valley was not really his fault because it was "wholly disaffected and traitorous." After leaving the Valley, Wise, his former fire-breathing rhetoric notwithstanding, was ready to give up on western Virginia, reporting that the region was lost and that there was no way to persuade the people there "that Virginia can or will ever reconquer the northwest." Floyd, however, believed that Wise's precipitate retreat had contributed to the Confederates' problems by producing "very injurious effects upon the public mind, even in the true and faithful portions of the country."[10]

Wise's movement out of the Kanawha Valley had been especially difficult for the Twenty-second and Thirty-sixth Virginia. Many of the men in the two regiments were of the opinion that they had enlisted to defend their homes and, when ordered to leave the Valley, simply deserted and went home to their families. Sympathetic officers in the regiments who opposed Wise's decision to retreat exacerbated the problem by furloughing large groups of men in their companies. In the Twenty-second Virginia, the entire company from Boone County went home, although most of them did return to the regiment in August. As the Twenty-second passed through Gauley Bridge, its commander, Tompkins, thought of his nearby farm and the family still living there. On a brief visit home he wrote a letter to Cox the day after the bridge burning to request the Federal commander's assistance in protecting his family and property from "abuse of private rights."[11]

Floyd, the senior of the two feuding novice generals, assumed command of all the Confederate forces operating in and near the Kanawha Valley on August 11, including Wise's Legion and the two Kanawha regiments under his command, the Twenty-second and Thirty-sixth Virginia. These two regiments frequently found themselves moved between Wise and Floyd because the two generals went to great lengths to keep the regiments they had personally raised under their own command. Two days after Floyd took command he asked Wise to send the Thirty-sixth to Lewisburg. Wise did not comply, explaining that the regiment was "in a state of great dilapidation and destitution, from the many resignations of its officers and desertions of its men." The regiment, Wise wrote, numbered "less than 550 men, many of whom have the measles." The condition of the Thirty-sixth was typical of the forces under Wise. When Floyd ordered a battery of artillery, Wise again failed to comply. The reason this time was that the horses were not properly shod because there were no smiths, shoes, or nails available. Floyd's overall assessment of Wise's force at the time was that it was so disorganized as to be of little use.[12]

While Floyd and Wise feuded, the Federals strengthened their defensive line. From his headquarters in Clarksburg, Rosecrans ordered telegraph lines constructed to Westover, and from there south to Gauley Bridge. Captain Theophilus Gaines and his company from the Fifth Ohio were detailed to protect Fuller and his construction party. Upon reaching Westover, Gaines, a militia officer on his first independent command, sent the first military message on the line to report that, threatened by armed local opposition forces, he had entrenched his company on a hilltop where they would hold out until help arrived. Rosecrans may have been concerned with defense, but that did not mean stopping at every perceived threat. He promptly wired back to Gaines that he had been "sent into the field to become a terror to the enemy, and not be terrorized by them. March out of that entrenchment and disperse those rebels." The telegraph construction continued with no further delays by Captain Gaines.[13]

Rosecrans had already sent the Seventh Ohio under Colonel Erastus B. Tyler down the Gauley Bridge and Weston Pike ahead of the telegraph party to open a line of communication with Cox. The Seventh arrived in Summersville on August 7 and was shortly joined there by the Thirteenth and the Twenty-third Ohio. On the 13th, Tyler and the Seventh Ohio moved further south to Cross Lanes, where a road from Carnifex Ferry on the Gauley River intersected with the Gauley Bridge and Weston Pike. From Carnifex Ferry, the Sunday Road provided access to the James River and Kanawha Turnpike, joining it at Dogwood Gap, about fifteen miles east of Gauley Bridge. Tyler's mission at Cross Lanes was to provide early warning of any Confederate movement along the Sunday Road that threatened to turn Cox's position at Gauley Bridge or cut the road to the Federal supply depot that had been established at Weston.[14]

Hearing rumors of a Confederate advance up the Wilderness Road that linked Summersville with the James River and Kanawha Turnpike at Meadow Bluff, the commanders of the Thirteenth and Twenty-third Ohio took it upon themselves to follow Tyler to Cross Lanes on the 15th. When Cox learned of the move, he urged the two regiments to return to Summersville where, in the event of a Confederate attack, they would be in a more favorable position to move north to Sutton. Tyler, however, was to maintain his position at Cross Lanes. Rosecrans confirmed Cox's directions and on August 17 instructed Tyler to hold the ferries as long as possible and, when the position became untenable, fall back toward Gauley Bridge.[15]

By repositioning the Thirteenth and Twenty-third Ohio to be ready to retreat in case of attack rather than leaving them where they could engage an advancing force early, both Rosecrans and Cox confirmed the Federal shift from an offensive campaign to a defensive posture, thus giving the initiative to the Confederates. Before the Federal defeat at Manassas Junction, the situation had been reversed. McClellan's invasion of western Virginia and his relatively swift advance to the Allegheny Mountains had kept the Confederate defenders off balance and disorganized. But the gloom of defeat had pervaded Rosecrans and the other Federal commanders in the theater since Manassas Junction, and they believed that Lee's presence in western Virginia marked the beginning of a major Confederate offensive. The consequent loss of initiative on Rosecrans's part gave the Confederates a chance to bring reinforcements into the theater and the hope of regaining their lost territory.

Floyd, who was among the reinforcements, did not let his feud with Wise overwhelm his desire to force the Federals out of the Kanawha Valley. Even as Cox and Rosecrans were keeping their lines of withdrawal open, Floyd was on the move toward Carnifex Ferry where he saw an opportunity to cut the Federal north-south line of communications between Gauley Bridge and Weston. Both the Wilderness Road and the Sunday Road offered routes from the

James River and Kanawha Turnpike that would give Floyd the
opportunity to break the link between Cox and Rosecrans and out-
flank Cox's position at Gauley Bridge. Followed by a reluctant
Wise, Floyd marched west from Lewisburg toward Gauley Bridge.
On August 19 the advance guard reached Dogwood Gap where the
Sunday Road intersected with the turnpike, and the next day Heth's
Forty-fifth Virginia skirmished with troops of the Eleventh Ohio
patrolling to Cox's front.[16]

Learning of the skirmish at Dogwood Gap, Cox believed it was
the beginning of the much-anticipated Confederate offensive. He
moved the Seventh Ohio from Cross Lanes to a position about six
miles north of Gauley Bridge to guard a road that passed to the rear
of the Federal defenses. Once satisfied the attack had been repulsed,
Cox sent Tyler back to Cross Lanes. But Tyler's return was delayed
for a couple of days while the Ohio men received a long-delayed
issue of clothes and shoes. The Seventh did not get back to its position at Cross Lanes until August 24, by which time Floyd had
moved across the Gauley River at Carnifex Ferry.[17]

On the Confederate side, the day after the skirmish at Dogwood
Gap, Floyd and Wise met at the foot of Gauley Mountain to discuss
what they should do next. There they decided that Wise and his
legion would move up the Sunday Road and attack Carnifex Ferry
while Floyd waited with his brigade along with the Twenty-second
and Thirty-sixth Virginia at Dogwood Gap to guard their supplies.
In an effort to demonstrate that Floyd was indeed in command of
both forces, Lee had ordered, on August 21, that the two regiments
be assigned to Floyd. Early on the morning of August 22 Wise
started north with seventeen miles of ankle-deep mud the only
obstacle in the way of his legion. In the meantime, unknown to
Wise, Floyd had learned that the Federal position at Cross Lanes
was unoccupied and moved quickly on a forced march along
another road. He reached the ferry site soon after Wise. Tyler's
troops had sunk the ferry boats before they left, but they had not

destroyed them, and the Confederates were able to use them to cross the Gauley River with little delay. Once across the river, Floyd changed the plan agreed to at Gauley Mountain and ordered Wise back to Dogwood Gap while he remained at Carnifex Ferry. Wise, disgusted, complied.[18]

Tyler, returning to Cross Lanes with the Seventh Ohio on August 24, was five miles from the village when he learned that Floyd had already crossed the river. Tyler immediately retreated two miles to spend the night and report the situation to Cox. Cox ordered Tyler to "make a dash at them." Ever mindful of the defensive posture the Federals had adopted, Cox also cautioned Tyler to take care to keep his "force well in hand so as to keep your retreat safe." Still thinking defensively, Cox also sent half a regiment to hold Peters Creek, some six miles from Cross Lanes, to keep a line of retreat open to Gauley Bridge should the Seventh need it. Tyler took to heart the injunction to proceed with caution. Leaving one of his companies and a company of Virginians, the Snake Hunters, to guard the baggage trains, Tyler and the rest of the regiment spent most of the 25th cautiously moving the seven miles to Cross Lanes, even though they encountered no opposition along the way.[19]

The Seventh Ohio was a new three-year regiment with no combat experience, and Tyler, a trapper and fur merchant before the war, was new to the responsibilities of command. Coming within a half mile of Floyd's position, he elected to halt his regiment for the night before attacking. During the night Confederate scouts located the Federal encampment. When he learned of Tyler's location, Floyd sought Heth's counsel, asking him what he should do. Heth was quick to answer. "Do," he said, "[t]here is but one thing to for you to do, attack them at daylight tomorrow morning." Floyd did. Tyler and the Seventh Ohio received their initiation to the chaos of battle when Floyd's brigade, led by the Heth's Forty-fourth Virginia, fell upon them while they breakfasted on locally gathered green corn, roast beef, crackers, and coffee. Although completely surprised and thoroughly routed, most of the Seventh Ohio lived to fight another day, and the regiment exacted some measure of revenge in March 1862 when it routed the forces of "Stonewall" Jackson at Kernstown in the Valley of Virginia shouting, "Cross Lanes!"[20]

Tyler and about two hundred of his men eventually straggled back to Gauley Bridge. Major John S. Casement managed to gather another four hundred of the confused soldiers and lead them west across the mountains to safety in Charleston. The regimental trains reached the covering detachment at Peters Creek just ahead of the Confederates and escaped intact. Heady with his small victory at Cross Lanes, Floyd moved to Carnifex Ferry to fortify positions there and sent the Thirty-sixth Virginia north to occupy Summersville. In reporting to Lee that he had "certainly cut off effectually all communications between General Cox and the forces toward the north," Floyd expressed the belief that he had prevented Cox and Rosecrans from joining forces. If the Confederates could keep the Federals separated, they had a better chance of regaining the Kanawha Valley.[21]

Cox was less concerned about being cut off from Rosecrans than he was puzzled by Floyd's actions following the battle at Cross Lanes. He "fully expected" that the Confederates would follow the same route that Casement and the remnant of the Seventh Ohio had taken to escape to Charleston, but Floyd simply entrenched his forces at Carnifex Ferry. If his success at Cross Lanes made Floyd content to wait for the Federals to attack, Rosecrans was ready to oblige. Upon learning of Tyler's defeat, Rosecrans set out from Clarksburg to secure the Federal line of communications between the northern and southern portions of the theater. After he assumed command of the Federal occupation forces in western Virginia, Rosecrans had set up a chain of defensive positions and a telegraph line from Weston to Gauley Bridge. In late August, upon leaving Clarksburg, Rosecrans marched along that line to engage Floyd. Near the town of Sutton, Rosecrans and his army caught up with

Fuller and his telegraph construction party. The road there was so narrow that the work had to stop while the troops passed by. Once the army had cleared the area, Fuller went back to work, and by September 10 the line was within four miles of Carnifex Ferry where Floyd hoped to prevent Rosecrans from joining Cox.[22]

In Sutton, where the Gauley Bridge and Weston Pike cross the Elk River, Rosecrans organized his forces into three brigades. The first brigade under Benham, the former engineer recently promoted to brigadier general, included the Tenth, Twelfth, and Thirteenth Ohio and a battery of Ohio artillery. Colonel R. L. McCook commanded the second brigade with his own Ninth Ohio as well as the Twenty-eighth and Forty-seventh Ohio, both newly organized regiments of three-year troops. In the third brigade Colonel Eliakim Parker Scammon had his own Twenty-third Ohio, half of the Thirtieth Ohio, and a battery of regular army artillery. Scammon, an 1837 West Point graduate who had been dismissed from the army for disobeying orders in 1856, had been teaching in a parochial school in Cincinnati until June 1861 when he received a colonel's commission in the Ohio Volunteers. The Twenty-third also had two future U.S. presidents in the regiment, Major Rutherford B. Hayes and Private William McKinley.[23]

Although Floyd did not move on Charleston as Cox had expected, the Confederates were not idle. On August 31, believing the Federals were preparing to abandon Gauley Bridge, Floyd ordered Wise to send one of his regiments to Carnifex Ferry and then take the remainder of his command to occupy the camp at the mouth of the Gauley River. Wise demurred, reporting that reduced troop strength caused by an outbreak of measles and a lack of forage for the horses left him with insufficient strength both to occupy Gauley Bridge and guard the James River and Kanawha Turnpike. When Floyd insisted, Wise left a regiment as rear guard at Dogwood Gap and started with the rest of his command toward Carnifex Ferry on September 1. As he reached the ferry, however,

Floyd sent a messenger with orders for Wise to remain at Dogwood Gap until further notice. A disgusted Wise turned around and retraced his path to Dogwood Gap where he spent the night, determined that he would advance on Gauley Bridge on his own.[24]

The next day, Wise moved from Dogwood Gap toward Gauley Bridge. On the way he encountered a Federal detachment consisting of troops from the Eleventh and Twenty-sixth Ohio and, in cooperation with local militia forces, launched an attack. The combined attack, accompanied by considerable cannonading from the Confederate guns, forced the Federals to fall back along the turnpike about thirteen miles. They eventually stopped Wise's advance at a place known alternately as Pig Creek or Big Creek. A cannon that had been rushed forward to support the Ohioans opened fire, but after a few shots a premature discharge sent the swab whirling toward the Confederates, wounding two of the Federal cannoneers. Frizell, finding the gun more of a threat to his troops than to Wise's, sent the faulty cannon to the rear. During the skirmish Wise maintained control of his forces and attempted to outflank Frizell by sending Lieutenant Colonel Frank Anderson and his Fifty-ninth Virginia, a legion regiment, around the Federal left. But when the flanking force lost its way in the heavy woods, the Confederates withdrew to Hawks Nest to protect Liken's mill, a source of ground wheat and corn. The affair produced no fatalities and no more than a dozen light wounds on either side. Reporting the day's events to Floyd on September 4, Wise suggested that he could "amuse the enemy in front" if Floyd would advance upon Gauley Bridge. But if Wise had any thoughts of cooperation with Floyd, they were gone by the next day when he sent a report of his recent activities to Lee along with a plea to be released from Floyd's command. Wise candidly admitted that if they remained together, they would "unite in more wars than one." Lee took no action on Wise's report. In the meantime, Floyd sent the Twenty-second Virginia back to Wise on August 6 in case Cox followed up the skirmish at Pig Creek.[25]

Lee, aware of the Federal movement from the north, had earlier advised Floyd to withdraw to the southern bank of the Gauley River to avoid being trapped between Rosecrans and Cox. In spite of Lee's advice, Floyd elected to remain in position at Carnifex Ferry where he constructed field fortifications along the north side of the Gauley with his back to the river. Behind the Confederate position, the Gauley River formed a horseshoe, allowing both ends of the defensive line to rest on the river's steep banks. While this protected the flanks from a Federal attack, it also made a rapid Confederate withdrawal difficult. In the short term, Floyd needed the flour from nearby mills, and in the long range, he still harbored hopes of severing communications between Cox and Rosecrans in anticipation of an advance he hoped to lead into the Kanawha Valley. On September 9, with Rosecrans drawing closer, he sought to reinforce his position by asking Wise to return the Twenty-second Virginia and send one of the legion's regiments to Carnifex Ferry. Wise sent the Twenty-second, but again citing the measles, refused to send any other troops to aid Floyd, believing that any further reduction in his forces at Hawks Nest would necessitate abandoning Liken's mill and the ground he had gained a week earlier. Wise was also worried about losing the line of communications he had established with local militia forces. While he did provide some rationale to Floyd for keeping his legion intact at Hawks Nest, Wise actually believed he "had been already fooled twice in going to Carnifex, and there was great danger in my falling back at all, with the probability of being ordered again to remain in camp."[26]

Four days after Wise's encounter with the Federals around Gauley Bridge, Colonel McCausland, commanding the Thirty-sixth Virginia, notified Floyd that the Federals were just twelve miles from his position in Summersville. McCausland had sent Captain Henry M. Beckley and his company to Sutton some days earlier to lend their support to the local recruiting effort and watch for Federal movement. On September 8 Beckley encountered an advance

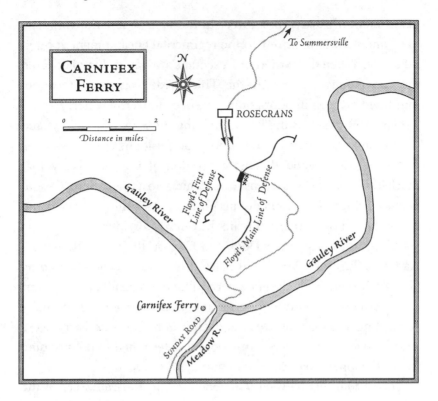

detachment of Rosecrans's force. In the face of superior numbers the Confederates withdrew to the regimental encampment at Summersville. When he learned of Rosecrans's advance, Floyd ordered the understrength regiment—the Thirty-sixth was down to about four hundred men in poor condition—back to Carnifex Ferry.[27]

Gauley Bridge was the key to holding the Kanawha Valley, and the Confederates were deployed in good positions to move against it. Floyd held a good defensive position at Carnifex Ferry that blocked the route Rosecrans would have to take to join Cox at Gauley Bridge. The Confederate position at Carnifex Ferry could be reinforced by Wise moving up the Sunday Road from Dogwood Gap. From his position at Dogwood Gap on the James River and Kanawha Turnpike, Wise could also threaten the Federals holding Gauley Bridge. From Carnifex Ferry, Floyd too could move against Cox's position. Unfortunately for the Confederates, the mutually supporting positions at Dogwood Gap and Carnifex Ferry were held by two commanders who seemed determined to do anything to avoid cooperating with each other.

The skirmishing between Confederate and Federal forces in the area of Gauley Bridge continued until September 10. Cox, unaware of the antagonistic relationship between Floyd and Wise, and thinking that Wise's attack might be part of a coordinated movement with Floyd, sent two companies up the Gauley River toward Carnifex Ferry to protect the Federal left flank. Floyd, however, remained ensconced in his Carnifex Ferry defenses, and Cox remained in a defensive posture at Gauley Bridge.[28]

When Rosecrans reached Summersville, he received reports from local citizens that Floyd was positioned along the north side of the Gauley River near Cross Lanes with a considerable force. But Rosecrans was unconcerned with numbers; he wanted to "whip or pass" Floyd and unite with Cox. Rosecrans started moving toward Floyd, taking the road between Cross Lanes and Carnifex Ferry at 3 A.M. on September 10. By 1 P.M. he had moved fifteen miles to halt two miles short of the Confederate defenses, meeting only a few skirmishers along the way. While he rested his infantry for a few minutes, Rosecrans sent his staff and two cavalry companies forward to reconnoiter the entrenchments.[29]

The reconnaissance revealed no significant opposition, and the Federals resumed the advance at about 2:30 P.M. Shortly thereafter the Tenth Ohio, led by Colonel William Haines Lytle who had been a company commander in the Ohio militia in Mexico, came upon the recently abandoned camp of the Fiftieth Virginia, commanded by Colonel Alexander Welch Reynolds, an 1838 West Point graduate who had joined the Confederate army in March without first having bothered to submit his resignation from the U.S. army. The Fiftieth had moved back from its forward position to strengthen the main Confederate defensive line at Carnifex Ferry. Reynolds led his regiment through a wooded area marked by multiple paths and moved into a position alongside the Fifty-first Virginia in the center of the defensive line. Floyd had deployed his brigade across a bend of the Gauley River. The right end of his entrenched line was anchored on steep cliffs above the river, but there was a gap on the left because the line was too long to be adequately covered by the forces Floyd had available. The Forty-fifth held the Confederate right flank between the river and the road that led from Cross Lanes to the ferry site, and Captain John H. Guy's battery of artillery, about to receive their baptism of fire, was on its left near the center of the line. The Fiftieth and Fifty-first, both raised by Floyd for his brigade, held the center. The Twenty-second, arriving just before Rosecrans launched his attack, held the left flank. The Thirty-sixth held a line on a bit of high ground forward of the main defenses on the left. It was a strong position, but Floyd was outnumbered by the Federals. Heth, making a realistic estimate of the situation facing the Confederate brigade, took the precaution of having a rope bridge constructed across the Gauley River at the ferry site.[30]

As the Federals approached the Confederate defensive line, the entrenchments could not be clearly detected through the dense foliage. Rosecrans directed Benham, commanding the lead brigade containing what Rosecrans considered three of his best regiments, to advance into the woods with caution and feel out the Confederate defenses that had thus far remained unseen. Benham, however, in the excitement of his first engagement as a brigade commander, caused his regiments to advance into the forest without deploying skirmishers. It was to prove an unfortunate oversight by Benham. As the Tenth approached the entrenchments, an unexpected volley of musket and artillery fire had a paralyzing effect on Lytle's Ohioans, bringing the regiment to a complete halt. With the Tenth immobilized, Benham ordered the Twelfth and Thirteenth to move to the left and continue the advance while calling on Rosecrans for assistance. In the opening moments of battle, commanders near the firing on both sides quickly suffered its effects. Lytle of the Tenth was wounded in the initial assault, and Colonel Lowe was killed by heavy fire from the Confederate right as he led his Twelfth Ohio into action. On the Confederate side, Floyd received a musket ball in his right arm in the opening exchange of fire and was taken to the rear. A surgeon from the Forty-fifth, Doctor Samuel Gleaves, bandaged the wound and Floyd was soon back on the field.[31]

Responding to Benham's request for assistance, Rosecrans ordered his other two brigades forward, and he moved to the front to look over the defenses for himself. McCook, meanwhile, ordered part of his Ninth Ohio to the right of the Federal assault where it attracted the fire of the Thirty-sixth Virginia, holding a position just in front of the main Confederate defensive line. By now Rosecrans had realized that the only way to continue the attack was by a frontal assault. He therefore concentrated the Thirteenth Ohio and four companies of the Twelfth, reinforced by the Twenty-eighth Ohio and four companies of the Twenty-third, on the Federal left where they would have a covered route to within fifty yards of the right side of the Confederate defensive line. The plan of attack entailed moving units from all three Federal brigades. By the time the Ohioans finally launched their assault, it was almost sunset. Although the Federal attack forced the Forty-fifth Virginia to move toward the center of the defensive line, darkness, fatigue, and the rugged terrain forced the Federals to halt the attack before they could turn the Confederate right flank. When the assault against the Confederate right bogged down, Rosecrans withdrew to the open fields near Cross Lanes. The Federal attack had caused the regiments to become scattered among the three brigades, and they needed time to get reorganized. Rosecrans planned to resume the attack the next morning with an assault on the center of the Confederate line with three regiments of McCook's brigade.[32]

During the night Floyd too assessed his situation. Remarkably, no Confederates had been killed in the fighting. Although his men had fought well and remained in control of an excellent defensive position, Floyd had too few troops to man the extensive entrenchments effectively and he was outnumbered by the Federals. That evening Heth advised Floyd that while the right flank was secure, the left remained open with no men to fill the gap. At first Floyd swore that he would never surrender a foot of country, but after an hour or so of contemplation he decided to take advantage of the Federal pause in the attack and withdraw under cover of darkness. At about 10 P.M. the withdrawal across the Gauley River began, using Heth's rope footbridge and several small boats at Carnifex Ferry. In spite of the difficult mile-and-a-half winding descent to the river, the Virginians executed the movement in good order. The three regiments of Floyd's brigade led the way out, while the Twenty-second and Thirty-sixth covered the crossing. The Twenty-second was the last to cross the river. They destroyed the boats before departing and passing through the Thirty-sixth. The Thirty-sixth then took a position as the rear guard of the column as it moved back down the Sunday Road toward the James River and Kanawha Turnpike.[33]

Meanwhile, back at Hawks Nest, Wise had been active, but uncooperative. At midday on September 10, as Rosecrans was approaching Carnifex Ferry, Wise had received a message from Floyd that expressed surprise, if not outrage, that more troops were not moving to reinforce him. Floyd also demanded that one thousand infantry and a battery of artillery be dispatched immediately to Carnifex Ferry. Wise quickly replied that he needed all of his forces to hold the turnpike and prevent a movement upon Floyd's rear. He was, he wrote, taking the responsibility to "exercise a sound discretion whether to obey your very peremptory orders of to-day or not."[34]

Some twelve hours later Floyd sent word of the successful defense at Carnifex Ferry and responded to Wise's earlier message with a bit of sarcasm: "You are hereby peremptorily ordered to dispatch to me, immediately on the receipt of this, all of your disposable force, saving one regiment." Whether or not Wise was moved by Floyd's wit, he complied with the instructions without comment. On the morning of September 11, Wise and his legion once again set out for Carnifex Ferry, but as had happened in each of their previous attempts, about halfway to their destination Wise received orders to turn around and retrace their steps down the Sunday Road to Dogwood Gap. When the two men met later that day, Floyd seemed dazed by the experience of his first battle, and he was unable to respond to Wise's request for instructions. The next day, the two generals held a lengthy conference where they decided to withdraw their combined forces seventeen miles east to Big Sewell Mountain.[35]

While Wise was marching and countermarching, Rosecrans discovered that Floyd had made good his escape during the night, destroying both the footbridge and ferry as he withdrew. McCook, who had prepared his brigade for the attack planned for that morning, received orders to clear the far bank of the Gauley River of skirmishers and hold the ferry site, while Benham, the former engineer, was ordered to repair the crossing site as soon as possible. Rosecrans also sent word to Cox to cross the Gauley River and initiate a

careful pursuit of Wise along the James River and Kanawha Turnpike until the two Federal columns could be united. The repair
work to the ferry was considerable. One of the small boats was sal-
vaged, however, and by September 14 McCook's brigade was
across the river and on its way to join Cox at Dogwood Gap where
he had established an encampment after the Confederate withdrawal to Sewell Mountain. Rosecrans remained at Cross Lanes
waiting for Benham to finish repairing the ferry site and for his
ammunition and supply wagons to catch up with him. The rain and
poor mountain roads from Weston had combined to delay the logis-
tic trains much longer than had been anticipated.[36]

On September 15 Cox rode up to meet Rosecrans at Cross
Lanes. In spite of his interest in meeting with Rosecrans for the first
time since becoming the theater commander, it was a sad day for
Cox. He had just learned of the death of his youngest child in Ohio.
Because of the war he had seen his infant son only once, and the
campaign in the Kanawha would not permit him to return home
anytime soon. At Cross Lanes Cox met the other brigade commanders and became reacquainted with Rosecrans, having not seen him
since their days at Camp Dennison in Ohio. While getting to know
one another was an important part of the conference, logistics and
future operations headed the list of things the Federal officers discussed. The Federal supply line that now extended across the
mountains from Clarksburg was proving inadequate to the task.
Cox had accumulated a considerable store of provisions and ordnance at Gauley Bridge and was ready to turn the supply line that
ran up the Kanawha Valley to Gallipolis over to the quartermaster
and commissary departments of Rosecrans's staff. Although Rosecrans was hesitant to make the change, Cox assured him that the
large ferry operation at Gauley Bridge would support the Federal
logistical requirements much better than the overworked, inadequate Clarksburg line. As it turned out, the rains that had been
plaguing the area for weeks turned the mountain roads into mud

and delayed Rosecrans's wagons for nine days, making Gauley Bridge by default the primary Federal supply depot. The immediate operational decision was to continue pursuing the withdrawing Confederates along the James River and Kanawha Turnpike. McCook was to report to Cox and the two brigades were to advance east along the turnpike.[37]

After agreeing on September 12 to withdraw, Floyd and Wise quickly returned to their antagonistic relationship. Three days later the two met again at Floyd's headquarters, a short distance from where Wise held Sewell Mountain. There, Wise advised Floyd to consolidate their forces on Sewell and establish a defensive position. After promising to inspect the position the next morning, Floyd ended the meeting. Shortly after departing, however, Floyd informed Wise that he was moving further east. Wise was to join Floyd by bringing up the rear of the move. Once again, Wise was upset that Floyd had changed what had been mutually agreed upon without consulting him. Mounting his horse and riding in front of his assembled troops, Wise rose in the stirrups and called, "Men, who is retreating now? John B. Floyd . . . the bullet-hit son of a bitch, he is retreating now." When Floyd moved, Wise stayed put. Two days later, encamped at Meadow Bluff, Floyd inquired why Wise had not yet followed as ordered, and Wise explained that he had to remain in place to protect the baggage Floyd had left behind, that the weather was wet and disagreeable, that most of his men were sick, and that the roads were impassable as a result of Floyd's recent move. With a flair that described his attitude toward both Floyd and the Federals, Wise dubbed his position at Sewell Mountain Camp Defiance.[38]

By now the rift between Floyd and Wise had become a public scandal. A member of the general assembly from Greenbrier County had written to Davis informing him that the Kanawha Valley was not big enough to hold both men. Davis's correspondent stated that a recent visit to both camps had convinced him "that each of them would be highly gratified to see the other annihilated." Davis was unable to do anything from Richmond. His only hope to reconcile the differences between Floyd and Wise lay with Lee. The rivalry had already led to the abandonment of the Kanawha Valley, and neither Floyd nor Wise appeared ready to call a halt to their internal hostilities, even in the face of the Federal advance.[39]

While Floyd and Wise squabbled, Cox and McCook established Camp Lookout on September 16 a few miles west of Sewell Mountain. Cox sent an advance guard of five companies under Major Hines to scout the area to the east. Hines went as far as the summit of Sewell Mountain where he reported that Wise had set up camp and that Floyd had retreated to Meadow Bluff where the Wilderness Road to Summersville joined the James River and Kanawha Turnpike. Both positions had merit. But by occupying both, the Confederate forces on the turnpike were divided, offering the Federals a chance to defeat them one at a time. By the 20th Hines had occupied a position on Sewell Mountain with the Confederates on a parallel ridge one mile to the east. Cox reported the situation to Rosecrans who authorized a further advance to Sewell Mountain. However, he directed Cox to remain on the defensive and avoid any engagements until the Federal forces still waiting to cross the Gauley at Carnifex Ferry could join him. As September drew to a close, the James River and Kanawha Turnpike from Sewell Mountain to Gallipolis on the Ohio River remained firmly in Federal control.[40]

It took considerably longer for Rosecrans to get his forces across the river at Carnifex Ferry than he had anticipated. But the delay did not materially affect the situation in the Kanawha Valley. With Cox following the Confederate withdrawal and establishing a defensive position on Big Sewell Mountain, the Valley remained firmly in Federal hands. In any case, with Floyd and Wise spending most of their time sniping at one another, there was no threat from the Confederates at the moment. The inability of the strongly independent and hard-headed Confederate commanders to respond to the direction of a single theater commander was a boon to the Federals. As time went by, more of the region fell under the influence, if not control, of pro-Union political forces, who would do much to solidify Union support as the October 24 referendum on forming a new state neared. Meanwhile, the Confederate withdrawal from the Kanawha Valley disillusioned people who had believed that Richmond could protect them from the Federal invasion. Thus far, Lee's presence in western Virginia had had little impact. He had been unable to quell the bitter fighting between Floyd and Wise, and he had his hands full trying to cope with Loring's unwillingness to move quickly against the Federals on Cheat Mountain. Lee's ambiguous instructions to coordinate and consult gave him no command authority over the Confederate commanders in western Virginia, and thus far those commanders had shown no willingness to cooperate with Lee or each other. The lack of a single Confederate theater commander in western Virginia continued to plague military operations, and there was very little that Lee could do about it.

CHAPTER ELEVEN

Lee's Plan Goes Awry

W HILE FLOYD AND Wise managed to throw away any further Confederate opportunities in the Kanawha Valley with their constant bickering, Lee tried to keep Confederate hopes alive along the Staunton-Parkersburg Turnpike, where an opportunity to regain control of that critical line of communications remained. Opening the pass at Cheat Mountain would give the Confederates an opportunity to move back into the region and discourage the pro-Union politicians of northwestern Virginia by demonstrating that their recently acquired Federal protection was tenuous at best. A Confederate victory at Cheat Mountain, coming after the triumph at Manassas, might also sway undecided residents of the western counties toward pro-Virginia sympathies.

When Lee had arrived in the theater in late July, he was not received warmly by either Loring or the weather. Neither the one-armed general nor the weather changed in August. Loring remained aloof, and the cold rain continued to fall. Loring seemed content to concentrate on building up a supply base at Huntersville before thinking about advancing toward the Federal defenses at Cheat Mountain. The seemingly endless rains had turned the roads into ribbons of mud, slowing wagons, tiring horses, and demoralizing men, and further delaying Loring's move toward Cheat Mountain. In a situation where the Confederate forces had a fleeting opportunity to take the initiative in the western counties, Loring's leisurely approach to war was disastrous.[1]

Loring's delay gave the Federals time to strengthen their position on Cheat Mountain and wasted Confederate resources. The depot Loring was developing at Huntersville would be only a temporary measure if the Confederates managed to capture the pass and assume control of the Staunton-Parkersburg Turnpike. Once the turnpike was in Confederate hands, there would be a direct line of communications from Staunton to Huttonsville, and moving supplies and equipment along the roundabout route through Huntersville would no longer be necessary. Nonetheless Loring pressed on with matters of logistics, leaving operations aside for the moment.

While annoyed at Loring's delays, Lee did nothing overt to hurry him along. Neither Lee nor the Confederate high command had yet developed the ability to employ stern measures when dealing with a recalcitrant commander. To avoid unpleasantness with Loring, Lee fell back on his oral instructions from Davis–that he was to consult and coordinate. Rather than attempt to overrule Loring and quickly take the offensive against the Federal position at Cheat Mountain, Lee chose to wait for Loring's jealousy to pass, trying to coax, rather than push, Loring into action. Lee had been raised in a privileged atmosphere where consideration for others was considered a virtue, but his inability to handle Loring was embarrassing and somewhat bewildering. Lee's reluctance to confront Loring further weakened the Confederate command structure in western

Virginia. Rather than giving the Confederates a strong leader in the theater, Lee allowed the fragmented system to continue.[2]

Thus Lee turned away from the unpleasantness to something he understood. On August 6 he removed himself from the immediate vicinity of Loring by going to Valley Mountain, the Confederate position north of Huntersville on the road to Huttonsville, to establish a headquarters of his own. He took with him the squadron of cavalry commanded by his eldest son, "Rooney" Lee, for scouting and reconnoitering the area around Cheat Mountain. Lee knew that the Federal position at Cheat Mountain was too strong to take in a frontal assault, so, falling back on his only personal experience with war, Lee spent much of his time in August as he had during the Mexican War, looking for routes that would provide an opportunity to attack the defenders on a flank. Virtually every day Lee, accompanied only by his aides, Washington and Taylor, was reconnoitering possible approaches to turn the flank of the Federal position. Lee and his small staff frequently ventured well out in front of the Confederate picket lines, and on at least one occasion were mistaken for Federal scouts by a captain in the Forty-eighth Virginia, who sought to make them his prisoners. The attempt came to an abrupt end when the captain, after quietly approaching the unsuspecting Confederate officers with pistol drawn, came face to face with a surprised General Lee.[3]

Although he was supposed to be in command of all Confederate forces in Virginia, Lee was not yet thinking above the tactical level. He remembered the importance of his reconnoitering services for Scott in Mexico, but now, senior officer himself, in another army facing a similar situation, where the native population held divided loyalties and maps of the wild terrain were nonexistent, Lee failed to grasp that in western Virginia he was the equivalent of Scott in Mexico. Although he did not hold the clear command position that Scott had had in Mexico, Lee should have been thinking in terms of a theater commander. Someone else, not the senior general, should have been doing the tactical function of route reconnaissance. In addition, while Lee's reconnoitering did provide the useful information that the Federal position was too strong to attack in a frontal assault, it had little effect on prodding the laggardly Loring to take the offensive.

The Federal defenses at Cheat Mountain were under the command of Brigadier General John J. Reynolds. Reynolds had organized a three-month regiment, the Tenth Indiana, and was its colonel when it was mustered into Federal service in April. When he received a commission as a brigadier general in May, he turned the regiment over to Colonel Mahlon D. Manson for the remainder of its enlistment. When Rosecrans replaced McClellan as the Federal theater commander, Reynolds was responsible for defense of the Staunton-Parkersburg Turnpike. In light of the Confederate victory at Manassas that had prompted the Federals to abandon the offensive posture and concentrate on defending the western counties, Cheat Mountain pass had been reinforced in the expectation of a Confederate attack. Rosecrans was confident Reynolds could hold the pass with the forces he already had there. The pass, a narrow gap near the top of the mountain, had had its natural strength as a defensive position increased by the addition of fortifications. Rosecrans also expected that as soon as Reynolds received the additional three-year regiments that were on the way from Ohio, he would begin harassing the Confederates to his front. By the end of July there were four three-year regiments on Cheat Mountain; the Fourteenth Indiana, the Twenty-fourth Ohio, the Twenty-fifth Ohio, and the Thirty-seventh Ohio. None of these regiments had seen action thus far in the war. Reynold's responsibilities also included holding the road between Huntersville and Huttonsville where the Federals had established a supply depot. By August, the Federal defense included a line of field works at Elkwater, a small town located about seven miles south of Huttonsville. The Cheat Mountain pass controlled the Staunton-Parkersburg Turnpike, while Elkwater blocked the road from Huntersville. About ten miles separated the Confederate position at Valley Mountain and the Federal position at Elkwater. While both Federal positions had a good line of communications with the supply depot at Huttonsville, there was only a small path through the wooded mountains between them. If Lee could find a way to cut both positions off from Huttonsville and get a force of his own between them, they could be defeated separately.[4]

When Lee arrived at the Valley Mountain camp, Colonel William Gilham's Twenty-first Virginia and Colonel Lee's Sixth North Carolina were already there. Gilham, an 1840 graduate of West Point, had been ordered there by Jackson after the defeat at Rich Mountain. Jackson believed the Valley Mountain position offered an opportunity to turn the flank of the Federal position at Cheat Mountain. When Loring arrived to take command, he concurred with Jackson's assessment. Loring planned to use Valley Mountain as the starting point for initiating offensive operations against Cheat Mountain. The regiments encamped there would provide the nucleus for an attack. The Confederate position provided an opportunity for attacking Cheat Mountain, but it also argued for a rapid advance against the pass. The Federals could not ignore a large Confederate force so close to their positions indefinitely. Even with their newly adopted defensive attitude, the Federals had more regiments moving into the theater, which would eventually attack any Confederates that posed a threat.[5]

For the month of August, however, the greatest threat to the Confederates around Cheat Mountain was not the nearby Federals but the rain. The narrow mountain roads were nearly impassable, wagons moved through hub-deep mud with the greatest difficulty, and men succumbed to all manner of camp diseases. Within weeks nearly one-third of the army was not fit for action because of typhoid fever and measles. Treating the sick was made even more difficult by the problems of moving food and other supplies. Confederate morale was rapidly being washed away in the rain. But

Lee, proving as indefatigable in western Virginia as he had been in Mexico, maintained his good humor as he daily sought a way to assail the Federal position at Cheat Mountain without a costly frontal assault by his weakened, weary soldiers. Lee's constant movement through the area made him highly visible to the soldiers, and they developed a strong affection for him as they watched him ride through their camps with his small staff. Sam Watkins of Company H, First Tennessee, remembered a visit by Lee during which the soldier felt like walking up to Lee and saying, "Good evening, Uncle Bob." Watkins thought Lee "looked like some good boy's grandpa," and he "fell in love with the old gentleman." Lee may have been having difficulties with his generals in western Virginia, but the troops adored him. Ironically, as Lee toiled in the rain and mud, the Southern press was showering him with praise over a series of mythical successes over the Federals. Lee's reputation was soaring in Richmond even if there were not yet any tangible gains from his leadership in western Virginia.[6]

While Lee won the hearts of his soldiers, Confederate offensive preparations continued to move slowly under Loring's direction. By August 12 Loring had finally established his base at Huntersville and moved all of the forces under his immediate command forward to Valley Mountain. Jackson was moving his forces closer to Cheat Mountain by establishing Camp Bartow on the Greenbrier River. But Lee had not yet found a way around the Federal flank. During the month of August the number of Confederate forces around Cheat Mountain grew, but the weather continued to take its toll. Many men of the Eighth and Sixteenth Tennessee at Huntersville died of malaria and typhoid in the damp, wet conditions of the camps. Winter arrived early. By mid-August the temperature dropped below freezing. Watkins, in the First Tennessee, reported that "the biggest white frost fell that [he] had ever saw in winter." In the Third Arkansas, half the regiment was sick, and the troops were referring to the encampment as "Camp Measles."[7]

On the Federal side the weather was causing problems too. The Fourteenth Indiana, on Cheat Mountain since July 16, found that the "dreams of recruitment times were melting away like cotton candy in the drizzling rains." The Fourteenth had yet to see any action, and "many soldiers decided to fold their dreams of glory, pack them away among the cotton batting, and look out for the first opportunity to get out." By August 24 the men of the regiment, having seen the Sixth Indiana leave Virginia, were ready to go home, arguing that they could not be held beyond three months, even though they had signed up for three years. At that point Reynolds visited them and decided that the best way to take their minds off going home was to keep them busy getting their camp organized. So "in a great flurry of ditching, paving of streets and orderly pitching of tents [that] set the post in order," the men finally decided they were in the war to stay, no matter the hardships. While the Fourteenth Indiana grappled with the reality of a long war, the Ninth Indiana, originally a three-month regiment, had gone home to be reorganized into a three-year regiment. By late August the Ninth was back in western Virginia holding a portion of the line at Elkwater, or as the recently promoted Sergeant Bierce saw it with an old soldier's cynicism, they were "holding a road that ran from Nowhere to the southeast." The Third Ohio, which had enlisted for three years, was also at Elkwater, still waiting for its first battle. The closest they had come in August was when a detachment of the regiment captured Captain De Lagnel, the Confederate artilleryman who had been on the run since the battle at Rich Mountain.[8]

August finally ended and September brought an improvement in the relations between Lee and Loring and a welcome break in the weather. On August 31 Lee was confirmed as a full general, the highest rank in the Confederate army. He was listed third on the first promotion list of five officers. Samuel Cooper, the adjutant and inspector general of the Confederate army, and Albert Sidney Johnston were senior to Lee; Joseph E. Johnston and P. G. T. Beauregard, heroes of Manassas, were his juniors. Lee received the news of his confirmation along with a letter from Cooper assuring him that Davis fully approved of his actions in western Virginia. Knowing he still had Davis's confidence made Lee feel better, but the practical result of his confirmed rank was that Loring became much more amenable to Lee's suggestions. Gradually, Lee took charge of the campaign while Loring, ever conscious of rank, became a willing subordinate.[9]

Finally, the endless reconnaissance trips paid off. Early in September Lee found a narrow path that led to a point on the Staunton-Parkersburg Turnpike about two miles west, or behind, the Federal position on Cheat Mountain. This discovery was followed by a report from a local surveyor that he had located another route that wound through the mountains from Camp Bartow on the Greenbrier River to a point that overlooked the Federal defenses. The surveyor had twice made the trip to the summit undetected. On the second trip Rust, commander of the Third Arkansas, accompanied him and confirmed to Jackson that the route did indeed lead to a position that would turn the Federal position. Rust and the surveyor reported their findings to Lee and Loring in person, and during the meeting they were adamant in their insistence that an attacking force could move along the route and open a surprise attack on the exposed Federal flank without being detected. The news was good, but there were other factors to consider.[10]

On the negative side, the ground along the route Rust proposed was extraordinarily difficult. It was treacherously steep and covered with a dense undergrowth of laurel that would certainly impede, if not halt altogether, a large body of troops trying to move through it. Lee was uncertain of the size of the Federal forces he would be facing, and although he had about fifteen thousand Confederates in the vicinity of Cheat Mountain, almost half of those were unavailable because of sickness. The Federals were concentrated in two relatively close positions, Elkwater on the Huttonsville-Huntersville

Pike and the Cheat Mountain pass, under a single commander, Reynolds. But the two positions were not mutually supporting and could be isolated from one another. The Confederates were also in two different encampments, but Loring and Jackson were separated by Cheat Mountain, and it would be virtually impossible to maintain any close coordination between forces attacking from Valley Mountain and Camp Bartow. Finally, on the list of difficulties facing Lee, the provisions available in Huntersville would not allow for an extended offensive. In spite of the potential problems, however, there was no real alternative to attacking if the Confederates were to have any chance of recovering the western counties. With the wet weather, widespread sickness, and resupply difficulties facing him, if Lee did not take the offensive, he would have to withdraw. He decided to attack.[11]

For what would be his first battle as a commander, Lee issued a detailed plan on September 8 for an attack that would take place four days later. Wanting to avoid any further ill will, Lee issued the order in Loring's name. The plan, while carefully thought out between Lee and Loring, was horrendously complex, especially since it was going to be executed by formations new to the chaos of battle. The Confederates, organized into six brigades, were to move in five separate columns, from two widely separated bases, against two different objectives, and simultaneously initiate a surprise attack against an entrenched Federal force of undetermined size. To Lee's credit, the plan clearly explained to all commanders their expected role. But such a plan would need experienced leaders to execute. In his unbounded concern for other people's feelings, Lee had acceded to Rust's request to lead the forces that were to turn the Federal flank at Cheat Mountain. Rust was a big, strong, impressive-looking man with a keen intellect, who convinced Lee of his ability to play the key role in the attack because he was the only commander who had already covered the route to the pass. But Rust was untested in battle. There were other, more experienced regimental

commanders who could have been given the task had Lee been
willing to do so, but he put his faith in Rust. Responsibility for the
most critical element of the complex plan, therefore, lay with the
least experienced colonel.[12]

According to Special Order No. 28 the movement of Confederate forces would begin on September 11, so all five columns would
be in position to begin the attack at daylight on the 12th. The key
brigade, commanded by Rust for this operation, was to depart from
Camp Bartow on the Staunton-Parkersburg Turnpike and follow the
narrow path to the summit of Cheat Mountain. Rust was to lead the
brigade consisting of his Third Arkansas and the Twenty-third,
Thirty-first, and Thirty-seventh Virginia along the route he had earlier reconnoitered and launch a surprise attack on the flank of the
Federal position at Cheat Mountain. Jackson was to move forward
with his brigade along the turnpike to take a position on the eastern
slope of Cheat Mountain to occupy the Federals from their front
and cooperate with Rust's attack "should circumstances permit."
The other three columns were to depart from Valley Mountain.
Brigadier General Samuel Read Anderson, commanding a brigade
of three Tennessee regiments, was to move down the Tygart's Valley
River along the west slope of Cheat Mountain and take the path Lee
had earlier found to occupy a position on the turnpike west of the
pass where he could intercept reinforcements, cut the telegraph line
between the Federal positions, and aid in the attack by Rust if necessary. Lee cautioned Anderson to keep the movements of his
brigade unobserved. Brigadier General Daniel Smith Donelson was
to take his two Tennessee regiments along the right side of the
Tygart's Valley River to gain a favorable position in the rear of the
Federal position at Elkwater. Both Anderson and Donelson had
been commissioned as major generals in Tennessee on May 9. Two
months later when the Tennessee troops transferred to Confederate
service, they both became brigadier generals in the Confederate
army. Anderson had been born in Virginia but served with the First

Tennessee in the Mexican War. Donelson, a native of Tennessee, was a West Point graduate but had resigned after less than a year of active service, although he had maintained an active role in the Tennessee militia. While in state service Donelson had selected the site for the fort that bore his name on the Tennessee River. The fifth column, a brigade commanded by Colonel Jesse S. Burks, was to move down the left side of the river and clear that side of the Valley. Loring would direct Burks and retain control of a reserve brigade under Colonel William Gilham at Valley Mountain. Lee planned to accompany Burks. The final paragraph of the order cautioned all commanders to ensure their officers and men took precautions not to fire on their own troops, especially on Cheat Mountain where forces would be moving toward each other as they approached the Federal position through difficult terrain. The well-drafted, though complicated, plan promised great success if the troops and commanders could actually carry it off.[13]

Lee may have issued the movement order in Loring's name on September 8, but on the same day he also published a short order intended to inspire his troops. He signed that order as "General commanding." Lee had finally assumed command of the Confederate forces at Cheat Mountain. Although he did not have the flair for the bombastic rhetoric that McClellan had used to such good advantage earlier in the campaign, Lee did use the order to take "the opportunity of exhorting the troops to keep steadily in view the great principles for which they contend." He finished his first message to the troops about to go into combat under his command with an admonition that the "progress of this army must be forward." Lee was about to fight his first battle as a senior commander. As the Confederates prepared to take the offensive in western Virginia, the rainy weather finally broke. The sunshine, however brief it might prove to be, raised hopes that Lee's elaborate plan would bring a much longed-for Confederate success in western Virginia.[14]

Success depended on timing, however, and the key to coordinating

the surprise assaults of the five columns rested entirely in Rust's inexperienced hands, assuming all the brigades involved were in the right
place at the right time. Rust was to be in position to open the attack at
daylight on September 12. Upon hearing the sound of his guns, the
other brigades would open their supporting attacks. But that could
only happen if the other four Confederate columns reached their
assigned attack positions at approximately the same time, a feat that
would require some extraordinary efforts with the distances, terrain,
and uncertain weather facing the troops. Because of the varying distances the brigades began their approach marches at different times.
Once the commanders received their orders and began moving to
their objectives, they were on their own to get into position on time
and ready to fight—not an easy task for veterans, virtually impossible
for the untried forces Lee was relying on. But each of the brigade commanders was determined to carry out his portion of the plan.

Anderson's Tennessee brigade was the first column to move into
position. The Tennessee regiments had all been together briefly at
Valley Mountain before they initiated their approach marches on
the 10th. It had been a fine, bright morning with a layer of fog over
the Valley. As they marched out, Loring rode along the lines on a
white horse, giving many of the soldiers their first look at the man.
The Tennessee troops who saw him that day remembered that "his
appearance inspired the fullest confidence in his ability." The Fourteenth Tennessee, part of Anderson's brigade, had cooked five days'
rations on the 9th in anticipation of the move. That brigade had the
furthest distance and the most difficult terrain to traverse, and their
difficulties were compounded on the night of the 10th with a return
of the rain. After moving single file during the night of September
11 along the stock trail Lee had found, they reached and occupied a
position on the turnpike west of the pass behind the Federal
defenses on Cheat Mountain about sunrise. The troops, without
tents or blankets, had nowhere dry to sleep as the rain poured down
on them. But the rain let up toward morning and the march got

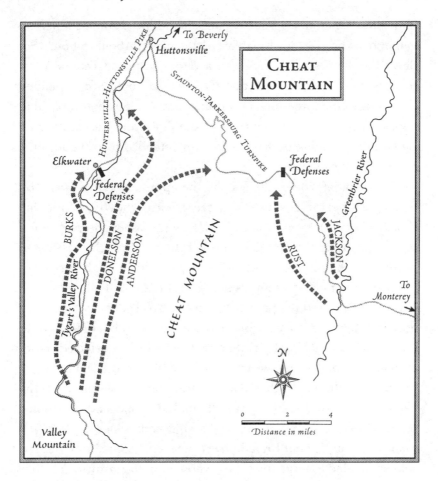

To Beverly

Huttonsville

HUNTERSVILLE-HUTTONSVILLE PIKE

STAUNTON-PARKERSBURG TURNPIKE

CHEAT MOUNTAIN

Elkwater

Federal Defenses

Federal Defenses

Greenbrier River

BURKS

DONELSON

ANDERSON

Tygart's Valley River

CHEAT MOUNTAIN

RUST

JACKSON

To Monterey

N

Valley Mountain

0   2   4

Distance in miles

under way again at a leisurely pace that allowed some soldiers to gather blackberries for a breakfast on the move. About an hour after dawn the Tennesseeans captured a rather surprised Federal engineer who confirmed that the Confederate presence remained unknown to the forces defending the pass. Anderson and his Tennesseeans then settled down to await the shots from Rust that would signal the beginning of the charge they intended to make into the Federal fortifications.[15]

On the other side of the Valley, the approach march was a bit more exciting for Donelson's green troops who began moving shortly after Anderson. The rugged, heavily wooded terrain found the troops using the abundant growth to get through the steeper portions of the route by "letting themselves down by the branches of trees and pulling themselves up as occasion might require." When they crossed the path between the two Federal positions on the 11th, they noticed signs of recent movements, but there was no indication that the Confederate advance had been detected. Later in the day they encountered two Federal outposts manned by troops from the Fifteenth Indiana, encamped at Elkwater, but the Tennessee troops quickly overran them. In the Sixteenth Tennessee there was considerable interest in seeing and talking to "the first Yankee that any of our brigade has ever seen." Sometimes the new soldiers tended to forget that they were not in the army to socialize with their opponents, but to do them bodily harm. That night the brigade was so close to Federal pickets that Donelson allowed no fires, in spite of the torrents of rain that drenched the men. At daybreak the brigade was anxiously awaiting the sounds of gunfire from Cheat Mountain.[16]

Rust, approaching Cheat Mountain from the east, had had a more difficult time reaching his objective. For most of the approach march, Rust's men traveled single file through dense stands of mountain laurel climbing steep mountain slopes. They crossed the Cheat River wading for a half mile in waist-deep water, cold as ice.

Troops had to scramble up the slippery mountainside. Like their Tennessee comrades on the other side of the mountain, they used the dense growth to assist them climbing "almost perpendicular slopes by grasping the Myrtle brushes and hand over hand" struggled from one level place to the next. At about sunset, the exhausted column arrived in position and prepared to spend a quiet night in anticipation of the next day's attack. The tired troops had little or nothing to eat as they settled in for the night. Their discomfort was compounded when a cold, pouring rain began to fall at about nine o'clock and continued for the remainder of the night. At dawn, as the rain ended and the sun started to make an appearance, the optimistic and indefatigable Rust, who had passed the night standing calmly under a tree, began to gather his wretched, wet troops into formation to approach the Federal fortifications.[17]

In what was nothing short of a miraculous performance by the brigade commanders, all five columns had managed to be in the right place at the right time with no indication that the Federals were aware of the impending attack. The first phase of Lee's plan had gone well in spite of the return of cold, rainy weather during the night before the attack. The rain, however, may actually have helped. Rainy nights tend to make defenders somewhat complacent, as the Confederate veterans of Philippi had learned the hard way. In any case the tired, wet Confederates appeared on the verge of gaining revenge for the Federal surprise that rainy night at Philippi. The night of September 11, with its rain and fog, did not dampen Confederate spirits. Commanders and troops all believed they were about to attain a victory. After days of marching and short rations, every one of the columns was in exactly the right place and ready to attack when dawn broke on September 12. As the tension and excitement mounted throughout Lee's small army, everyone was ready for the signal from Rust that would initiate the attack.[18]

Meanwhile, on Cheat Mountain, the Third Arkansas, leading Rust's brigade, came upon two Federal pickets at breakfast who were completely unaware of the approaching Confederates. When called on to surrender, the startled pair tried to run but were quickly shot dead. As other surprised pickets reacted to the shooting, the Confederates captured a few prisoners from the Twenty-fifth Ohio, who upon interrogation, exaggerated the number of Federal defenders. Rust, believing the prisoners, and after taking a look at the defenses, decided they were too strong for his force, especially since the beating of drums in the Federal encampment led him to surmise that he had lost the critical advantage of surprise. The other regimental commanders in the brigade agreed with his assessment, and Rust, holding the key to Confederate success, withdrew with no further action. Taliaferro, commanding the Twenty-third, and Fulkerson, commanding the Thirty-seventh, were both senior to the Arkansas colonel and had considerably more military experience, but they had agreed to serve under his command for the operation in deference to Lee's decision to allow Rust the honor of leading the attack. Neither of them moved to countermand Rust's decision.[19]

As the morning wore on, concern over Rust's fate grew. Excitement soon turned to disillusionment among the waiting troops, many of whom had been eager to participate in their first battle. But the wide dispersion of the brigades precluded any timely exchange of information, so there was nothing to do but wait. From their position on the Staunton-Parkersburg Turnpike, Anderson's men wanted to attack the Federal position without waiting for Rust's signal, but Anderson stood by the letter of the orders he had received and waited for the sound of a volley from the pass. In the Tygart's Valley River, Lee sensed potential failure as the minutes ticked by with no signal from Rust. At ten o'clock Lee decided to attack the Elkwater position in an attempt to salvage something from the elaborate preparations. Lee ordered Donelson to begin the attack, and he sent word to Anderson to retire from the turnpike where he would be vulnerable to a Federal attack. A company commander in the Sixteenth Tennessee recorded in his diary that Lee himself, a "gallant officer and most exemplary man, fearing to risk a courier on this occasion," rode to the brigade and personally delivered the order. But the long march, wet night, and short rations had finally caught up with the tired Confederates. When the long-awaited signal from Rust did not come as expected, men and officers seemed to lose their enthusiasm and morale plummeted. A listless, haphazard attack by the weary Confederates briefly cut communications between the Federal positions at Elkwater and Cheat Mountain, but the line was quickly reestablished with a Federal counterattack that met little Confederate resistance. In the Federal position at Elkwater, the men of the Third Ohio, still awaiting the chance to participate in a battle, could only hear the sounds of the skirmish. They were disappointed, but not so much as Lee. His first battle was over before it had even begun.[20]

By now alerted to the Confederate activity, Reynolds sent reinforcements from Elkwater to Cheat Mountain early on the morning of September 13. That same day, having heard nothing from either Rust or Jackson, who was to have occupied the Federals east of the pass, Lee determined that any attempt to open the turnpike would simply be an exercise in futility. He did hope, however, that with a night's rest behind them, his troops could be persuaded to hold their positions in the Tygart's Valley River. In an effort to find a way to flank the Federal right at Elkwater, Lee sent reconnaissance parties to seek out suitable routes.[21]

In one party, Lee's senior aide, Colonel John A. Washington, and "Rooney" Lee, along with a few cavalry troopers, set out along the right branch of the Elkwater Fork. When the group unexpectedly came upon a concealed Federal picket line, Washington was shot from his horse, hit by three musket balls in the first volley. Leaving the colonel's body behind, "Rooney" Lee narrowly escaped on Washington's horse, his own having been downed in the gunfire. Washington's death devastated Lee. He sent messengers toward the Federal lines under a flag of truce to ask for information about

Washington's body on September 14. On the way the messengers met a party of Federals who were returning the body to Lee. The campaign had now claimed the second of the staff officers who had worked closely with Lee during the mobilization of the Virginia militia—first Garnett, now Washington. Thus far, in his first campaign as a senior commander, Lee had not met with very much success.[22]

With supplies running low, the Federals now on full alert, and Confederate morale sagging, the saddened Lee had no real choice but to retire to Valley Mountain. He had nothing to show for the gallant efforts of his troops. Lee had been in western Virginia for about six weeks, and the Confederate forces held no more ground than when he arrived. The Federals, in the meantime, had consolidated their defenses in the Alleghenies and opened lines of communications between their forces in the northern and southern portions of the theater of operations. Lee wrote Letcher from Valley Mountain to explain what had happened at Cheat Mountain. In the letter, Lee praised the troops who "traversed twenty miles of steep, rugged mountain-paths, and the last day through a terrible storm, which lasted all night, and in which they had to stand drenched to the skin in the cold rain." Ever the gentleman, Lee did not attempt to lay responsibility for the failed attack on anyone. He explained that the rain and the roads combined to paralyze the efforts of his army.[23]

Lee's performance at Cheat Mountain must be faulted on several counts. His first failure was his reluctance to push Loring into action in early August. When Lee finally brought the Confederate forces to battle, his inexperienced subordinates managed to execute the most difficult part of his elaborate plan. But Lee erred grievously in allowing Rust to lead the most critical part of the attack. Rust completely misinterpreted the situation facing him at the critical moment of decision, and failed most reprehensibly in simply walking away from his responsibilities. His brigade could have easily swept through the Federal position on Cheat Mountain, which was neither as large nor as well prepared as Rust's prisoners had led him to believe. When Rust failed to act, Taliaferro and Fulkerson, the two more senior and experienced regimental commanders on the scene, chose to accept Rust's decision. But Lee did not reprimand or censure Rust for the error that cost him victory, nor did he question the actions of any other commander on Cheat Mountain that day. Lee was finally able to step in and take command from Loring, but he was not ready to criticize the actions of his subordinates.

Lee's first battle stands in notable contrast with McClellan's, both in the results and their reactions to their subordinates' performance. In both battles Lee and McClellan drew on their experience at Cerro Gordo to attempt to turn a flank of an entrenched defense to avoid a costly frontal assault. In doing so, each had to rely on a subordinate to conduct a critical flanking attack. At Rich Mountain, McClellan was fortunate to have Rosecrans in that role; at Cheat Mountain Lee allowed Rust, a man of no military experience, to play the most important role of the day. But where Lee was reluctant to fault Rust or anyone else on Cheat Mountain, McClellan was equally reluctant to credit Rosecrans with the victory at Rich Mountain. Indeed, at Rich Mountain it was McClellan who hesitated and Rosecrans who carried the day, while at Cheat Mountain, when Rust hesitated, Lee attempted to continue the attack only to be thwarted by subordinates who pleaded that their men were too tired. In their first battles as senior commanders, both Lee and McClellan demonstrated they had learned their lessons of theoretical warfare well. They avoided the dreaded frontal assault, but in so doing had to rely on the efforts and initiative of others. Where Lee tended to treat his subordinates' failures kindly, McClellan was quick to complain about any mistakes, real or perceived, his subordinates made. There was a risk in both approaches.

But Lee had little time to worry over the failure at Cheat Mountain. In the aftermath of Carnifex Ferry, Rosecrans and Cox were about to join forces at the head of the Kanawha Valley, while, on Sewell Mountain, Floyd and Wise remained preoccupied with their own private feud. Thus far the anticipated Confederate offensive in western Virginia had not seriously threatened the Federal defenses in the theater of operations. If any hope remained for the Confederates to regain the western part of the Old Dominion, Lee had to reconcile Floyd and Wise and unite their forces in order once more to attempt to go on the offensive. On September 20 Lee set out for Floyd's camp at Meadow Bluff. Loring and five of the regiments at Valley Mountain—the First, Seventh, and Sixteenth Tennessee and the Forty-second and Forty-eighth Virginia—followed him a few days later. Jackson remained at Camp Bartow, still holding the Staunton-Parkersburg Turnpike.[24]

With Lee now clearly in command, for the first time in the campaign the Confederates had unity of command of all their forces in the theater. It remained to be seen what that meant to the campaign, however. With the end of summer, the weather in the mountains promised no improvement; supply shortages continued to be a major problem; and with little success to show for their efforts against the Federals during the campaign, Confederate morale remained low. With Cheat Mountain behind him, Lee set out for Meadow Bluff to meet with Floyd and Wise.

CHAPTER TWELVE

"If They Would Attack Us . . ."

WHILE LEE EXPERIENCED the chaos of war in his first battle as a senior commander at Cheat Mountain, Rosecrans had to endure some frustrating delays before he was able to continue his advance to join forces with Cox. It took twelve days to repair the boats that Floyd had destroyed during the nighttime withdrawal from Carnifex Ferry. While some of the Federal force had managed to cross the Gauley River and join Cox, the supply wagons that were to follow Rosecrans found the roads in such bad condition that they took nine days to reach him. Even if the ferry had been operational, the delayed arrival of the ammunition and rations carried on the supply wagons would have caused the bulk of Rosecrans's force to remain idle. But, while Rosecrans was forced to wait, Cox had followed the withdrawing Confederates and established a defensive position where he could keep an eye on Floyd and Wise at Sewell Mountain.[1]

When Lee reached Floyd's headquarters at Meadow Bluff on September 21, he found the feud between the two political generals still going strong. At immediate issue was the relative strengths of the two separate encampments they occupied. Lee had earlier instructed Floyd to secure the Confederate rear along the James River and Kanawha Turnpike in the strongest position west of Lewisburg. Floyd had selected Meadow Bluff and moved there with his brigade along with the Twenty-second and Thirty-sixth Virginia, the two regiments from the Kanawha Valley. Wise, however, had elected to keep his legion on Sewell Mountain, twelve miles to the west. Wise believed it was better to defend the turnpike on the high ground at Sewell Mountain, while Floyd wanted to hold Meadow Bluff where the Wilderness Road intersected with the James River and Kanawha Turnpike to prevent the Federals from getting behind him. On September 19 Wise had informed Floyd that the Federals were advancing toward Sewell Mountain. Floyd replied that since Wise had not obeyed the earlier order to move to Meadow Bluff, disaster could only come to the divided command and urged Wise to join him if time permitted before the Federal attack. Wise, however, remained at Camp Defiance on Sewell Mountain, and the day before Lee arrived at Meadow Bluff, Cox's advance guard occupied a ridge two miles west of the mountain's crest.[2]

Lee's first inclination upon arriving at Floyd's headquarters was to unite the two forces, but since he had not seen either position before arriving at Meadow Bluff, he was unable to determine where best to consolidate them. The advantage of Meadow Bluff was that it forced the Federals to advance along an extended line, and it controlled the intersection where the Wilderness Road to Summersville joined the James River and Kanawha Turnpike. Lee initially accepted Floyd's assessment and sent a rather dramatic message to

Wise advising him to join Floyd and begging "that the troops be united, and that we conquer or die together." Wise was unshaken in his belief that he held the stronger position. In any case, he argued, the forces were practically united since he could join Floyd whenever Lee ordered. Wise invited Lee to inspect his position on Sewell Mountain, and on September 22 Lee rode up the turnpike to visit Wise and assess the situation for himself.[3]

After inspecting the ground at Sewell Mountain, Lee agreed that the position Wise had selected was a good one. Should the Federals attack along the turnpike, Wise held higher ground than Floyd back at Meadow Bluff. In that case it made sense to bring Floyd to Sewell Mountain. Still, Lee knew that there was always the possibility of a flank attack along the Wilderness Road. Rosecrans had done it at Rich Mountain; Lee had almost done it at Cheat Mountain. Should Rosecrans decide to attempt to turn the Confederate position at Sewell Mountain, then leaving Meadow Bluff unguarded could open the Wilderness Road to a Federal movement against the Confederate rear. A number of small roads that could be used to turn the Confederate defenses also ran to the north and south of Wise's position on Sewell Mountain. Leaving Wise to his own devices for the moment, Lee returned to Meadow Bluff without making any comments or giving instructions.[4]

Whatever he thought of Sewell Mountain as a defensive position, Lee returned to Meadow Bluff appalled at the condition of Wise's command. The men existed in wretched conditions, with little or no shelter from the cold rain that continued to plague the campaign. In Lee's view, no one on the mountain understood his duty or knew where anything was. There was "no order, organization." In contrast to his general ineptness as a commander, Wise was able to communicate with his troops, who admired him. He had managed to convey clearly his dislike of Floyd to his officers and men, infecting them with an intense distrust of his rival and making any cooperation between the two commands extremely difficult.[5]

Lee had to choose between the feuding generals, something he was not by nature comfortable doing. His instructions from Davis had been to smooth over differences among the Confederate generals in the theater of operations, and Lee was still trying to do that. Even after the recent unfortunate experience at Cheat Mountain where Lee had sacrificed time in consideration of Loring's feelings, the "General commanding" still did not want to offend either Floyd or Wise. After inspecting Sewell Mountain, Lee wrote a tactful note to Floyd suggesting that Wise had selected the better defensive position. In the note, Lee asked "how would it do to make a stand here [Sewell Mountain]?" But it was well short of a definitive order that would unite the two commands. The lack of unity of command in western Virginia continued to create problems for the Confederates.[6]

Leaving the Floyd-Wise feud unresolved, Lee once again conducted personal reconnaissances while the Federals strengthened their position in front of the Confederates. Since September 16 Cox and McCook had remained encamped on the turnpike twelve miles west of Sewell Mountain at Camp Lookout. From there Federal scouts could keep track of the movements of both Floyd and Wise. When Cox reported that Wise had stopped on Sewell Mountain, Rosecrans authorized him to move forward but cautioned him to remain on the defensive until the Federal forces stuck at Carnifex Ferry could move forward to join him. Rosecrans did not want Cox to make an attack on the Confederate position until they had joined forces. Neither Lee nor Rosecrans would be in a position to move against the other until they could unite their respective divided forces.

While they waited to consolidate their forces, both sides sent reconnaissance parties. A detachment of five companies from the Forty-sixth and Fifty-ninth Virginia set out from Camp Defiance to probe the Federal lines on the evening of September 20. After a brief skirmish with Ohio troops, the Confederates spent the night camped between the lines and returned unscathed the next day. Two days later, a patrol from the Ninth Ohio at Camp Lookout had less success in finding the Confederate lines. After marching for two hours they found themselves about to attack their own camp. They had marched in a circle and were approaching their own position from the rear. The next day, the 23rd, Cox and McCook moved their brigades forward to Sewell Mountain.[7]

On September 23 Wise reported Cox's advance to Floyd. With Loring bringing reinforcements and with no report of any movement on the flanks, Lee decided to move forward to meet the Federal threat at Sewell Mountain with part of Floyd's command. The day after Cox established a defensive position on Sewell Mountain, he sent Federal skirmishers to probe the Confederate line. Wise responded by sending his own skirmish line from the Forty-sixth and Fifty-ninth Virginia. The ensuing action prompted one Virginia soldier to write that "it was nothing but an Indian fight–Virginians behind trees fighting Ohioans behind trees." While Wise was occupied with the Indian skirmish, Floyd, accompanied by four regiments, arrived to reinforce the defenses. The 25th brought more action as the Eleventh Ohio probed the right of the Confederate line against the Forty-ninth Virginia, and again Wise went forward to the action. As long as the Federals continued to probe the defenses, perhaps Lee could convince Floyd and Wise to unite against a common foe. But before Lee had to deal with an open confrontation between the two men, the problem was resolved from afar. Floyd forwarded a dispatch to Lee that included a message from Richmond with instructions for Wise. According to the instructions from the acting secretary of war, Wise was to "turn over all the troops heretofore immediately under your command to General Floyd, and report yourself in person to the Adjutant-General in this city with the least delay." It further stipulated that Wise was to transfer "everything under your command" to Floyd. Lee sent the order to Wise without comment.[8]

Upon receipt of the order, Wise debated whether to comply with its very explicit instructions. He had already defied direct orders from Floyd, and Richmond was farther away. Wise wrote Lee for advice, expressing his desire to wait until after the battle at Sewell Mountain before relinquishing his command. Lee urged Wise to obey the order. After drafting a farewell to his troops, the head-strong general heeded Lee's advice and departed for Richmond. Privately, Wise maintained that he had left his command only because of Lee's advice. In any case, with Wise's recall, Lee, who not taken sides in the feud, was relieved of having to deal with the problem of his dueling generals. Upon Wise's departure, Colonel James Lucius Davis, a graduate of West Point and commander of the Forty-sixth Virginia, assumed temporary command of the legion. When Wise arrived in Richmond, he took to his bed for two months with a bad case of pneumonia.[9]

With Wise gone, Lee had one less problem to distract him, and he proceeded to reinforce the defensive positions on Sewell Mountain in anticipation of a Federal attack. On the other side of the mountain more Federal forces were moving forward. On the 26th, Scammon's brigade moved into a position close enough to provide support for Cox's forces, and Rosecrans arrived the same day to take personal command. The two forces now occupied defensive positions on naturally strong ridges separated by a depression about a mile wide. It was rugged terrain. With the exception of the James River and Kanawha Turnpike, the land between the ridges could be traversed only with great difficulty. On the Confederate side of the mountain, Loring arrived at Sewell Mountain with the five regiments from Valley Mountain on the 29th. Lee used them to strengthen the defensive line and form a strong reserve under Colonel Savage of the Sixteenth Tennessee.[10]

While he was at Sewell Mountain, Lee was not too busy to notice Major Thomas L. Broun of the Third Regiment of Infantry in Wise's Legion occasionally riding a distinctive four-year-old gray horse. The animal belonged to Broun and his brother Joseph, a captain and quartermaster of the same regiment. The brothers had recently purchased the horse in Greenbrier County, and the mount was well known in the regiment for "his rapid, springy walk, his high spirit, bold carriage, and muscular strength." Lee took a fancy to the horse and learned from its owners that it had taken the first premium at the Lewisburg fairs in 1859 and 1860 under the name Jeff Davis. The general started referring to the horse as "my colt" whenever he saw one of the brothers riding it. Admiring the horse and chatting occasionally with its owners was one of the few bright spots for Lee as he prepared his defenses to stop the Federal offensive at Sewell Mountain. In February 1862 Lee saw Captain Broun riding the horse in South Carolina, and recognized it immediately. Upon inquiring about "his colt," the younger Broun offered it to Lee as a gift. The general declined, but offered to buy the animal after he had a chance to learn its qualities. Lee found the mount suited him, and the Brouns agreed to sell him the horse for $200 in currency, the price they had paid for it. Lee sent them $225 to make up for the depreciation in currency from September 1861 to February 1862. The horse, renamed Traveller, became Lee's favorite and remained with him until after the war.[11]

Near the end of September, both sides were forced to endure a common enemy. The uncommon rains that had plagued the campaign from its beginning dampened the spirits of Federals and Confederates alike. One of the worst storms in the history of western Virginia caused the Gauley River to rise to fifty feet, sweeping away great quantities of Federal stores, forage, and clothing and damaging much of the rest. In Rosecrans's headquarters alone, eighteen horses perished in one night. The roads became impassable. In the thirty-eight miles between Gauley Bridge and Sewell Mountain what little forage had been available was now all but gone, washed away. Within a few days of the onset of the cold, wet weather, sickness had considerably reduced the number of effective troops in the

Federal brigades concentrated at Sewell Mountain. Supplies were scarce. Every available wagon was put to work hauling supplies and ammunition across the muddy, slippery roads, but they were not up to the task of keeping the army adequately supplied sixty miles from the closest head of steamboat navigation, Gauley Bridge.[12]

In the Ninth Ohio, the troops found "foraging not exactly a snap" in the abominable weather conditions and turned to a local delicacy, snakes, to supplement their short rations. They discovered that the many snakes that populated the rugged mountains could be a "sumptuous (under the conditions)" meal if prepared right, and the regiment soon had a number of "snake-hunters" known for their ability to find and cook the creatures. In addition to short rations, the volunteer Federal soldiers at Sewell Mountain had to cope with the regular army bureaucracy. At the end of September Major Adam Jacoby Slemmer, the acting assistant inspector general of the Department of the Ohio, arrived to inspect the regiments. Not surprisingly, the troops were of mixed feelings about the inspections, depending on what the inspecting officer found. The Ninth Ohio felt "duly praised," but the Eleventh Ohio was "*disappointed*" when Slemmer criticized their appearance, believing that he had not allowed "for long marches and severe duty in the rain and mud."[13]

The Confederates suffered as well. The downpour swept away bridges and turned the roads into morasses, cutting off the troops at Sewell Mountain from their base of supply at Meadow Bluff. Entire sections of roadway disappeared to be replaced by gullies ten feet deep. With Loring's arrival, Lee now had the forces available to resist a Federal attack or even launch an offensive of his own, but weather remained the greater threat. Lee needed supplies from Meadow Bluff, and the troops did their best to forward them under the grim conditions. The offensive became less likely as Lee's men were barely able to keep themselves and their horses alive, much less build up enough stocks to support an advance. Floyd continued to press Lee to return to Meadow Bluff, which would force the

Federals to negotiate the twelve miles of very bad road if they wanted to continue their own offensive. Lee, however, held firm at Sewell Mountain, hoping for a Federal attack that would be blunted on the Confederate defenses. A newspaper correspondent with Lee summarized the situation succinctly: "If they would attack us, we could ship them without, perhaps, the loss of a man; but, if we have to attack them, the thing will be different."[14]

While they waited for the generals to decide on a course of action, the Confederate soldiers, like their Federal counterparts, tried to supplement their short rations. In Company D of the Forty-sixth Virginia, a group of soldiers struck a deal to buy a quart of flour for fifty cents, but the only money they had was a five-dollar bill. Seeing Lee close by, one of the soldiers, a large man with a hand that had once been mangled by a hog, took the bill and proceeded to greet the general. Offering his disfigured hand to Lee, he asked for change. Lee took the huge hand, apologized for not having the necessary currency, and asked his nearby staff to help. When one of the officers produced the correct change, the soldier thanked Lee and returned to his horrified comrades to complete the flour purchase. Lee's accessibility to the troops was becoming legendary. On another occasion, two brothers of the same company, Sergeant Eugene Cox and Private Leroy Cox, trying to get a better look at the Federal position opposite them, encountered Lee and Loring doing the same thing. The generals had field glasses, and after a moment Lee offered his to the brothers so they too could get a better look at their opponents. Private Cox reported that Lee "was the handsomest man [he] had ever seen." Such encounters made Lee enormously popular with the troops.[15]

The waiting continued. By September 30, as Lee was beginning to despair of a Federal attack and was contemplating an attack of his own, Rosecrans was nervously looking over his shoulder at the tenuous supply from Gauley Bridge. On October 5 the Kanawha River helped Rosecrans decide on a definite course of action. At

Charleston the river had risen above its forty- to fifty-foot-high banks and was standing five feet deep inside buildings local residents had always considered safe from flooding. The Federal quartermaster tried to keep the supplies moving up the river, but it was extremely difficult to protect the "the piles of barrels and boxes of bread and sacks of grain" with no warehouses at Gauley Bridge. After assessing the possibility of further offensive operations, Rosecrans elected to withdraw his forces to Gauley Bridge, where he could replace the equipment and clothes they had worn out in four months of continual marching far removed from supply depots. On the 5th, Rosecrans started moving spare baggage and sick troops back to Camp Lookout. At 10 P.M., under the cover of darkness, the main body struck their tents and an hour later the trains were moving west, followed shortly by the infantry regiments. Rosecrans left Cox's brigade as a rear guard until the main column cleared Sewell Mountain. The night was clear and the excitement of the clandestine withdrawal heightened the sentinels' imagination. Every noise from the Confederate side of the gulch separating the two armies sparked rumors of discovery. But at 1:30 in the morning Cox led his brigade safely off the mountain, leaving a thin line of pickets to follow a few hours later. Although there was no interference from the Confederates, the withdrawal was not without its problems. The supply trains and artillery batteries had great difficulty negotiating the washed-out roads, causing numerous halts. The men of the Eleventh Ohio would long remember Rosecrans riding frantically up and down the main column, "ordering mess chests and officer's baggage thrown out, fires built under wagons stalled in the mud." Each time the long column halted, the rear guard had to deploy in battle formation and then, upon receiving word that the move was again under way, gather in the pickets and resume the march. It was a very tedious operation, and by daybreak on October 6 Cox and his brigade had moved only three or four miles and were settled into defensive positions to await the Confederate response.[16]

The Confederates quickly detected the increased activity in the Federal camp, but at first they interpreted it as preparations for the long-awaited attack. Pickets heard and reported the sounds of creaking wagon wheels in the clear night and concluded that the Federal artillery was repositioning to support an attack. Excitement rose in the Confederate camp, and they were ready to bring their own artillery to bear. At dawn, all remained quiet. At first the silence was ominous, but the nervous defenders soon became suspicious. By full light it was obvious that the Federals were no longer across the valley. Lee immediately ordered a pursuit, but the weakened horses of the cavalry were not up to the pursuit. When the Confederate cavalry encountered the Federal rear guard only a few miles up the turnpike, they were easily repulsed. The tired, hungry infantry regiments were barely on the move when they met the returning cavalry, forcing Lee to call the whole thing off. The lack of provisions at Sewell Mountain made any further action impossible, and the weary Confederates returned to their defensive positions with an air of resignation to await further developments.[17]

Lee, discouraged that another of his plans had failed because of circumstances beyond his immediate control, went back to work. When he learned of the Federal withdrawal, he drafted and delivered the preliminary orders for another advance. The new plan called for Floyd to move from Meadow Bluff to a point south of the New River and then advance west through Fayetteville to intercept and cut the Federal line of communications at Gauley Bridge. When Floyd was in position, Lee and Loring would advance from Sewell Mountain toward Hawks Nest and drive the Federals from the Kanawha Valley. But again, events beyond Lee's control would force him to change his plan.[18]

Back at Cheat Mountain, Reynolds had moved against Camp Bartow on the Greenbrier River on September 26, but the attack had been aborted because of an ice storm. On October 3 Reynolds tried again. He led nine regiments of Ohio and Indiana infantry reinforced with artillery and cavalry in a reconnaissance in force against Jackson's six Confederate regiments. The Federals started down Cheat Mountain at about 1 A.M., and the advance guard reached the first Confederate pickets about six hours later. Alerted to the Federal movement by his cavalry patrols, Jackson sent a company of the Third Arkansas to meet the attack on the turnpike. He deployed his other regiments along the defensive line his forces had been preparing. The First and Twelfth Georgia were on the right, the Forty-fourth and Twenty-third Virginia held the center, and the Third Arkansas and the Thirty-first Virginia secured the left. As the Third Arkansas moved into position, the Federal artillery opened fire on the regiment, "creating a terrific din but raising no harm." The Danville Artillery returned fire along with the Eighth Star Artillery, which had finally received its own cannon in late September. The short artillery duel caused no significant damage to either side, and the Third Arkansas held off the Ohioans' charge. Reynolds then attempted to turn the Confederate right, but heavy artillery fire drove the attackers back in confusion. At 2:30 P.M. the Federals broke off the attack and returned to Cheat Mountain.[19]

Although the encounter had little immediate impact, it had a profound effect on the campaign as a whole. It alerted Lee to the possibility of a renewed Federal offensive along the turnpike into the Valley of Virginia that would threaten the Virginia Central Railroad's terminus at Staunton. Even as Lee prepared to send Floyd on his way west to attempt a flanking attack on Rosecrans, he was contemplating sending Loring back to reinforce Jackson at Greenbrier. On the Federal side, the unsuccessful foray caused Reynolds to overestimate the Confederate strength on the Greenbrier River. As a result, he had no further thoughts of returning to the offensive.

Although Floyd was less than enthusiastic about Lee's latest plan, he nonetheless set out to do what he could. Floyd did, however, exercise his discretion and leave Wise's obstreperous legion behind at Sewell Mountain. He had found it "to be in such a state of insubordination and so ill-disciplined as to be for the moment unfit for military purposes." Heth, commanding the Forty-fifth Virginia, after serving under Floyd for a number of months had considerable reservations about Floyd's abilities to exercise independent command. Taking advantage of his special relationship with Lee, Heth discussed the situation and offered the opinion that Floyd "was as incapable of taking care of his men or fighting them as a baby." Lee was unmoved. After Floyd left, the situation on Sewell Mountain continued to deteriorate. The cold weather persisted, and sickness thinned the ranks daily. Floyd had taken the wagons that had been moving supplies from Meadow Bluff to Sewell Mountain, further exacerbating the already poor living conditions. Two weeks after drafting his latest plan, Lee was finally forced to give up the idea of an offensive. He finally abandoned the barely tolerable Sewell Mountain position. On October 20 Lee ordered Loring to reinforce Jackson at Greenbrier and sent Wise's Legion to Meadow Bluff. It was the best he could do under the circumstances. With the Federal withdrawal to Gauley Bridge, there was no good reason to maintain the Sewell Mountain position. By reinforcing Greenbrier and holding Meadow Bluff, the Confederates could at least prevent any further Federal moves east.[20]

Like Lee, Rosecrans was preparing to defend. When Rosecrans withdrew from Sewell Mountain, he deployed his four brigades in depth along the James River and Kanawha Turnpike. Schenck's brigade remained closest to Sewell Mountain, some ten miles from Gauley Bridge; McCook's brigade was two miles west of Schenck, where the road to Fayetteville intersects the turnpike; Benham held a position six miles from Gauley Bridge; and Cox's brigade covered Gauley Bridge and the surrounding area long the Kanawha. Rosecrans and Cox both located their headquarters at the Tompkins farm. Rosecrans expected a Confederate move south to attack his line of communications from the rear, so he ordered McCook to lead his brigade south across the New River to Fayetteville. Finding only some guerrilla activity, McCook recrossed the river, but he left no guards to watch the area. Some days later, when he attempted to rectify the error, it was too late. When McCook's detachment approached the town, it came under fire from Confederate sharpshooters holding positions in the cliffs and along the shore. Floyd had occupied Fayetteville, and for the moment the Federals were content simply to watch the Confederate activities across the river.[21]

Operating south of New River, Floyd objected to Lee's change of plan. Floyd argued that the Confederates could have captured Rosecrans's forces if Lee had made an advance on Gauley Bridge from Sewell Mountain in coordination with his own movement into the Kanawha Valley behind the Federals. But Lee thought otherwise and left Floyd on his own. Floyd's movements went uncontested by the Federals. Confederate cavalry patrols were in Cabin Creek, a small town on the Kanawha River, on October 24, but other than disrupting the referendum on forming a new state, they accomplished very little. Shortly thereafter, Rosecrans learned of Lee's withdrawal from Sewell Mountain. Now that the possibility of a Confederate attack along the turnpike had been considerably reduced, Rosecrans began to make plans to capture Floyd's brigade.[22]

By the end of October, Floyd had taken advantage of a lapse on the part of the Federals and occupied Cotton Hill, the steep mountain that dominated Gauley Bridge from across the Kanawha River, in force. Troops from the Fifty-first Virginia worked for days to move a rifled cannon to the top of the hill. On November 1 Floyd made his presence known by cannonading the Federal supply depot and ferry below. Rosecrans, who had put no forces on the high ground that now provided Floyd such a convenient platform for his guns, was surprised. The unexpected attack caused him to lose his composure. Cox recalled that because Rosecrans had expected an attack from Lee along the James River and Kanawha Turnpike, the artillery fire into the Federal rear "so startled him as to throw him off his balance." For the moment, the Confederates had gained the upper hand, forcing the Federals hurriedly to protect the ammunition and supplies stockpiled along the river. But when Cox moved from his headquarters and took command at Gauley Bridge, he soon found that the Confederate artillery fire, while inconvenient, was not formidable. He located a site for Federal guns that would silence the Confederate fire and, after making arrangements to move the ammunition out of range during the night, went to bed. When he arose the next morning, he found the weather foggy but clearing rapidly. But contrary to his instructions, the ammunition had not yet been moved. The loaded wagons were neatly lined up on the road while the drivers patiently waited for a recalcitrant team of mules near the head of the column to move out of the way. As the fog began to lift, those troops not directly involved with transporting the ammunition started to edge away from the loaded wagons. They realized that the gunners on Cotton Hill would soon spot them. The wagon drivers, stuck behind their teams, grew more nervous as they too realized they were in imminent danger. The quartermaster officer in charge replaced the balky team and got the wagons moving just as the Confederates opened fire. The first cannon balls, apparently solid shot, bounced harmlessly on the road, however, and no harm was done.[23]

Meanwhile, Rosecrans had regained his composure by November 2 and developed a plan to capture Floyd's little army. Rosecrans planned to use his four brigades to surround the Confederates on Cotton Hill. Benham was to move his brigade west along the James River and Kanawha Turnpike, cross the Kanawha River five miles below Gauley Bridge, and attack Floyd's left flank. At the same time Schenck would lead his brigade along the north side of New River and cross at Townsend's Ferry to strike the Confederate right flank. Cox's brigade would cross the Kanawha River just below Gauley Bridge and conduct a frontal attack on Cotton Hill. Finally, McCook would hold his brigade in position at Miller's Ferry near

Fayetteville where he had Floyd's rear under observation and would be prepared to conduct a feint to distract the Confederates.[24]

Rosecrans's plan was somewhat complex, but his forces had the advantage of being able to move into their attack positions with little Confederate interference. Except for a short stretch of the turnpike that was under artillery fire during daylight hours, the Federal forces controlled all of the roads they would need to prepare for the attack. Floyd took no further action to interfere, content to await Rosecrans's reaction. But the primary difficulty facing the Federal plan was coordinating the attacks of the four separate columns that all faced river crossings in horrid weather conditions.

Heth had already warned Floyd that although Cotton Hill afforded a good position for artillery, it also offered Rosecrans an excellent opportunity to cut off and capture the Confederate brigade. Floyd could not bear the thought of being captured. Remembering his ignoble departure from the War Department the previous year, he told Heth that he feared being put "in an iron cage" and put on exhibit as if he "were a wild beast." Heth was not the only officer in Floyd's command who had serious concerns about being surrounded by the Federals on Cotton Hill. A number of them signed a petition requesting that the brigade be moved to a safer location. Tompkins, commanding the Twenty-second Virginia, was in a particularly difficult dilemma because the Confederate artillery fire from Cotton Hill posed a threat to his own family who was still living at his farm, Gauley Mount. Fortunately, Rosecrans, Tompkins's old friend from earlier days in the Kanawha Valley coal mining business, intervened. Rosecrans gave the Tompkins family a safe conduct pass to travel through Federal lines to Richmond. Gallantly, he even sent a letter with the colonel's wife wishing her husband well. In a return letter, Tompkins thanked Rosecrans for the kindnesses to his family and for taking care of his farm. The two men, both graduates of West Point, for a moment overcame their national loyalties. The brief exchange between Rosecrans and

Tompkins encapsulated the situation for many people, military and civilian, in western Virginia. Long-standing personal relationships were not easily put aside by the arbitrary demands of war.[25]

Rosecrans had instructed his brigade commanders to be ready to attack between November 5 and 10. Benham crossed the Kanawha on November 6, but unfavorable high water conditions at Townsend's Ferry prevented Schenck from crossing the New River as planned. On the 7th Cox sent Captain Lane of the Eleventh Ohio, his bridging expert, across the Kanawha to make a reconnaissance in preparation for the attack. Three days later, Cox managed to get the Eleventh Ohio and First Kentucky across the Kanawha. Colonel DeVilliers, back in command of the Eleventh Ohio after a sojourn as a Confederate prisoner in Richmond following his capture at Scary Creek, led his regiment up Cotton Hill and forced an enemy artillery battery from its position. Joined by a detachment from the First Kentucky, the Ohioans were able to hold the crest and send a reconnoitering party along the road to Fayetteville where no enemy was found. During the night Cox sent the Second Kentucky across the river and joined them the next day. Rosecrans ordered Schenck to remain in position until Floyd was forced to attack Benham, giving the Federals room to maneuver after crossing the New River. Benham, however, was beginning to demonstrate that he was a better engineer than a line commander. His actions reflected the wisdom of his pre-war decision to remain a captain in the Corps of Engineers rather than accept an appointment as a major in the infantry. He knew of Cox's advances but spent a day studying the topography before he managed to get his brigade under way.

When the Federals began to move, Floyd finally agreed with his officers and ordered a withdrawal to begin the next day, November 11. Faced with trying to move heavy wagons over muddy roads, he issued orders for the troops to burn what they could not easily carry, and tents, overcoats, and blankets went under the torch. With the Thirty-sixth Virginia covering the rear, the brigade headed for

Fayetteville. As Benham approached, Heth encouraged Floyd to escape with most of the brigade before they were surrounded. But Benham's delayed movement allowed the entire brigade to escape the cul-de-sac of Cotton Mountain. Floyd turned to Heth for advice, expressing his concern that the withdrawal was about to turn into a rout. Conferring with Heth in the rain at midnight, all the tents having been burned, Floyd proposed assembling the command to tell them reinforcements were on the way. Heth persuaded Floyd that the men needed sleep more than a pep talk, and, besides, they would quickly realize that Floyd was lying about the reinforcements. Heth's assessment of Floyd's limited capabilities as a commander would appear to have been sound.[26]

Benham did not arrive on the scene until the 12th, and by that time Floyd had already retired to Fayetteville. Rosecrans then abandoned the planned river crossing at Townsend's Ferry and sent Schenck up the James River and Kanawha Turnpike to join Benham and pursue Floyd. On the 14th, the Thirteenth Ohio, the leading regiment of Benham's brigade, finally caught up with Floyd's rear guard at McCoy's Mill where it had stopped to cover the withdrawal of the Confederate trains. The Seventh Ohio, back together after its embarrassing incident at Cross Lanes, and the Thirty-seventh Ohio quickly advanced and dispersed the Confederates. But Benham, with no train or provisions, had to stop the pursuit on the 15th some fifteen miles east of Fayetteville.[27]

Benham's sluggish performance infuriated Rosecrans. He reported that "Benham had been instructed *ad nauseam* to look to . . . cutting off the enemy's retreat," and then went on to use Benham's own report to highlight the delays that had allowed Floyd's brigade to slip out of the Federal trap. The Confederate retreat began at 9 P.M., but Benham, according to his report, did not know it until 4:30 the next afternoon. The time lag prompted Rosecrans to note that Benham's "boldest scouts were desperately engaged from daylight until late in the afternoon in finding their way over a distance of two and a half miles that separated his bivouac from the enemy's deserted intrenchments." Heth, inside the trap, recalled that Benham "came within a quarter of a mile, or a half mile of the mouth of the cul-de-sac, and for reasons best known to himself came no further."[28]

Floyd continued to retreat until early December when the brigade reached Newbern in the Valley of Virginia. Rosecrans did not pursue. Floyd's activities had gained the Confederates little. Had he not had the good fortune to have Benham, an equally maladroit brigade commander, conducting the encircling movement, Floyd might have lost his brigade. Richmond also recognized Floyd's ineptness. The cynical reaction to Floyd's operation was that he "had shown the Federals the great importance of Cotton Hill, and then had turned it over to them to fortify."[29]

The Confederate withdrawal left the Federals with uncontested control of the Kanawha Valley at year's end. Both sides were consolidating their defensive positions and putting their troops into winter quarters. Lee had returned to Richmond, having turned command over to Floyd on October 30. With the onset of winter and troops already suffering from the ravages of an exceptionally cold, wet autumn, both sides began to redeploy forces out of western Virginia in response to the demands of a widening war. The campaign season for the first year of war was over, and even the political generals understood that their soldiers were worn out. The Federals controlled all of western Virginia, but they had been unable to move into the Valley of Virginia. While the triumph at Manassas Junction had helped the Confederates halt the Federal advance, they had not been able to mount an offensive to regain the western counties. All that was left for the armies to do in western Virginia was to consolidate their positions and prepare for what was going to be a very long war.

CHAPTER THIRTEEN

The Lessons of Defeat

A S THE 1861 campaign season drew to a close in western Virginia, both the Federals and Confederates were ready to move into winter quarters. The Federals controlled western Virginia, but the Confederates retained the Valley of Virginia. The Allegheny Mountain range provided a natural defensive barrier between the two regions, and both sides deployed their forces to consolidate defensive positions along that line.

At Sewell Mountain, Lee, concerned about the possibility of Federal activity along the Staunton-Parkersburg Turnpike, had sent Loring back to Huntersville on October 20, and at Camp Bartow, Jackson moved his forces from the Greenbrier on November 22 to establish a position at the John Yeager farm on Allegheny Mountain, eight miles to the east. There four regiments prepared defensive positions and set up a winter camp, while the rest of Jackson's

brigade moved on to Monterey. On December 2 Jackson resigned
from the Confederate army to accept a commission as a major general with his home state of Georgia. Colonel Edward Johnson of the
Twelfth Georgia replaced Jackson at Camp Allegheny and continued to develop the fortifications there with the troops of the Twelfth
Georgia and the Twenty-fifth, Thirty-first, and Fifty-second Virginia. The Twelfth Georgia and Twenty-fifth and Thirty-first Virginia were veteran regiments that had already seen action in the
campaign, while the Fifty-second was still looking for its first battle.[1]

The Federals were also making changes. On October 11 the
United States War Department had created the Department of
Western Virginia, naming Rosecrans the commanding general. The
new department had three districts: the Railroad District in the
north under Kelley, who had been there since recovering from
the wound he received at Philippi; the District of the Kanawha,
commanded by Cox; and the Cheat Mountain District where
Brigadier General Robert Milroy, former commander of the Ninth
Indiana, replaced Reynolds who had returned home to settle affairs
after the death of his brother who was also his business partner. In
early December Milroy decided to move against Camp Allegheny.[2]

Armed with information from a pro-Union man named Slayton
who lived near Greenbrier River, Milroy made his move early on
the morning of December 13, the same day that Johnson was promoted to brigadier general in the Confederate army. Five Federal
regiments–the Ninth and Thirteenth Indiana, the Twenty-fifth and
Thirty-second Ohio, and the Second Virginia–moved off Cheat
Mountain on December 12 to make the attack. When they reached
the Greenbrier River, the force split into columns. Three regiments
moved down the turnpike to attack the Confederate right, the other
two moved by the way of Green Bank Road to hit the left and rear
of the defensive position. The Thirteenth Indiana and the two Ohio
regiments moved down the turnpike under the command of
Colonel J. A. Jones. Arriving early in the morning of the 13th to

within a mile of Camp Allegheny, Jones deployed the Ohio regiments to the left of the turnpike to wait until the other column under Colonel Gideon C. Moody was in position.[3]

In the meantime Johnson's cavalry patrols had reported the Federal movement, and two companies of the Fifty-second Virginia under Major John DeHart Ross were in position to ambush them at Camp Bartow. After a brief skirmish with the advance guard, the Confederates withdrew to Camp Allegheny with the information that "about one thousand yankees" were coming up the road. About 4 A.M. Confederate pickets fired on the Ohioans, rousing the entire camp. Jones deployed the Thirteenth Indiana, his reserve regiment, and advanced to the crest of the hill. Companies of the Twelfth Georgia and Twenty-fifth and Thirty-first Virginia twice advanced against the Federal center. After unsuccessfully trying the Federal right, a fourth Confederate attack led by Johnson "with a clubbed musket in the left hand and a long club in his right" against the Federal left finally forced Jones to withdraw and return to the turnpike. About the time Jones pulled back, Moody, delayed by a three-mile climb through slashed timber, belatedly attacked the Confederate left, only to be surprised to find the well-entrenched troops of the Fifty-second Virginia waiting for him. By 2 P.M. the Federals had had enough and withdrew back to Cheat Mountain.[4]

It was a minor encounter that encouraged the Confederate defenders and discouraged the Federal attackers, but it made no change in the overall situation in the theater of operations. Both Cheat Mountain and Camp Allegheny remained occupied through the winter with little action at either position. But for some participants there was something special about the battle. It had allowed the Fifty-second Virginia, a locally raised regiment, to taste battle for the first time since being organized that August in Staunton. The regiment had been on its way to reinforce the position at Camp Bartow when it was attacked by Reynolds in October, but that battle ended before they got there, leaving them, as one officer put it, a "crestfallen set of chaps." The battle also brought the war close to home for Privates William and Henry Yeager in the Thirty-first Virginia, who were literally fighting for their home and family. Camp Allegheny was located on the Yeager farm. The Federals, who had failed in their attempt to take the camp, took a more cynical view of the results. In the veteran Ninth Indiana that had unsuccessfully assaulted the trenches held by the Fifty-second Virginia, Sergeant Bierce wrote that "the regiment had its hardest fight in Western Virginia, and was most gloriously thrashed" at Camp Allegheny.[5]

The battle at Camp Allegheny marked the end of the fighting for 1861 in western Virginia. The forces that successfully defended the camp spent the winter there. For two months prior to the battle, however, Confederate and Federal forces had been deploying to other theaters of operations. The three regiments of the Wise Legion left Sewell Mountain on October 20 for Meadow Bluff where they remained for several weeks. There, measles continued to plague the troops, and although food was more readily available, uniforms were not. While at Meadow Bluff Colonel Charles Henningsen, commanding the Fifty-ninth Virginia, helped keep the Wise-Floyd feud alive by writing to Wise to tell him "that Floyd had lost the chief part of the baggage of 2 regiments, that 1 regiment was reduced to 200 and another to 125 men." He wrote again to plead with Wise "to prevent destruction of the Legion." Wise may not have been much of a commander, but he did inspire loyalty. On December 10 the men of the legion received the welcome news that they would move to Richmond for the winter. Their arrival in the capital on the 13th was less than inspirational. Wise's youngest son, John, recalled that "all the gilt and newness of their uniforms had disappeared. The hair and beards of the men had grown long, and added to their dirty appearance." The campaign in western Virginia had not been pleasant for the legion.[6]

On the same day that Wise's Legion departed Sewell Mountain, the Sixteenth Tennessee marched off the mountain to Huntersville.

The regiment spent a few days there and then moved to Lewisburg, arriving there on November 14. Snow fell on the 17th and 18th, but on the 19th a shipment of clothing arrived from home with "coats, shoes, hats, bed-clothing, and all the bodily comforts that the good people at home could devise." They were especially appreciative of the "several hundred bottles of splendid apple brandy." After a few days to warm themselves inside and out, the men of the Sixteenth were on the move again on December 1, their eventual destination, South Carolina, where they would once again serve with Lee.[7]

In Monterey, on November 23, Colonel Taliaferro received orders to form a new brigade that would serve under Major General Thomas J. Jackson, who was then commanding the Valley District. The brigade consisted of the Third Arkansas, First Georgia, and the Twenty-third and Thirty-seventh Virginia. After a leisurely march, the brigade arrived in Winchester on December 8, where it went into a semipermanent bivouac six miles north of town to spend the winter. Along the way to Winchester, Rust of the Third Arkansas, still a member of the Confederate Congress, received word that he was needed in the capital. He turned the regiment over to Major Manning and took the train to Richmond.[8]

Floyd reached Dublin Depot where the Virginia and Tennessee Railroad crossed the upper waters of the New River in the Valley of Virginia in early December. The brigade started building winter quarters, and Floyd held a grand review on December 15 at Newbern that included the five regiments of his brigade, the Twenty-second, Thirty-sixth, Forty-fifth, Fiftieth, and Fifty-first Virginia. Two days after the review Floyd was ordered to take his brigade and join General Albert Sidney Johnston in Kentucky. Just after Christmas three of the regiments left for Kentucky and eventually ended up in Fort Donelson. The Twenty-second, "poorly equipped, half-clothed, undernourished, and unpaid," was designated to stay behind at Lewisburg to protect Greenbrier and Monroe counties, mainly because it was in no condition to make the trip to Kentucky. The

Forty-fifth also stayed in Virginia to protect the Virginia and Tennessee Railroad. At least one man in the regiment thought they were "very well fixed in regular winter quarters" with "shanties made of planks and logs." The campaign had largely dimmed the enthusiasm for war that had caused so many men to join in the spring. The regiment had lost only four men in battle, but at least seventy had succumbed to disease, a tragic sign of the hardships suffered on that first campaign.[9]

The Forty-fourth Virginia left Camp Bartow on November 22 and settled into winter quarters near Monterey where the men named the encampment in honor of Colonel Scott. Scott, a member of the Virginia legislature, left to attend its convocation. Lieutenant Colonel Hubbard became acting commander for the winter. The regiment had raced to the assistance of Johnson at Camp Allegheny on December 13, but the battle was over before it arrived. The threat of increased Federal activity in the area, however, kept the regiment in western Virginia when Loring took the rest of his command to join General "Stonewall" Jackson in Winchester. Some of the regiment were sorry not to join Jackson, believing that if they got "to Winchester and have a battle successful to us the chance of a furlough will be good." A section of the Eighth Star Artillery stayed with the Forty-fourth. The battery had finally acquired a second cannon while at Camp Bartow, doubling its firepower. Although the battery still had only half its desired number of guns, it was making progress.[10]

The Federals were also busy moving forces in response to changing situations in other theaters of operations. As active operations decreased in the theater, troops previously promised to Rosecrans were sent elsewhere, and with the departmental reorganization in October, the War Department began to transfer Ohio and Indiana regiments out of the Cheat Mountain and Kanawha Districts of the Western Virginia Department.[11]

In the Kanawha Valley, the Seventh Ohio was on its way back to Charleston on the steamer *Marmora* on November 16. Ten days later the Ninth Ohio was also steaming down the Kanawha to Ohio, and the regiment arrived in Cincinnati on Thanksgiving where the troops were warmly welcomed home. After a short stay the regiment was on its way to Kentucky. On December 2 the Eleventh Ohio received orders to proceed to Point Pleasant where it spent the winter. The Third Ohio, at Elkwater in the Tygart's Valley River, was ordered to Kentucky in November and arrived at Louisville by steamer on the 30th of the month. The regiment, still waiting to participate in its first battle, "had neither killed anybody nor had been killed themselves." Based on its experience in western Virginia one member of the regiment noted afterward that "war was about the most wholesome business cheerful men could engage in." That was not a widespread sentiment among veterans of the first campaign on either side; the weather and sanitary conditions had made the whole affair something less than wholesome.[12]

After the debacle at Camp Allegheny in December, the Ninth Indiana returned to Cheat Mountain where it ended up spending the winter. It was reassigned to Tennessee in February where its new brigade commander complained that the men "seemed fixed in many vicious habits, acquired while in the three months' service in Western Virginia. To correct this, some severity was indispensable." The Ninth's fellow Indianans in the Fourteenth, who themselves had undergone increased discipline to correct their problems in November on Cheat Mountain, faced a different fate. Ordered off the mountain in December, they spent the holidays in Huttonsville and then set off to Romney where they soon found themselves chasing after "Stonewall" Jackson.[13]

As Indiana and Ohio regiments were departing the theater, the Reorganized Government of Virginia in Wheeling was raising troops for Federal service in the western counties. By October that state government had ten regiments of infantry and two of cavalry in various stages of organization. The First and Second Virginia Infantry, initially raised as three-month regiments at the beginning of the campaign, had both been reorganized and mustered in for three years of Federal service. In October, the First Virginia Infantry was with Kelley in the Railroad District, and the Sixth, Seventh, and Eleventh were all being organized there. The Second Virginia Infantry was in the Cheat Mountain District along with the Third Virginia Infantry and First Virginia Cavalry. The Fourth and Fifth Virginia Infantry were serving in the Kanawha Valley along with the Second Virginia Cavalry. The Eighth and Ninth Virginia Infantry were also getting organized in the Kanawha District.

At the end of 1861, with active operations at a halt and troops settling into winter quarters, the two men most responsible for the results of the first campaign were not in western Virginia. As a result of their performances as commanders in the theater, Robert E. Lee and George B. McClellan were in dramatically different situations. McClellan had attained the status of national hero, while Lee's reputation was at a low ebb. Indeed, at the end of the first campaign, Lee was in danger of being written off as one of the South's great disappointments of the war. In the aftermath of the great Confederate victory at Manassas Junction in July, public expectations ran high for all Southern generals to succeed against the Federals. Thus, when Lee stumbled in the wilds of western Virginia, his reputation plummeted. The Southern press was hard on him, chastising him for his "dilly-dally, dirt digging, scientific warfare." Newspaper editors dubbed him "Granny Lee," the "Great Entrencher," and the "King of Spades."[14]

When Lee returned to Richmond at the end of October, he found that, despite the press reports, Davis still retained faith in him. Lee had not prepared a written report of his experience in western Virginia, because it would have highlighted Loring's delays at Huntersville, Rust's mistake at Cheat Mountain, and the Floyd-Wise feud in the Kanawha Valley. He was not one to clear his name at the expense of others. When Davis pressed for at least an oral report, Lee agreed only after exacting a promise that it would not be made public. The report left Davis unshaken in his "confidence in [Lee's] ability, zeal, and fidelity." After hearing Lee's recitation of his part in the first campaign, Davis decided to send him to examine coastal defenses in South Carolina, Georgia, and eastern Florida in the wake of Federal amphibious operations along the Confederate Atlantic coast. It was an assignment appropriate to Lee's engineering skills. Lee accepted the offer, although the experience in western Virginia had taught him to ask Davis to spell out exactly what would be expected of him before he left Richmond. Davis did. When Lee left Richmond on November 6, he carried orders naming him commander of a newly created military department. But it was a mark of his low standing in the South that Davis felt compelled to send a letter to the governor of South Carolina reassuring him of Lee's abilities.[15]

In the first campaign Lee had demonstrated a remarkable ability to gain the confidence of the enlisted troops, but he had failed to assert himself as a leader of generals. His habit of issuing broad orders and leaving details to subordinates had led to a series of lost opportunities as the Confederate military leaders in western Virginia delayed and bickered. Burdened with political generals who cared more about reputations than tactics, Lee's first performance as a battlefield commander left much to be desired. While his plans for the offensive were complex and beyond the capabilities of his inexperienced commanders, perhaps his private assessment of failure led to the genius for defensive operations he exhibited later in the war. His thinking had remained at the tactical level during the campaign, and he was never able to achieve unity of command over the various Confederate commanders in the theater. Misunderstanding the political situation, he did not concern himself with western Virginia early in his planning when he might have been able to prepare a stronger foundation for the defense of the area rather than rely on local militia to rally to protect the Old Dominion. However, Lee had more than western Virginia to worry about.

That part of the state was but one of four potential avenues of approach he had had to consider in the spring.

But the campaign in western Virginia had been a formative experience for Lee. While there, he was promoted and became the third ranking general in the Confederate army. His dark hair turned gray, perhaps not surprising under the circumstances, and he grew a beard of the same shade, giving him the grandfatherly look the troops remembered so well. His reputation among the troops of the Confederate army grew with the anecdotes of his gentle attitude toward soldiers brash enough to approach him. Lee's concern for his men became well known in the Confederate army, and it engendered a common bond between the general and his soldiers that lasted the entire war. He also observed and remembered the sense of frustration that developed when an army was posed to attack and then did not. The memory of the eagerness of the men before the Cheat Mountain attack, and their demoralization when the operation fell apart, remained with him. He resolved never again to shrink from decisive action when opportunities presented themselves.[16]

In contrast to Lee, McClellan was suddenly a national hero who had captured the popular imagination of soldiers and citizens alike. As he took command of the army of the Potomac, they looked to him to end the terrible war quickly. The press lauded him as "the Napoleon of the Present War." His campaign in western Virginia was praised as being "military workmanship by a master hand." When McClellan arrived in Washington in July, his presence had an inspiring effect on the dispirited troops who had been routed at Manassas Junction. A member of the army remembered that "shout upon shout went out into the stillness of the night; and it was taken up along the road and repeated by regiment, brigade, division and corps" as the news of McClellan's assumption of command swept through the ranks. It was a heady moment for the young general, and he believed his press releases. His ego swollen, McClellan wrote his pregnant wife in Cincinnati that by "some strange opera-tion of magic I seem to have become *the* power of the land."[17]

McClellan had not embraced Lee's gentlemanly code of behavior. In the flush of success, he had no qualms about criticizing the actions of the subordinates in western Virginia that had helped him get to Washington. Of Rosecrans at Rich Mountain, McClellan wrote that he "failed to carry out his orders to move on the rear of Pegram's works," and that had he "been able to follow his instructions, and moved direct upon Pegram, none of his command would have escaped." Strong words from the man who simply sat on his horse during the battle, unable to decide what the sound of the guns meant! In reflecting upon his rapid rise to prominence, McClellan later wrote that it "would probably have been better for me personally had my promotion been delayed a year or more." But he quickly dis-abused himself of any false humility by writing in the same sentence that he did "not know who could have organized the army of the Potomac as [he] did." Organizational skills no doubt he had. It was commanding in the field that caused him problems.[18]

McClellan planned and conducted the first campaign at the strategic level. By designating a theater of operations in which he commanded all the Federal troops, McClellan developed a unity of command that allowed him to coordinate the military operations in the area. He understood the political goal, and his military opera-tions were designed to support it. Unlike Lee, McClellan had the luxury of focusing on preparing and commanding the troops that fought the first campaign. He was able to concentrate his energies on an offensive campaign, whereas Lee had to plan to defend along four different avenues of approach. McClellan's proposed plan to invade Virginia along the Kanawha was the first attempt at an overall Northern strategy to end the war. Although Scott dismissed the plan as too complex and historians have since tended to agree, it should be noted that Scott was pushing for acceptance of his own strategic plan when he critiqued McClellan's efforts. Furthermore, the rainfall that plagued the Kanawha Valley's operations during August and September was among the heaviest ever recorded there, and the river itself crested at Charleston on October 5 at a record high.

Cox, who conducted the bulk of the operations in the Kanawha, came away from the campaign impressed by the difference between war in the abstract and the reality of battle. "It was easy," he wrote, "sitting at one's office table, to sweep the hand over a few inches of chart showing next to nothing of the topography, and to say, 'We will march from here to here.' " But in the Kanawha Valley, as "the natural obstacles began to assert themselves, . . . one general after another had to find apologies for failing what ought to never have been undertaken."[19]

The 1861 campaign in western Virginia was a significant Federal success. With relatively little loss of life, Federal forces retained control of critical east-west lines of communication and created a political environment that allowed the residents of Trans-Allegheny Virginia to create a new state that became a permanent part of the Union. Although the Confederacy could claim partial victory at the end of the campaign in that it had denied Federal forces access to the Shenandoah Valley, the so-called breadbasket of Virginia, that was due as much to Northern military leaders not understanding the importance of the Valley to the Southern cause as to Confederate defenders. They had not realized that this would be a war of attrition, waged against the Southern economy, not just the Confederate army.

The campaign also introduced some elements of modern warfare. The telegraph that followed the Federal forces provided first McClellan, then Rosecrans, the capability of communicating with both higher and lower headquarters during the military operations in western Virginia. By the end of the campaign, telegraph lines had been constructed to connect Federal garrisons from Gauley Bridge to Gallipolis in the Kanawha Valley, reaching north to Clarksburg where they joined the lines along the railroads. Steam power in the form of railroad trains and river steamers was another significant element of modern war. It gave the Federals a strategic mobility in the theater of operations that the Confederate forces could not match. Still, when the rivers and railroads ended, the Federals had to rely on horse-drawn wagons to move supplies. As Cox experienced it, "long lines of communications over forest-clad mountains, [are] dependent upon wagons to carry everything for man or beast."[20]

For both sides, the strategic objective of the first campaign was essentially the same—control of the western counties of Virginia. It was a political objective that required military force to achieve. The military leaders on both sides had a variety of experience planning and conducting war, ranging from none to considerable. The outcome of the campaign was decisive, although at the time it went largely unnoticed. The Federal invasion and occupation of the western counties of Virginia that began in May of 1861 did not cause the formation of West Virginia, but the invasion certainly helped pro-Union politicians accomplish that feat. When McClellan moved into Virginia, he may not have had the creation of a new state in mind, but he did grasp that the political unrest in the western counties presented an opportunity to keep some of Virginia in the Union. The campaign he initiated ultimately produced a state born of war. Lee, unaware of the nature of the political climate in the western portion of the state, was initially confident that the people who lived in the region shared his love of Virginia. By the end of the campaign, however, he was all too aware of how the westerners felt and was happy to leave their mountains.

In the first campaign the Federals gained a significant strategic advantage, while the Confederates incurred a significant disadvantage in western Virginia. Ironically, neither side realized the importance of the campaign at the time. Virginia lost the western counties forever. But the Old Dominion retained the Shenandoah Valley, a primary source of agricultural products for the South, until the very end of the war when the North finally understood the nature of modern warfare and sent Sheridan to destroy Virginia's granary. The Confederates were also able to use the Valley as an invasion route into Maryland and Pennsylvania. Although Federal forces could have used western Virginia as a base of operations to occupy the Shenandoah Valley, the North did not capitalize on that advantage. Federal forces failed to press eastward out of the mountains, and so allowed the Confederacy to reap the annual harvest of the rich Shenandoah unmolested throughout three long years of war.

Early in the war, the Federal occupation of western Virginia created a buffer zone for the states of Ohio and Pennsylvania, allowing them to concentrate on providing troops for Federal service without having to worry about keeping their militia forces at home to defend themselves. But by halting in the summer of 1861, the Federals lost the initiative in western Virginia. The battle at Manassas Junction in July 1861 did more than the Confederate defense to stop the Federal advance before it reached the Valley. Fearful of an offensive capability the Confederates did not actually have, Rosecrans was convinced he had to go on the defensive and consolidate the Federal position in the Allegheny Mountains rather than continue moving east. Thus the Federals failed to take full advantage of the first great strategic triumph of the war. Other theaters of operations attracted a high level of attention, and the forces in western Virginia became an army of occupation, on the defensive for the remainder of the war. Western Virginia remained in Federal hands for the rest of the war, but it was subject to periodic raids from Confederate forces operating out of the Valley of Virginia.

Both sides faced similar problems during the first campaign. They had politically appointed generals who were untested in battle, ill-trained but enthusiastic militia, short-term enlistments, and inadequate logistical support. While the strategic leadership on each side was generally aware of the strategic objective during the campaign, the military commanders in the theater tended to have a shorter view of operations, especially on the Confederate side where they never managed to attain unity of command in the theater. The campaign ended not with a bang, but a whimper. There was no parade to mark victory. Each side surrendered to nature and went into winter quarters. The generals were finished for the moment; it was time for the politicians to capitalize on the military successes of the first campaign. In spite of its political significance, the campaign in western Virginia was soon overshadowed by larger, bloodier battles.

West Virginia provides a lasting legacy to the first campaign of the Civil War. Had it not been for the Federal invasion of western Virginia, the state of West Virginia would not exist in its present form. The economic and social differences that caused friction between the eastern and western portions of Virginia might have eventually caused the counties nearest Ohio and Pennsylvania to attempt to form a separate state. But much of what is now West Virginia had strong ties to the Old Dominion. Of the fifty counties in West Virginia, twenty-four voted to ratify the secession ordinance in May 1861. It is doubtful that any of them would have followed the pro-Union counties into West Virginia had it not been for the Federal army that occupied western Virginia during the statehood process. The success of the Federal invasion, made possible by regiments provided by Ohio and Indiana and fueled by McClellan's rhetoric, enabled pro-Union politicians in western Virginia to form the new state. West Virginia owes its existence as much to the military forces provided by Northern states as it does to the pro-Union people who lived in western Virginia.

The creation of West Virginia, however, did not solve the problem of competing loyalties in the western counties. Throughout the war many West Virginians served in both armies. Out of a population of fewer than 400,000, about 30,000 served in Federal units while between 10,000 and 12,000 fought for the Confederacy. Units on both sides saw service outside western Virginia. West Virginia regiments were at Gettysburg and Vicksburg and saw service as far away as the Dakotas. When Lee surrendered the Army of Northern Virginia in 1865, regiments raised in western Virginia were under his command.

The military campaign in western Virginia, the first campaign of the war, had lasted only about eight months. It had begun in April when McClellan ordered Federal troops into western Virginia, and it had ground to a halt in December at Camp Allegheny when both sides settled into their defensive lines along the Alleghenies. At this point Federal military forces controlled virtually all of the territory that would become the state of West Virginia. Although there were periodic Confederate forays into various parts of this territory, after December 1861 there was never a real military threat to the formation of West Virginia. Even so, it took another eighteen months of political activity before Lincoln issued the proclamation that made the state of West Virginia part of the Union.

Less than a year after the campaign in western Virginia dissolved in the mud, Lee and McClellan again matched wits in a confrontation in the Peninsula Campaign in eastern Virginia. In the spring of 1862, when General Joseph E. Johnston, commanding the Army of Northern Virginia, was wounded, Davis, as he had in western Virginia, called on Lee to rescue a failing defense. But this time Davis made it clear that Lee was in command. Unlike the situation in western Virginia, on the peninsula Lee was blessed with talented subordinates who could respond to his style of command and translate his broad campaign guidance into the appropriate tactical action. After replacing Johnston in command, Lee stopped McClellan's advance toward Richmond. As in western Virginia, McClellan initiated the campaign with an invasion of the Old Dominion, and Lee arrived in the theater of operations well after the beginning of the Federal offensive. This time the two generals were on the field at the same time as McClellan directed the attack toward Richmond up the peninsula between the York and James Rivers. Although he conducted the campaign with his customary propensity for detailed preparations and use of maneuver to avoid frontal assaults whenever possible, McClellan failed to understand the necessity of providing a periodic victory to maintain public enthusiasm for the war. In western Virginia McClellan demonstrated his ability to think big and take advantage of favorable circumstances, along with an unfortunate tendency to hesitate at crucial moments. He owed his rapid rise to command to the positive public response to his victory in western Virginia, but in eastern Virginia he forgot about the importance of good press.

The first campaign propelled McClellan to glory, but it left Lee stuck in the mud. During the campaign the press on both sides freely offered assessments of the two generals for their readers. McClellan was lionized in the North, while Southern newspapers belittled Lee. In spite of their very different popular images in 1861, however, Lee and McClellan had one important thing in common—they both had the confidence of their respective commanders in chief. On November 1 Lincoln appointed McClellan to command all the Union armies, replacing Scott; Davis gave Lee command of a newly created military department in South Carolina a few days later. Lee's later performances as commander of the Army of Northern Virginia would fully repay Davis's trust, but McClellan would squander his chance for greatness.

How They Fared After the First Campaign

HENRY WASHINGTON BENHAM (1813–1884)

Benham fell into disfavor with Rosecrans after his laggardly performance at Cotton Hill and was sent to South Carolina. After a resounding defeat at Secessionville, South Carolina, he was removed from command and his commission revoked in August 1862. Lincoln reinstated Benham as a general officer in early 1863 after he had been posted to engineering duty in Massachusetts. Benham fared better as an engineer and spent the rest of the war directing the engineer troops of the Army of the Potomac, receiving brevet promotions to major general in both the volunteers and regular army. After the war he remained in the Corps of Engineers until his retirement in 1882 as a colonel.

AMBROSE GWINNETT BIERCE (1842–1914?)

Bierce remained with the Ninth Indiana until the end of the war. He was wounded at Kennesaw Mountain in 1864. After the war he settled in San Francisco where he became a writer and editor. His wartime experiences provided the material for his 1891 book, *Tales of Soldiers and Civilians.* In 1896 he moved to Washington, D.C., and continued writing for newspapers and magazines. As a newspaper columnist, he specialized in attacks on frauds of all sorts. Bierce went to Mexico in 1913, then in the midst of a revolution led by Pancho Villa. His end is a mystery, but he is presumed to have been killed in the siege of Ojinaga in January 1914.

JOHN SNYDER CARLILE (1817–1878)

Carlile stayed in the Senate until his term expired in March 1865. His opposition to the Willey Amendment destroyed his political career. He moved to Maryland and unsuccessfully attempted to reenter national politics. Carlile returned to Clarksburg in 1868 to practice law. President Grant nominated him for a diplomatic post in Sweden, but the Senate did not confirm the appointment. Carlile died in Clarksburg in October 1878.

JACOB DOLSON COX (1828–1900)

Cox remained in western Virginia until August 1862. During the rest of the war he held a variety of division and corps command positions including the Department of the Ohio for most of 1863. He ended the war a major general, and before he left active service was elected governor of Ohio. After one term as governor he became Grant's secretary of the interior in 1869. Cox resigned that post one year later and returned to the practice of law. He wrote widely on his experiences in the war and was an expert on Gothic cathedrals.

JEFFERSON DAVIS (1808–1889)

Davis continued to have difficulties with his generals throughout the war. He had constant feuds with Beauregard and Johnston, and often defended his favorite generals in spite of their poor performances. His attempts to consolidate control of the war effort in Richmond were constantly thwarted by the states, which maintained that dissatisfaction with a strong central government was one of the causes of the war. When Richmond fell, he fled south with the government and was captured in Georgia. After two years in prison, charged with treason, he was released on bail, never having had a trial. He lived the remainder of his life in Mississippi and made no attempt to regain his U.S. citizenship.

WILLIAM DENNISON (1815–1882)

After providing much of the political support and military wherewithal for the first campaign, Dennison lost his bid for reelection as governor of Ohio. Leaving office in 1862, he resumed his law practice and became an advisor to the new governor. He chaired the Republican national convention in 1864 and became Lincoln's postmaster general later that year. Two years later he found he could not support Andrew Johnson's policies and resigned the post to return to his legal, banking, and railroad interests in Ohio.

JOHN BUCHANAN FLOYD (1806–1863)

Floyd went on to command Fort Donelson, Tennessee, in February 1862. With three other brigadier generals there, the command situation was as confusing as it had been in western Virginia. Under indictment by a Federal court for alleged indiscretions involving War Department bonds, Floyd greatly feared capture by Federal forces. As General Grant neared the fort, he turned command over to General Gideon Pillow, who in turn quickly relinquished it, and both generals fled with Floyd's Virginia brigade before the fort surrendered. As a result, Davis revoked Floyd's commission in March 1862. Floyd was appointed major general of the Virginia State Line two months later. He was to organize partisan bands to operate in the southwestern part of the state, but his health broke and he died near his home in Abingdon in August 1863. He is buried in Abingdon.

ROBERT SELDEN GARNETT (1819–1861)

Garnett was the first general officer to be killed in the war. His body was returned to his family, and he was buried in the Greenwood Cemetery in Brooklyn, New York.

RUTHERFORD BIRCHARD HAYES (1822–1893)

Beginning his military service as a major in the Twenty-third Ohio, Hayes was one of six Civil War soldiers who would go on to become president of the United States. He became the colonel of the regiment in October 1862. During the course of the war he rose to the rank of brevet major general of volunteers before he resigned in June 1865. He served two terms in the House of Representatives and two terms as governor of Ohio before being elected to the presidency in 1876.

HENRY HETH (1825–1899)

After the first campaign Heth was promoted to brigadier general and went to Tennessee where he commanded a division. Lee requested his services in the Army of Northern Virginia in 1863 where he initially commanded a brigade and later a division. He was wounded at Chancellorsville and again at Gettysburg where his division opened the fighting. He surrendered with Lee at Appomattox and was in the insurance business after the war.

JEDEDIAH HOTCHKISS (1828–1899)

After the first campaign Hotchkiss fell ill with typhoid fever. Upon his recovery, he joined Stonewall Jackson's staff in March 1862 as chief topographical engineer. He served throughout the war, rising to the rank of major. Many of the Confederate maps in the *Official Records* were drawn by Hotchkiss.

HENRY ROOTES JACKSON (1820–1898)

Jackson resigned his commission as a brigadier general in the Confederate army in December 1861 to become a major general in the Georgia Militia. In September he was again commissioned in the Confederate army when the state forces were absorbed into the national service. He commanded a brigade until he was captured at Nashville and held in Boston until July 1865. Upon his release he resumed practicing law in Georgia and served as a diplomat in Mexico.

WILLIAM LOWTHER JACKSON (1825–1890)

After the campaign in western Virginia Jackson joined the staff of Thomas J. "Stonewall" Jackson as a volunteer aide where he became known as "Mudwall" Jackson to distinguish him from his more famous cousin. In 1864 he raised a cavalry brigade and became its colonel. He ended his military career as a brigadier general and disbanded his command in April 1865 and fled to Mexico rather than surrender. He eventually returned to practice law in Kentucky and was again named a judge.

BENJAMIN FRANKLIN KELLEY (1807–1891)

After recovering from his wound at Philippi, Kelley guarded the Baltimore and Ohio Railroad between Harpers Ferry and

Cumberland. He was breveted a major general in August 1864. In 1865, both he and his superior, General George Crook, commanding the Department of West Virginia, were taken prisoner and held briefly. Kelley resigned from the army in June 1865. He died in Oakland, Maryland, in July 1891 and is buried in Arlington National Cemetery.

FREDERICK WEST LANDER (1821–1862)

While commanding a brigade in the Army of the Potomac, Lander was severely wounded in the leg at Ball's Bluff. When he returned to duty in early 1862, he received command of a division. Shortly thereafter he requested relief due to ill health to which he received no reply. He came down with what was termed a "congestive chill" and after nearly twenty hours of morphine treatment, he died of pneumonia in March 1862.

ROBERT EDWARD LEE (1807–1870)

Lee led the Army of Northern Virginia for the remainder of the war, until he surrendered to Grant at Appomattox Court House in April 1865. Just two months before the surrender he had been confirmed as general in chief of the Confederate armies, giving him the highest rank of any officer in Confederate service. After the war his reputation, like his rank, increased. Refusing a number of offers that would have brought him considerable wealth, Lee accepted the presidency of Washington College at Lexington, Virginia, in the Shenandoah Valley. Lee's wartime prestige in both the North and South soared and he became a legendary figure. He died in October 1870. Lee's remains are interred at Lexington on the grounds of what is now Washington and Lee University.

WILLIAM HENRY FITZHUGH "ROONEY" LEE (1837–1891)

Robert E. Lee's oldest son rose to the rank of major general and commanded a cavalry corps by war's end. He was captured after the cavalry battle at Brandy Station while recuperating from wounds and held until March 1864, during which time his wife died. After the war he was a farmer, served in the Virginia legislature and U.S. Congress, and was president of the state agricultural society.

JOHN LETCHER (1813–1884)

As governor of Virginia during the first campaign, Letcher failed to convince the people of the western region to stay with the Old Dominion when it seceded from the Union. He was a loyal Confederate and rarely wavered in his support of the war effort. His cooperation with the Confederate government in Richmond made him unpopular with many Virginia residents, and he lost his bid for reelection in 1863 because he was considered too much a Confederate and too little a Virginian. After an unsuccessful bid for a seat in the Second Confederate Congress, he took his family to Lexington in January 1864 where he continued to support the war as a private citizen. His house was burned by Federal troops in June, and in May 1865 he was arrested and held in Washington for almost seven weeks. When his parole ended, he returned to Lexington to resume practicing law, and in the mid-1870s he served a term in the state legislature. Letcher died at home in January 1884 after a period of declining health.

WILLIAM WING LORING (1818–1886)

After the first campaign Loring was assigned to General Stonewall Jackson's command where he soon found himself in violent disagreement over the conduct of operations around Romney, Virginia. Richmond supported Loring, prompting Jackson to submit his resignation. Jackson was persuaded to stay, and Loring was promoted. Loring received command of a division in late 1862 and by the end of the war was the senior major general in the Confederate army. At the end of the war he went abroad and entered the Egyptian army where he rose to the rank of general of division and was twice decorated. Returning to the United States in 1879, he died in New York in December 1886. He is buried at St. Augustine, Florida.

JOHN McCAUSLAND (1836–1927)

After moving with Floyd to Kentucky, McCausland commanded the Virginia brigade that escaped from Fort Donelson just before it surrendered to General Ulysses S. Grant. He spent the next two years defending the Virginia and Tennessee Railroad in southwestern Virginia. He was promoted to brigadier general in May 1864, blaming his late rise in rank to his connection to the Fort Donelson debacle. While commanding a brigade of cavalry in the Valley of Virginia, he was sent to demand $100,000 in gold from the residents of Chambersburg, Pennsylvania. When he was unable to collect the money, he ordered the town burned. He returned to his home in the Kanawha Valley, but he felt increasingly mistreated by his neighbors and the press for his role in the war. He died in 1927, a recluse on his farm.

GEORGE BRINTON McCLELLAN (1826–1885)

While Lee's reputation grew during the war, McClellan's fell. After the failed Peninsula Campaign, he met Lee again in the Maryland Campaign. At Antietam, fighting a smaller army, McClellan made tactical blunders that allowed Lee to escape with the Army of Northern Virginia intact. With Lincoln growing weary of McClellan's failures, the War Department sent the general home to Trenton, New Jersey, to await orders that never came. McClellan ran against

Lincoln in 1864 on a Democratic party "peace at any price" platform. Union victories during the presidential campaign lessened the nation's war weariness, and McClellan carried only three states. He resigned from the army on election day. He served as governor of New Jersey from 1878 to 1881. McClellan died at Orange, New Jersey, in October 1885 and is buried in Riverview Cemetery in Trenton.

ROBERT LATIMER McCOOK (1827–1862)

One of the fighting McCooks of Ohio–seventeen members of the family served as soldiers and sailors in the Union army and navy during the war–McCook was wounded in early 1862 at Mill Springs. He was taken ill later in the year and was confined to an ambulance as his brigade advanced along the Memphis and Charleston Railroad. On August 5, while on a scouting mission, his ambulance was overtaken by a band of irregulars and he was shot as he tried to escape capture. He died of his wounds the next day.

WILLIAM McKINLEY (1843–1901)

McKinley was one of two future presidents serving in the Twenty-third Ohio in the first campaign. He enlisted as a private and rose to the rank of captain, remaining with the regiment until it was mustered out of service in July 1865. After the war he was admitted to the bar in 1867 and entered politics four years later. He was elected to the presidency in 1896 and was shot and mortally wounded in September 1901, becoming the third president of the United States to be assassinated in office.

GEORGE SMITH PATTON (1833–1864)

Patton stayed with the Twenty-second Virginia and was promoted to colonel and command of the regiment in January 1863. While leading a brigade in the third battle of Winchester in 1864, he was severely wounded in the leg but refused to allow the surgeon to amputate the useless limb. He died a few days later from loss of blood. He was survived by his son, named for him, who became the father of the General George S. Patton of World War II fame.

FRANCIS HARRISON PIERPONT (1814–1899)

After the state of West Virginia was admitted to the Union with Arthur I. Boreman as the governor, Pierpont moved the offices of his Reorganized Government of Virginia to Alexandria. After the war, President Andrew Johnson recognized the legitimacy of the Reorganized Government of Virginia, and Pierpont served as Reconstruction governor of Virginia in Richmond. He was displaced in April 1868 by General John M. Schofield, and he returned to West Virginia where he served in the legislature and as a tax collector. He died in Pittsburgh in 1899.

ALLAN PINKERTON (1819–1884)

Pinkerton went with McClellan to Washington and was with him during the Peninsula and Maryland Campaigns. He was responsible for gathering information about the size and disposition of the forces facing McClellan. While he was successful in gaining information, he was unable adequately to consolidate and interpret the many reports he received, resulting in estimates of opposing forces far in excess of their real numbers. Ironically, his tendency to overestimate reinforced McClellan's propensity to believe himself constantly outnumbered. When McClellan was sent home, Pinkerton returned to Chicago and resumed running his detective agency where his military activities were confined to investigating charges of fraud in army supply system and among government contractors. After the war he continued to build his reputation, becoming involved with the hunt for Jesse James and the Younger brothers and working for the railroads and large industrial corporations as a "union-buster."

GEORGE ALEXANDER PORTERFIELD (1822–1919)

After the court of inquiry both praised his actions at Philippi and censored him for lack of forethought, Porterfield was relegated to staff jobs until May 1862. Capture and parole by Federal forces the next month ended his military career. After the war he was a successful banker in Charles Town, West Virginia.

WILLIAM STARKE ROSECRANS (1819–1898)

Rosecrans held a variety of command positions after the first campaign and had mixed success. In June 1863 he maneuvered a Confederate army out of Chattanooga, but in September that year he suffered a crushing defeat at Chickamauga. He was replaced by General Ulysses Grant in October. He commanded the Department of Missouri in 1864 and resigned his regular army commission in March 1867. President Johnson appointed him minister to Mexico in 1868, but Grant removed him in 1869. He spent most of the rest of his life on his ranch in California, taking time to serve in Congress from 1880 to 1885. He died at his ranch in March 1898 and was buried at Rosedale Cemetery in Los Angeles. His remains were reinterred in Arlington National Cemetery in May 1902.

ALBERT RUST (1818–1870)

After his failure at Cheat Mountain, Rust redeemed himself during operations around Romney and was promoted to brigadier general in March 1862. He spent most of the remainder of the war in various commands in the western theater of war. But by March 1865 he found himself without a job, apparently as a result of pro-Union sentiments and criticism of the Confederate government. After the war he returned to serve in the House of Representatives.

WAITMAN THOMAS WILLEY (1811–1900)

Having taken Mason's vacated seat as a U.S. senator in July 1861, Willey remained in the office when West Virginia became a state in 1863 and was reelected two years later. He left office in 1871, choosing not to run again. In 1882 he returned to his prewar position as a court clerk and held that job until retirement in 1896.

HENRY ALEXANDER WISE (1806–1876)

Shortly after returning to Richmond near the end of the first campaign, he received command of a brigade in North Carolina. He was in command of Roanoke Island when it was captured in February 1862. His son, Obediah Jennings Wise, was mortally wounded in the same action. He held a variety of posts and, during the retreat to Appomattox, he handled his command well and kept it together during Sayler's Creek. Two days before the surrender at Appomattox, Lee appointed him to command a division, but the war ended before he received a promotion to major general. After the war Wise practiced law in Richmond, seeking neither amnesty nor restoration of his civil rights. He died in Richmond in September 1876 and is buried in Hollywood Cemetery there. His brother-in-law, General George Gordon Meade, commanded the Federal troops at Gettysburg.

NOTES

PREFACE

1. Charles H. Ambler, "General R. E. Lee's Northwest Virginia Campaign," *West Virginia History,* vol. V, no. 2, January 1944, 101–115.
2. Joseph W. Thomas, "Campaigns of Generals McClellan and Rosecrans in Western Virginia, 1861–1862," *West Virginia History,* vol. V, no. 4, July 1944, 245–308.
3. Frank Klement, "General John B. Floyd and the West Virginia Campaigns of 1861," *West Virginia History,* vol. VIII, no. 3, April 1947, 319–333.
4. Jack Zinn, *R. E. Lee's Cheat Mountain Campaign* (Parsons, West Virginia: McClain Printing Company, 1974).
5. Robert W. Branwell, "The First West Virginia Campaigns," *Confederate Veteran,* vol. 38, April 1930, 148–151, and May, 186–189.
6. Martin K. Fleming, "The Northwestern Virginia Campaign of 1861," *Blue & Gray Magazine,* August 1993, 10–17, 48–65.
7. Stephen W. Sears, ed., *The Civil War Papers of George B. McClellan* (New York: Ticknor & Fields, 1989), May 30th letter to Lincoln, 29.
8. Carl von Clausewitz, *On War,* ed. and trans. by Michael and Peter Paret (Princeton, New Jersey: Princeton University Press, 1976), 579.
9. Antoine Henri Jomini, *The Art of War,* trans, by G. H. Mendell and W. P. Craighill (Westport, Connecticut: Greenwood Press, 1971; originally published in 1862 by J.B. Lippincott & Co., Philadelphia), 67–68.
10. James J. Schneider, "Theoretical Implications of Operational Art," in Clayton R. Newell and Michael D. Krause, eds., *On Operational Art* (Washington, D.C.: U.S. Government Printing Office, 1994), 17–31.

CHAPTER ONE

1. George Ellis Moore, *A Banner in the Hills: West Virginia's Statehood* (New York: Appleton-Century-Crofts, 1963), 31–32.
2. Richard Orr Curry, *A House Divided: A Study of Statehood Politics and the Copperhead Movement in West Virginia* (Pittsburgh: University of Pittsburgh Press, 1964), 28.
3. *Acts of the General Assembly of the State of Virginia,* 1861, Extra Session (Richmond, 1861), 337; Curry, 29.
4. Curry, 28–29.
5. Curry, 20–21; Moore, *Banner,* 15–17.
6. Curry, 31.
7. Moore, *Banner,* 41; Craig M. Simpson, *A Good Southerner: The Life of Henry A. Wise of Virginia* (Chapel Hill: University of North Carolina, 1985), 240.
8. Moore, *Banner,* 39.
9. Curry, 30.
10. Shelby Foote, *The Civil War: A Narrative, Fort Sumter to Perryville* (New York: Random House, 1958), 47.
11. Ibid., 48.
12. Stephen D. Lee, "The First Step in the War," *From Sumter to Shiloh: Battles and Leaders of the Civil War—Volume I* (South Brunswick, New York: Thomas Yoseloff, 1956), 77–80; Clifford Dowdey, *The History of the Confederacy: 1832–1865* (New York: Barnes & Noble Books, 1992), 90.
13. Foote, 51.
14. Charles H. Ambler and Festus P. Summers, *West Virginia: The Mountain State* (Englewood Cliffs, New Jersey: Prentice-Hall, 1958), 193.
15. B. A. Botkin, *A Civil War Treasury of Tales, Legends and Folklore* (New York: Promontory Press, 1981), 21; Moore, *Banner,* 45.
16. Curry, 18–21; Moore, *Banner,* 1–2.
17. Curry, 34, 160.
18. Charles H. Ambler, *Francis H. Pierpont: Union War Governor of Virginia and Father of West Virginia* (Chapel Hill: The University of North Carolina Press, 1937), 82; Virgil A. Lewis, *How West Virginia Was Made: Proceedings of the First Convention of the People of Northwestern Virginia* (Charleston, West Virginia: New-Mail Company Public Printers, 1909), 33–34; Otis K. Rice, *West Virginia: A History* (Lexington, Kentucky: The University Press of Kentucky, 1985), 117.
19. Ambler, *Pierpont,* 83–84.
20. Curry, 29–31.
21. Ibid., 36.
22. Ibid., 35.

CHAPTER TWO

1. James M. McPherson, *What They Fought For, 1861–1865* (Baton Rouge: Louisiana State University Press, 1994).

2. Jacob Dolson Cox, "War Preparations in the North," *From Sumter to Shiloh: Battles and Leaders of the Civil War–Volume I* (South Brunswick, New York: Thomas Yoseloff, 1956), 86.
3. Russell R. Weigley, *The American Way of War: A History of United States Military Strategy and Policy* (New York: MacMillan Publishing Co., Inc., 1973), 87–90.
4. W. Glenn Robertson, "First Bull Run, 19 July 1861," *America's First Battles: 1776–1965* (Lawrence, Kansas: University Press of Kansas, 1986), 85–87.
5. Ambler and Summers, *West Virginia,* 151–153.

CHAPTER THREE

1. Emory M. Thomas, *Robert E. Lee: A Biography* (New York: W.W. Norton & Company, 1965), 43, 55.
2. Douglas Southall Freeman, *R. E. Lee* (New York: Charles Scribner's Sons: 1934), 82; Thomas, *Lee,* 52.
3. Freeman, *Lee,* 82; Thomas, *Lee,* 54.
4. Thomas, *Lee,* 111.
5. Freeman, *Lee,* 203.
6. Ibid., 218–219.
7. Freeman, *Lee,* 246–248; Thomas, *Lee,* 127.
8. Freeman, *Lee,* 295–298.
9. Thomas, *Lee,* 140–141.
10. Ibid.
11. Ibid., 152, 158.
12. Freeman, *Lee,* 428.
13. Thomas, *Lee,* 175–176.
14. Freeman, *Lee,* 396.
15. Thomas, *Lee,* 184–186.
16. Freeman, *Lee,* 441; Thomas, *Lee,* 88.
17. Freeman, *Lee,* 457–458.
18. Sears *Papers,* 5.
19. Freeman, *Lee,* 17; Stephen W. Sears, *George B. McClellan: The Young Napoleon* (New York: Ticknor & Fields, 1988), 2.
20. John C. Waugh, *The Class of 1846: From West Point to Appomattox: Stonewall Jackson, George McClellan and Their Brothers* (New York: Warner Books, 1994), 66–67, 530.
21. Sears, *McClellan,* 12.
22. Ibid., 17–19.
23. Ibid., 20–21, 26.
24. Ibid., 33; John C. Waugh, *Class of 1846,* 162.
25. Ibid., 36.
26. George B. McClellan, *The Armies of Europe* (Philadelphia: J.B. Lippincott, 1861), 25.
27. Ibid., 13, 482.

28. Ibid., 6.
29. Jacob Dolson Cox, *Military Reminiscences of the Civil War,* vol. I, April 1861–November 1863 (New York: Charles Scribner's Sons, 1900), 90.
30. Sears, *Papers,* 12–13.
31. Ibid., 13, note 1.
32. Ibid., 12–13.
33. George B. McClellan, *Report on the Organization and Campaigns of the Army of the Potomac: To Which Is Added an Account of the Campaign in Western Virginia* (Freeport, New York: Books for Libraries Press, 1970, reprint of the 1864 edition), 8.

CHAPTER FOUR

1. Moore, *Banner,* 56; Curry, 48.
2. Freeman, *Lee,* 474, 486.
3. Ibid., 493.
4. Ibid., 495–496.
5. Granville Davisson Hall, *Lee's Invasion of Northwest Virginia in 1861* (Chicago: The Mayer & Miller Company, 1911), 32.
6. Stan Cohen, *The Civil War in West Virginia: A Pictorial History* (Charleston, West Virginia: Pictorial Histories Publishing Company, 1995), 13; Hall, 33; Moore, *Banner,* 49–50.
7. Charles J. Rawling, *History of the First Regiment, Virginia Infantry* (Philadelphia: J.B. Lippincott Company, 1887), 16–18.
8. Thomas, "Campaigns," 250–251.
9. James Birney Shaw, *History of the Tenth Regiment Indiana Volunteer Infantry, Three Months and Three Years Organizations* (Lafayette, Indiana, 1912), 11; Roy Morris, Jr., *Ambrose Bierce: Alone in Bad Company* (New York: Crown Publishers, Inc., 1995), 23; A. J. Grayson, *History of the Sixth Indiana Regiment in the Three Months Campaign in Western Virginia* (undated), 6–7.
10. Hall, 35–36.
11. Moore, *Banner,* 59–60.
12. Ibid., 60–61; Curry, 44.
13. Moore, *Banner,* 62.
14. John M. Ashcraft, *31st Virginia Infantry* (Lynchburg, Virginia: H.E. Howard, Inc., 1988), 1; Eva Margaret Carnes, *The Tygarts Valley Line: June–July 1861* (Philippi, West Virginia: First Land Battle of the Civil War Centennial Commemoration, Inc., 1961), 17–18.
15. Hall, 38.
16. Ibid., 39.
17. Fleming, 12; Richard L. Armstrong, *25th Virginia and 9th Battalion Virginia Infantry* (Lynchburg, Virginia: H.E. Howard, Inc., 1990), 1–2.
18. Freeman, *Lee,* 480–484, 501.
19. Ibid., 502.
20. Curry, 46–53.

21. Armstrong, 2.
22. McClellan, *Report*, 8; Sears, *McClellan*, 70–71.
23. Rawling, 19–20; Thomas, "Campaigns," 252.
24. Cox, "Preparations," 96; John Beatty, "A Regiment in Search of a Battle," *Sketches of War History* (Military Order of the Loyal Legion of the United States, Ohio, vol. III, 422–452), Cincinnati, Ohio: Robert Clarke & Co., 1890, 425.
25. Cox, "Preparations," 97.
26. McClellan, *Report*, 11.
27. Sears, *McClellan*, 74.
28. Moore, *Banner*, 68–69.
29. Sears, *Papers*, 11.
30. Moore, *Banner*, 69.
31. Sears, *Papers*, 25, *McClellan*, 78; Moore, *Banner*, 70.
32. Armstrong, 2; Ashcraft, 12.
33. Sears, *Papers*, 26.
34. Albro Martin, *Railroads Triumphant: The Growth, Rejection, and Rebirth of a Vital American Force* (New York: Oxford University Press, 1992), 23–24.
35. W. G. Fuller, "The Corps of Telegraphers Under General Anson Stager During the War of the Rebellion," *Sketches of War History* (Military Order of the Loyal Legion of the United States, Ohio, vol. II, 392–404), Cincinnati, Ohio: Robert Clarke & Co., 1888, 395–396; William R. Plum, *The Military Telegraph During the Civil War in the United States* (Chicago: Ansen, McClurg & Company Publishers, 1882), 93.
36. Sears, *Papers*, 28–29.

CHAPTER FIVE

1. Rawling, 23.
2. Ibid.
3. Grayson, 17–18; Morris, 24.
4. Thomas, *Lee*, 197; Freeman, *Lee*, 507–508, 514.
5. U.S. Government, *The War of the Rebellion: A Compilation of the Official Records of the Union and Confederate Armies* (Washington: Government Printing Office, 1880), Series I, vol. II, 66.
6. Morris, 25; Grayson, 20–21; Peter Cozzens, "The Tormenting Flame," *Civil War Times Illustrated,* vol. XXXV, no. 1, April 1996, 45; E. R. Monfort, "From Grafton to McDowell Through Tygart's Valley," *Sketches of War History* (Military Order of the Loyal Legion of the United States, Ohio, vol. II, 1–21), Cincinnati, Ohio: Robert Clarke & Co., 1888, 3.
7. Rawling, 24.
8. Armstrong, 4–5; J. N. Potts, "That Battle at Philippi," *Confederate Veteran,* vol. VI, no. 9, September 1898, 424.
9. Armstrong, 5; Carnes, *Valley,* 41–42.
10. Fleming, 14–15.

11. Carnes, *Valley,* 44.
12. Jack Waugh, "Long Distance Victory: McClellan's First Battles," *Civil War Times Illustrated,* vol. XXII, no. 7, November 1983, 12.
13. Carnes, *Valley,* 45.
14. Armstrong, 5; Fleming, 14.
15. Carnes, *Valley,* 47–48.
16. Ibid.
17. Fleming, 15.
18. Carnes, *Valley,* 48.
19. Carnes, *Valley,* 55–56; Cozzens, 47.
20. Carnes, 55–56.
21. Morris, 26.
22. *Frank Leslie's Illustrated Newspaper,* June 22, 1861, 102–103.
23. U.S. War Department, *The War of the Rebellion: A Compilation of the Official Records of the Union and Confederate Armies,* 70 vols (1880–1901), Series I, vol. II, 69–70. Hereafter cited as O. R.
24. Ibid., 72.
25. Moore, *Banner,* 76–79.
26. Ibid., 80.
27. H. W. Flourny, ed., *Calendar of Virginia State Papers* (Richmond, 1893), XI, 152–153.
28. *Ordinances of the Convention, Assembled at Wheeling, on the 11th of June, 1861* (Wheeling, Virginia, 1861), 5–6; Curry, 71.
29. Ambler, *Pierpont,* 96–98.
30. Moore, *Banner,* 84; Ambler, *Pierpont,* 102–103.
31. Moore, *Banner,* 85; Ambler, *Pierpont,* 104–105.
32. Moore, *Banner,* 86.
33. Ibid., 88; Curry, 73.

CHAPTER SIX

1. Fleming, 14.
2. Freeman, *Lee,* 514–516.
3. Ibid., 529.
4. Ibid., 532–533; Fleming, 16; Armstrong, 7; Robert White, *West Virginia,* vol. II, *Confederate Military History,* Clement A. Evans, ed., 1899, 17; O.R., Series I, vol. 2, 243.
5. Moore, *Banner,* 2, 62.
6. Sears, *Papers,* 32.
7. Ibid.; *McClellan,* 83.
8. Fuller, 395–396; Plum, 97.
9. Sears, *Papers,* 33–35.
10. Ibid., 39.
11. Ibid., 41–42; Plum, 98; Robert Luther Thompson, *Wiring a Continent: The*

History of the Telegraph Industry in the United States, 1832–1866 (New York: Arno Press, 1972), 385.

12. Freeman, *Lee,* 531–532; W. Hunter Lesser, *Battle at Corricks Ford: Confederate Disaster and Loss of a Leader* (Parsons, West Virginia: McClain Printing Company, Inc., 1993), 3.

13. Sears, *Papers,* 43–44.

14. Ibid.

15. Ibid., 45; McClellan, *Armies,* 25.

16. John Beatty, *Memoirs of a Volunteer, 1861–1863* (New York: W.W. Norton & Company, 1946), 20; William Kepler, *History of the Three Months' and Three Years' Service From April 16th, 1861, to June 22d, 1864, of the Fourth Regiment Ohio Volunteer Infantry in the War for the Union* (Cleveland: Leader Printing Company, 1886; reprinted by Blue Acorn Press, Huntington, West Virginia, 1992), 31.

17. Fuller, 396; Plum, 98; Sears, *Papers,* 46.

18. Armstrong, 13; Ashcraft, 15; Thomas M. Rankin, *23rd Virginia Infantry* (Lynchburg, Virginia: H.E. Howard, Inc., 1985), 4; G. L. Sherwood and Jeffrey C. Weaver, *20th and 39th Virginia Infantry* (Lynchburg, Virginia: H.E. Howard, Inc., 1994), 12–13.

19. Rankin, 7.

20. P. S. Hagy, "The Laurel Hill Retreat in 1861," *Confederate Veteran,* vol. 24, 1916.

21. Carnes, *Valley,* 69–70; Dallas B. Shaffer, "Rich Mountain Revisited," *West Virginia History,* vol. XXVIII, no. 1, October 1966, 18.

22. Freeman, *Lee,* 533; O.R., Series I, vol. II, 241–243, 290–291.

23. Shaffer, 17; Armstrong, 14; Douglas Southall Freeman, *Lee's Lieutenants, Volume 1: Manassas to Malvern Hill* (New York: Charles Scribner's Sons, 1942), 27.

24. Fleming, 49; Jedediah Hotchkiss, *Make Me a Map of the Valley: The Civil War Journal of Stonewall Jackson's Topographer,* ed. by Archie P. McDonald (Dallas: Southern Methodist University Press, 1974), xxvi–xviii.

25. Fleming, 18; Armstrong, 13–14.

26. Constanin Grebner, *"We Were The Ninth," A History of the Ninth Regiment, Ohio Volunteer Infantry, April 17, 1861, to June 7, 1864* (Kent, Ohio: The Kent State University Press), 61–62; Kepler, 32–33; Fleming, 18; Robert B. Boehm, "The Battle of Rich Mountain, July 11, 1861," *West Virginia History,* vol. XX, no. 1, October 1958, 6.

27. Rankin, 10; Carnes, *Valley,* 97–99; J. W. Stokes, "The Retreat from Laurel Hill, West Virginia," *Southern Bivouac,* vol. III, September 1884–May 1885, 13.

28. Thomas, "Campaigns," 262; Shaffer, 20; Boehm, "Rich Mountain," 7.

29. Boehm, "Rich Mountain," 7; Shaffer, 20–21.

30. Beatty, *Memoirs,* 26.

31. Thomas, "Campaigns," 262.

32. Fleming, 50–51.

33. Armstrong, 14–15; Freeman, *Lieutenants,* 27–29; Boehm, "Rich Mountain," 13; Fleming, 51; Kevin C. Ruffner, *44th Virginia Infantry* (Lynchburg, Virginia: H. E. Howard, Inc., 1987), 10.
34. Boehm, "Rich Mountain," 8–9; Thomas, "Campaigns," 262–263.
35. Thomas, "Campaigns," 263–264; Fleming, 54; Armstrong, 17.
36. Freeman, *Lieutenants,* 31; Boehm, "Rich Mountain," 11; O.R., Series I, vol. II, 260.
37. McClellan, *Armies,* 482; Beatty, *Memoirs,* 27; Kepler, 33; Shaffer, 26; Fleming, 54.
38. Boehm, "Rich Mountain," 12.
39. Sherwood, 19–20; Armstrong, 19–20; Boehm, "Rich Mountain," 12; O.R., Series I, vol. 2, 257.
40. Freeman, *Lieutenants,* 34; Shaffer, 29; Boehm, "Rich Mountain," 12; Sherwood and Weaver, *20th and 39th Virginia,* 19–20; Armstrong, 19–20; O.R., Series 2, vol. I, 257, 266–267; *Rosecrans's Campaigns,* Extracted from: U.S. Congress Joint Committee on the Conduct of the War. Report of the Joint Committee on the Conduct of the War, 1863–1866 (Millwood, New York: Kraus Reprint Co., 1977), 50–51.
41. *Rosecrans's Campaigns,* 5, Thomas, "Campaigns," 264.
42. Freeman, *Lieutenants,* 32–33.
43. Boehm, "Rich Mountain," 14–15; Shaffer, 27; Ruffner, 10–12; O.R., Series I, vol. 2, 273–275.
44. Fleming, 54, Boehm, "Rich Mountain," 30.
45. Freeman, *Lieutenants,* 33.
46. Grebner, 63; Beatty, *Memoirs,* 29; Kepler, 34; Boehm, "Rich Mountain," 26; Sears, *Papers,* 51.
47. Fuller, 396; Plum, 98–99; Sears, *Papers,* 60–61.
48. Morris, 28.
49. Morris, 28; Stokes, 15; Grayson, 37; *Rosecrans's Campaigns,* 59.
50. Grayson, 39–40; Lesser, 11–15; *Rosecrans's Campaigns,* 61.
51. Lesser, 17; Freeman, *Lieutenants,* 35; O.R., Series I, vol. 2, 287.
52. Fleming, 60; Lesser, 20.
53. Thomas, "Campaigns," 269–271; Stokes, 64–66; Sears, *Papers,* 58.
54. Ibid.
55. Hagy, 172–173.

CHAPTER SEVEN

1. Moore, *Banner,* 101.
2. Val Husley, " 'Men of Virginia–Men of Kanawha–To Arms!' A History of the Twenty-second Virginia Volunteer Infantry Regiment, C.S.A.," *West Virginia History,* vol. XXXV, no. 3, 220; Roy Bird Cook, "First Battle in the Great Kanawha Valley," *Confederate Veteran,* vol. 39, April 1931, 143; Lee A. Wallace, *A Guide to Virginia Military Organizations 1861–1865* (Lynchburg,

Virginia: H.E. Howard, Inc., 1986), 118–119; J. L. Scott, *36th Virginia Infantry* (Lynchburg, Virginia: H.E. Howard, Inc., 1987), 2; C. L. Thompson, "The Battle of Scary," *Confederate Veteran,* vol. 26, 1918, 275; David L. Phillips, *War Diaries: The 1861 Kanawha Campaigns* (Leesburg, Virginia: Gauley Mount Press, 1990), 34–35, 53.

3. Wallace, 104, 118; Scott, *36th Virginia,* 2; Husley, 221; J. M. Ferguson, "The Battle of Scary, W.VA.," *Confederate Veteran,* vol. 25, 1917, 503; Stan Cohen, "Colonel George S. Patton and the 22nd Virginia Infantry Regiment," *West Virginia History,* vol. XXVI, April 1965, 178.

4. Wallace, 86, 104, and 118.

5. Cook, 144; E. Kidd Lockard, "The Unfortunate Military Career of Henry A. Wise in Western Virginia," *West Virginia History,* vol. XXXI, no. 1, October 1969, 41–42.

6. John M. Belohavek, "John B. Floyd and the West Virginia Campaign of 1861," *West Virginia History,* vol. XXIX, no. 4, July 1968, 283–284.

7. Freeman, *Lee,* 580; Henry Heth, *The Memoirs of Henry Heth,* ed. by James L. Morrison (Westport, Connecticut: Greenwood Press, 1974), 152; Klement, 323–324.

8. Cohen, *The Civil War in West Virginia,* 34; Curry, 142–144; Wallace, 150.

9. Barton H. Wise, *The Life of Henry A. Wise of Virginia: 1806–1876* (London: MacMillan & Co., Inc., 1899), 285.

10. Sears, *Papers,* 44; Lockard, 42–43; Simpson, *A Good Southerner,* 254.

11. Cox, *Reminiscences,* 59.

12. Sears, *Papers,* 42.

13. Cox, *Reminiscences,* 61; Thomas Speed, *The Union Regiments of Kentucky* (Louisville, Kentucky: Courier-Journal Job Printing Company, 1897), 274, 282.

14. Cox, *Reminiscences,* 62–63; Jacob D. Cox, "McClellan in West Virginia," *From Sumter to Shiloh: Battles and Leaders of the Civil War–Volume I* (South Brunswick, New York: Thomas Yoseloff, 1956), 138–139.

15. Robert H. Moore, *The Danville, Eighth Star New Market and Dixie Artillery* (Lynchburg, Virginia: H.E. Howard, Inc., 1989), 102; Lockard, 42; O.R. Series I, vol. 2, 291.

16. Cohen, "Patton," 180; Allan Pinkerton, *The Spy of the Rebellion* (Kansas City: Kansas City Publishing Co., 1884), 210–216.

17. Heth, 152; J. L. Scott, *45th Virginia Infantry* (Lynchburg, Virginia: H.E. Howard, Inc., 1989), 2–4; William W. Hassler, "Henry Heth–Lee's Hard Luck General," *Civil War Times Illustrated,* vol. V, no. 4, July 1966, 13.

18. Belohavek, 285; Klement, 324; Thompson, "Scary," 275.

19. Cox, *Reminiscences,* 64–67; Joshua H. Horton and Teverbaugh, *A History of the Eleventh Regiment, Ohio Volunteer Infantry* (Dayton, Ohio: W.J. Shuey, Printer and Publisher, 1866), 26–27.

20. Horton, 28; Cox, *Reminiscences,* 68–69.

21. Cook, 183; Cox, *Reminiscences,* 69.

22. Thompson, "Scary," 275; Cook, 183; Wallace, 105.

23. Thompson, "Scary," 276; Cook, 184.

24. Cook, 185; Cox, *Reminiscences,* 69–70.

25. Sears, *Papers,* 61; Cox, *Reminiscences,* 70; O.R., Series I, vol. 2, 288.

26. Cox, *Reminiscences,* 35; Horton, 29.

27. Cox, *Reminiscences,* 70–71; Sears, *Papers,* 61; Moore, *Banner* 103; Lockard, 43; Scott, *36th Virginia,* 3–4.

28. Horton, 30–31; Thomas, "Campaigns," 279; Terry Lowry, *22nd Virginia Infantry* (Lynchburg, Virginia: H.E. Howard, Inc., 1988), 15; O.R., Series I, vol. 2, 290–292.

29. Cox, *Reminiscences,* 72–73.

CHAPTER EIGHT

1. Foote, 70; W. Glenn Robertson, "First Bull Run, 19 July 1861," *America's First Battles: 1776-1965* (Lawrence, Kansas: University Press of Kansas, 1986), 88–89.

2. Robertson, 88; Foote, 56.

3. Robertson, 89.

4. Foote, 70; James B. Fry, "McDowell's Advance to Bull Run," *From Sumter to Shiloh: Battles and Leaders of the Civil War–Volume I* (South Brunswick, New York: Thomas Yoseloff, 1956), 175.

5. O.R., Series I, vol. 2, 284–285.

6. Sears, *Papers,* 58–59.

7. Sears, *McClellan,* 93; John C. Waugh, *The Class of 1846,* 264–265.

8. Sears, *McClellan,* 58, 62.

9. Freeman, *Lee,* 534–535.

10. Foote, 74–75; Robertson, 94–95; Fry, 178–179.

11. Moore, *Banner,* 124–125.

12. Thomas, "Campaigns," 271; Sears, *Papers,* 59–60.

13. Fry, 182–183.

14. Fry, 183; Foote, 76.

15. John D. Imboden, "Incidents of the First Bull Run," *From Sumter to Shiloh: Battles and Leaders of the Civil War–Volume I* (South Brunswick, New York: Thomas Yoseloff, 1956), 229; P. G. T. Beauregard, "The First Battle of Bull Run," *From Sumter to Shiloh: Battles and Leaders of the Civil War–Volume I* (South Brunswick, New York: Thomas Yoseloff, 1956), 203.

16. Foote, 84–84; Freeman, *Lee,* 537.

17. Robertson, 103–104; Freeman, *Lee,* 540.

18. Foote, 85–86; Thomas, *Lee,* 198–199.

19. Freeman, *Lee,* 539–540.

20. Sears, *McClellan,* 95, *Papers,* 66–67; *Rosecrans's Campaigns,* 7.

21. Steven E. Woodworth, *Davis and Lee at War* (Lawrence, Kansas: University of Kansas Press, 1995), 46.

22. Thomas, *Lee,* 198; Woodworth, 59; Walter H. Taylor, *Four Years with General Lee* (New York: D. Appleton and Company, 1877), 16.

CHAPTER NINE

1. Freeman, *Lee,* 543–544.
2. Thomas, *Lee,* 202; Ezra J. Warner, *Generals in Gray: Lives of the Confederate Commanders* (Baton Rouge: Louisiana State University Press, 1965), 193; William L. Wessler, *Born to Be a Soldier: The Military Career of William Wing Loring of St. Augustine, Florida* (Fort Worth: Texas Christian University Press, 1971), 6, 18.
3. Freeman, *Lee,* 547–548; A. L. Long, *Memoirs of Robert E. Lee: His Military and Personal History* (New York: J.M. Stoddart & Company, 1886), 117–118.
4. Calvin L. Collier, *"They'll Do To Tie To!" The Story of the Third Regiment, Arkansas Infantry, C.S.A.* (Little Rock, Arkansas: Eagle Press, 1988), 33–35.
5. Samuel R. Watkins, *"Co, Aytch:" Maury Grays First Tennessee Regiment or A Side Show of the Big Show* (New York: Collier Books, 1962), 24–25.
6. *Rosecrans's Campaigns,* 8; William M. Lamers, *The Edge of Glory: A Biography of William S. Rosecrans, U.S.A.* (New York: Harcourt, Brace & World, Inc., 1961), 39.
7. Lowry, *22nd Virginia,* 15; Cox, *Reminiscences,* 71; William Forse Scott, *Philander P. Lane: Colonel of Volunteers in the Civil War, Eleventh Ohio Infantry* (Privately Printed, 1920), 40.
8. Cox, *Reminiscences,* 71–74; Thomas, "Campaigns," 279–280.
9. Sears, *Papers,* 62, 65.
10. Grayson, 44–45; Shaw, *History of the Tenth Regiment Indiana Volunteer Infantry,* 12, 16.
11. Cox, *Reminiscences,* 75–76.
12. Ibid., 76–77.
13. Ibid., 77–79; Lockard, 44; Clarice Lorene Bailes, "Jacob Dolson Cox in West Virginia," *West Virginia History,* vol. VI, no. 1, October 1944, 19.
14. Thomas, *Lee,* 195, 201–202; Taylor, 16.
15. Taylor, 16; Freeman, *Lee,* 541–542; Ambler, "General Lee's Northwest Virginia Campaign," 107.
16. Thomas, *Lee,* 204; Freeman, *Lee,* 550; Long, *Memoirs of Robert E. Lee,* 120.
17. Freeman, *Lee,* 540; Ambler, "Campaign," 105.
18. Sears, *Papers,* 63–64; Edward Conrad Smith, *The Borderland in the Civil War* (New York: The MacMillan Company, 1927), 217–218.
19. Curry, 79–85; Moore, *Banner,* 129–135.
20. Ibid.
21. Curry, 133–134; Moore, *Banner,* 84–85.
22. Heth, 153; Klement, 324; Lockard, 44–45; Scott, *45th Virginia,* 6.
23. Thomas, *Lee,* 200; Taylor, 17.

CHAPTER TEN

1. *Rosecrans's Campaigns,* 8.
2. *Rosecrans's Campaigns,* 8; Lamers, 17–18.
3. Lamers, 54–55.
4. Thomas, "Campaigns," 282–283.
5. Cox, *Reminiscences,* 80–81; Phillips, *Diaries,* 291.
6. Scott, *Lane,* 41–42.
7. Cox, *Reminiscences,* 88–89; Thomas, "Campaigns," 282.
8. Horton, 35–36.
9. Cox, *Reminiscences,* 87; Bailes, 22–21.
10. Lockard, 44–45; Klement, 324–325.
11. Lowry, *22nd Virginia,* 16; Phillips, *Diaries,* 293.
12. Scott, *36th Virginia,* 5–6; Lockard, 46.
13. Plum, 101.
14. Cox, *Reminiscences,* 92–92; Thomas, "Campaigns," 283.
15. Cox, *Reminiscences,* 93.
16. Horton, 42; Cox, "McClellan," 143; Scott, *45th Virginia,* 7; Moore, *Danville,* 105.
17. Cox, *Reminiscences,* 94.
18. Lockard, 48; Moore, *Danville,* 106.
19. Cox, *Reminiscences,* 95; Bailes, 27; Lawrence Wilson, *Itinerary of the Seventh Ohio Volunteer Infantry, 1861–1864* (New York: The Neale Publishing Company, 1907), 70.
20. Scott, *45th Virginia,* 7–8; Wilson, 75–78; Robert G. Tanner, *Stonewall in the Valley* (Garden City, New York: Doubleday & Company, 1965), 119–124.
21. Scott, *36th Virginia,* 6; Bailes, 28–29; Moore, *Banner,* 106.
22. Cox, *Reminiscences,* 97, 106; *Rosecrans's Campaigns,* 9; Plum, 103.
23. *Rosecrans's Campaigns,* 9; Thomas, "Campaigns," 287.
24. Lockard, 48–49.
25. Horton, 42; Sherwood and Weaver, 24; Lockard, 49; Cox, *Reminiscences,* 99–100; O.R., Series I, vol. 5, 125–126.
26. Lockard, 50; Terry Lowry, *September Blood: The Battle of Carnifex Ferry* (Charleston, West Virginia: Pictorial Histories Publishing Company, 1985), 299.
27. Scott, *36th Virginia,* 6.
28. Cox, *Reminiscences,* 103.
29. *Rosecrans's Campaigns,* 9.
30. Heth, 154; Scott, *45th Virginia,* 8–9.
31. *Rosecrans's Campaigns,* 9; Scott, *45th Virginia,* 8; O.R., Series I, vol. 5, 130–132.
32. *Rosecrans's Campaigns,* 9; O.R., Series, I, vol. 5, 130–132.
33. Heth, 154; Scott, *36th Virginia,* 7; Husley, 223; Moore, *Danville,* 109; O.R., Series I, vol. 5, 146–147.
34. Lockard, 50.

35. Lockard, 51; Moore, *Danville,* 109.
36. Cox, *Reminiscences,* 103–104.
37. Cox, *Reminiscences,* 108–109; *Rosecrans's Campaigns,* 10.
38. Heth, 155; Lockard, 52.
39. Lockard, 53; Moore, *Danville,* 109; Klement, 329.
40. Cox, *Reminiscences,* 117.

CHAPTER ELEVEN

1. Freeman, *Lee,* 550–551.
2. Ibid., 552–553; Thomas, *Lee,* 204.
3. A. L. Long, "Lee's West Virginia Campaign," *The Annals of the War* (Philadelphia: The Times Publishing Company, 1879). Republished by Civil War Times, Illustrated, Gettysburg, Pennsylvania, 1974, 88–89.
4. Shaw, 11; *Rosecrans's Campaigns,* 8; Thomas, "Campaigns," 292.
5. Long, *Memoirs,* 117–119.
6. Ibid., 121; Watkins, 27; Freeman, *Lee,* 558–559; Taylor, 17.
7. Collier, 37; Watkins, 27; Thomas A. Head, *Campaigns and Battles of the Sixteenth Regiment, Tennessee Volunteers, In The War Between The States, With Incidental Sketches of the Part Performed by other Tennessee Troops in the same War, 1861–1865* (Nashville, Tennessee: Cumberland Presbyterian Publishing House, 1885), 28.
8. Morris, 29; Beatty, "A Regiment," 434; Nancy Niblack Baxter, *Gallant Fourteenth, The Story of an Indiana Civil War Regiment* (Traverse City, Michigan: Pioneer Study Center Press, 1980), 57–61.
9. Thomas, *Lee,* 54; Freeman, *Lee,* 559–560.
10. Long, *Memoirs,* 122–123; Freeman, *Lee,* 543.
11. Freeman, *Lee,* 561–562; Taylor, 21–22; Long, *Memoirs,* 122–123.
12. Collier, 7, 38.
13. Freeman, *Lee,* 562; Taylor, 24–26; Joe Bennett McBrien, *The Tennessee Brigade* (Chattanooga, Tennessee: Hudson Printing & Lithographing Co., 1977), 4–6.
14. Taylor, 26.
15. Head, 32; Watkins, 28–29; William McComb, "Tennesseeans in the Mountain Campaign," *Confederate Veteran,* vol. 22, May 1914, 210.
16. Head, 33–34; Watkins, 16; Thomas, "Campaigns," 292–293; Freeman, *Lee,* 565–566.
17. Ashcraft, 12; Collier, 38; Thomas, *Lee,* 206.
18. Thomas, "Campaigns," 293; Taylor, 27–28.
19. Ashcraft, 12; Collier, 38; Thomas, *Lee,* 206.
20. Baxter, 6; McBrien, 8; Beatty, "Regiment," 435–436; Freeman, *Lee,* 567–568; Long, *Memoirs,* 123.
21. Freeman, *Lee,* 568; Moore, *Banner,* 114.
22. Long, *Memoirs,* 126; Freeman, *Lee,* 569; Thomas, *Lee,* 207.

23. Long, *Memoirs,* 127; Freeman, *Lee,* 574–575.
24. McBrien, 10.

CHAPTER TWELVE

1. *Rosecrans's Campaigns,* 10.
2. Scott, *36th Virginia,* 7; Lowry, *22nd Virginia,* 19; Cox, *Reminiscences,* 114; Lockard, 53.
3. Lockard, 53; Freeman, *Lee,* 588–589.
4. Freeman, *Lee,* 589.
5. Taylor, 33; Thomas, *Lee,* 208; Freeman, *Lee,* 591.
6. Freeman, *Lee,* 592.
7. Cox, *Reminiscences,* 117; Grebner, 71; Darrell L. Collins, *46th Virginia Infantry* (Lynchburg, Virginia: H.E. Howard, Inc., 1992), 19; Sherwood and Weaver, *20th and 39th Virginia,* 26.
8. Sherwood and Weaver, 27; Horton, 46; Collins, 20; Freeman, *Lee,* 592–593; Lockard, 53.
9. Collins, 21; Sherwood and Weaver, 27; Freeman, *Lee,* 593; Lockard, 54; Taylor, 34.
10. McBrien, 11; Cox, *Reminiscences,* 118.
11. Thomas L. Broun, "Gen. R.E. Lee's War-Horse," *Confederate Veteran,* vol. VI, no. 7, 1898, 292.
12. *Rosecrans's Campaigns,* 10; Cox, *Reminiscences,* 120.
13. Horton, 47; Grebner, 73.
14. Freeman, *Lee,* 595–596.
15. Collins, 21–22.
16. Grebner, 74; Horton, 48–49; *Rosecrans's Campaigns,* 11; Cox, *Reminiscences,* 121–124.
17. McBrien, 11; Freeman, *Lee,* 597; James J. Womack, *The Civil War Diary of Capt. J. J. Womack, Co. E, Sixteenth Regiment, Tennessee Volunteers (Confederate)* (McMinnville, Tennessee: Womack Printing Company, 1961), 21.
18. Ambler, "Campaign," 112; Freeman, *Lee,* 598.
19. Baxter, 63; Collins, 44–45; Moore, *Danville,* 7–8 and 64; Thomas, "Campaigns," 294; Walter A. Clark, *Under the Stars and Bars or, Memories of Four Years Service with Oglethorpes, of Augusta, Georgia* (Augusta, Georgia: Chronicle Printing Company, 1900; reprinted by Freedom Hill Press, Inc., Jonesboro, Georgia, 1987), 31–32; Augustus M. Van Dyke, "Early Days; or, The School of the Soldier," *Sketches of War History* (Military Order of the Loyal Legion of the United States, Ohio, vol. V, 18–31), Cincinnati, Ohio: Robert Clarke & Co., 1903, 28.
20. Collins, 23; Heth, 156–157; Sherwood, 28; Freeman, *Lee,* 598–599.
21. Grebner, 76; Cox, *Reminiscences,* 126.
22. Thomas, "Campaigns," 297.

23. Cox, *Reminiscences,* 130, 135–136; Horton, 52; James A. Davis, *51st Virginia Infantry* (Lynchburg, Virginia: H.E. Howard, Inc., 1984), 6.
24. *Rosecrans's Campaigns,* 12; Cox, *Reminiscences,* 137–138.
25. Heth, 157; Phillips, *Diaries,* 353–354; Scott, *45th Virginia,* 12, *36th Virginia,* 8; Lowry, *22nd Virginia,* 21.
26. Heth, 158–159; Scott, *36th Virginia,* 8.
27. *Rosecrans's Campaigns,* 13; Cox, *Reminiscences,* 140–144.
28. Scott, *Lane,* 61–61; Horton, 53–54; Wilson, 108–109; Heth, 158; O.R., Series I, vol. 5, 257.
29. Bailes, 40.

CHAPTER THIRTEEN

1. Armstrong, 26; Ashcroft, 24; Thomas, "Campaigns," 295.
2. Morris, 30.
3. Thomas, "Campaigns," 295–296; Richard W. Oram, ed., "Harpers Ferry to the Fall of Richmond: Letters of Colonel John De Hart Ross, C.S.A.," *West Virginia History,* vol. XLV, 1984, 170.
4. Thomas, "Campaigns," 296; Ashcroft, 24–25; Armstrong, 26–27; Robert J. Driver, *52nd Virginia Infantry* (Lynchburg, Virginia: H.E. Howard, Inc., 1986), 6–7.
5. Morris, 30; Oram, 167.
6. Collins, 24–25; Sherwood and Weaver, 28.
7. Head, 53–56.
8. Collier, 47; Rankin, 18.
9. Davis, *51st Virginia,* 8; Lowry, *22nd Virginia,* 23; Scott, *36th Virginia,* 9, *45th Virginia,* 13.
10. Moore, *Danville,* 65; Ruffner, 19–20.
11. Thomas, "Campaigns," 301.
12. Beatty, "Regiment," 436–437; Grebner, 79; Horton, 55; Wilson, 113.
13. Baxter, 65–66; Van Dyke, 28–29; Morris, 32.
14. Woodworth, 85; Freeman, *Lee,* 603.
15. Freeman, *Lee,* 603; Taylor, 37; Thomas, *Lee,* 211; Woodworth, 85; Jefferson Davis, *The Rise and Fall of the Confederate Government* (Richmond, Virginia: Garrett and Massie, Incorporated, undated), 376.
16. Thomas, *Lee,* 210.
17. Sears, *McClellan,* 93; Bruce Catton, *The Army of the Potomac: Mr. Lincoln's Army* (Garden City, New York: Doubleday & Company, Inc., 1962), 51; John C. Waugh, *The Class of 1846,* 342–343.
18. George B. McClellan, *McClellan's Own Story* (New York: Charles Webster & Company, 1887), 56, *Report,* 30–31.
19. Cox, *Reminiscences,* 145.
20. Ibid.; Plum, 103.

SELECTED BIBLIOGRAPHY

Acts of the General Assembly of the State of Virginia, 1861, Extra Session (Richmond, 1861).

Ambler, Charles H., *Francis H. Pierpont: Union War Governor of Virginia and Father of West Virginia* (Chapel Hill: The University of North Carolina Press, 1937).

_____, *The Makers of West Virginia and Their Work,* reprint from vol. I of *Debates and Proceedings of the First Constitutional Convention of West Virginia (1861–1863)* (Huntington, West Virginia: Gentry Brothers, Printers, 1942).

_____, "General R. E. Lee's Northwest Virginia Campaign," *West Virginia History,* vol. V, no. 2, January 1944, 101–115.

_____, and Festus P. Summers, *West Virginia: The Mountain State* (Englewood Cliffs, New Jersey: Prentice-Hall, 1958).

Andre, Richard, and Stan Cohen and William D. Wintz, *Bullets & Steel: The Fight for the Great Kanawha Valley, 1861–1865* (Charleston, West Virginia: Pictorial Histories Publishing Company, Inc., 1995).

Andrews, J. Cutler, *The North Reports the Civil War* (Pittsburgh: University of Pittsburgh Press, 1985), paper.

_____, *The South Reports the Civil War* (Pittsburgh: University of Pittsburgh Press, 1985), paper.

Armstrong, Richard L., *25th Virginia and 9th Battalion Virginia Infantry* (Lynchburg, Virginia: H.E. Howard, Inc., 1990).

Arnold, Thomas J., "The Battle of Rich Mountain," *Confederate Veteran,* vol. 29, 1921, 342–343.

Ashcraft, John M., *31st Virginia Infantry* (Lynchburg, Virginia: H.E. Howard, Inc., 1988).

Bailes, Clarice Lorene, "Jacob Dolson Cox in West Virginia," *West Virginia History,* vol. VI, no. 1, October 1944, 5–58.

Baxter, Nancy Niblack, *Gallant Fourteenth, The Story of an Indiana Civil War Regiment* (Traverse City, Michigan: Pioneer Study Center Press, 1980).

Beals, Carleton, *War Within a War: The Confederacy Against Itself* (New York: Chilton Books, 1965).

Beatty, John, *Memoirs of a Volunteer, 1861–1863* (New York: W.W. Norton & Company, 1946).

_____, "A Regiment in Search of a Battle," *Sketches of War History* (Military Order of the Loyal Legion of the United States, Ohio, vol. III, 422–452). Cincinnati, Ohio: Robert Clarke & Co., 1890.

Beauregard, P. G. T., "The First Battle of Bull Run," *From Sumter to Shiloh: Battles and Leaders of the Civil War–Volume I* (South Brunswick, New York: Thomas Yoseloff, 1956), 196–227.

Belohavek, John M., "John B. Floyd and the West Virginia Campaign of 1861," *West Virginia History,* vol. XXIX, no. 4, July 1968, 283–291.

Boehm, Robert Blair, *The Civil War in Western Virginia: The Decisive Campaigns of 1861,* Ph.D. Dissertation, The Ohio State University, 1957.

_____, "The Battle of Rich Mountain, July 11, 1861," *West Virginia History,* vol. XX, no. 1, October 1958, 5–15.

Botkin, B. A., *A Civil War Treasury of Tales, Legends and Folklore* (New York: Promontory Press, 1981).

Briant, C. C., *History of the Sixth Regiment Indiana Volunteer Infantry* (Indianapolis: Wm. B. Burford, Printer and Binder, 1891).

Branwell, Robert W., "The First West Virginia Campaigns," *Confederate Veteran,* vol. 38, April 1930, 148–151, and May, 186–189.

Broun, Thomas L., "Gen. R.E. Lee's War-Horse," *Confederate Veteran,* vol. VI, no. 7, 1898, 292.

Carnes, Eva Margaret, *The Tygarts Valley Line: June–July 1861* (Philippi, West Virginia: First Land Battle of the Civil War Centennial Commemoration, Inc., 1961).

_____, "The Battle of Philippi," *American Heritage,* Vol. No. 3, 1952.

Carrigan, C. H., *Cheat Mountain: Unwritten Chapter of the Late War* (Nashville: Albert B. Tavel, Stationer and Printer, 1885).

Carrington, Henry Beebee, *Ohio Militia and the West Virginia Campaign, 1861,* Address to Army of West Virginia at Marietta, Ohio, September 10, 1870 (Boston: R.H. Blodgett & Co., Printers, 1904).

Catton, Bruce, *The Coming Fury* (Garden City, New York: Doubleday & Company, Inc., 1961).

_____, *The Army of the Potomac: Mr. Lincoln's Army* (Garden City, New York: Doubleday & Company, Inc., 1962).

Chapla, John D., *48th Virginia Infantry* (Lynchburg, Virginia: H.E. Howard, Inc., 1989).

Chase, John A., *History of the Fourteenth Ohio Regiment, O.V.V.I., From the Beginning of the War in 1861 to Its Close in 1865* (Toledo, Ohio: St John Print. House, 1881).

Clark, Walter A., *Under the Stars and Bars or, Memories of Four Years Service with Oglethorpes, of Augusta, Georgia* (Augusta, Georgia: Chronicle Printing Company, 1900; reprinted by Freedom Hill Press, Inc., Jonesboro, Georgia, 1987).

Clausewitz, Carl, *On War,* edited and translated by Michael and Peter Paret (Princeton, New Jersey: Princeton University Press, 1976).

Cohen, Stan, *The Civil War in West Virginia: A Pictorial History* (Charleston, West Virginia: Pictorial Histories Publishing Company, 1995).

_____, "Colonel George S. Patton and the 22nd Virginia Infantry Regiment," *West Virginia History,* vol. XXVI, April 1965, 178–190.

Collier, Calvin L., *"They'll Do To Tie To!" The Story of the Third Regiment, Arkansas Infantry, C.S.A.* (Little Rock, Arkansas: Eagle Press, 1988).

Collins, Darrell L., *46th Virginia Infantry* (Lynchburg, Virginia: H.E. Howard, Inc., 1992).

Cometti, Elizabeth, and Festus P. Summers, eds., *The Thirty-Fifth State: A Documentary History of West Virginia* (Morgantown: West Virginia University Library, 1966).

Connelly, Thomas L., *The Marble Man: Robert E. Lee and His Image in American Society* (Baton Rouge: Louisiana State University Press, 1977).

Cook, Roy Bird, "First Battle in the Great Kanawha Valley," *Confederate Veteran,* vol. 39, April 1931, 143–145, and May, 183–186.

Cooper, Charles R., *Chronological and Alphabetical Record of the Engagements of the Great Civil War* (Milwaukee, Wisconsin: The Caston Press, 1904).

Cox, Jacob Dolson, *Military Reminiscences of the Civil War,* vol. I, April 1861–November 1863 (New York: Charles Scribner's Sons, 1900).

_____, "War Preparations in the North," 84–98, and "McClellan in West Virginia," 126–148, *From Sumter to Shiloh: Battles and Leaders of the Civil War– Volume I* (South Brunswick, New York: Thomas Yoseloff, 1956).

Cozzens, Peter, "The Tormenting Flame," *Civil War Times Illustrated,* vol. XXXV, no. 1, April 1996, 44–54.

Crute, Joseph H., Jr., *Units of the Confederate States Army* (Midlothian, Virginia: Derwent Books, 1987).

Curry, Richard Orr, *A House Divided: A Study of Statehood Politics and the Copperhead Movement in West Virginia* (Pittsburgh: University of Pittsburgh Press, 1964).

Davis, James A., *51st Virginia Infantry* (Lynchburg, Virginia: H.E. Howard, Inc., 1984).

Davis, Jefferson, *The Rise and Fall of the Confederate Government* (Richmond, Virginia: Garrett and Massie, Incorporated, undated).

Doll, William H., *History of the Sixth Regiment Indiana Volunteer Infantry in the Civil War* (Columbus, Indiana: Republican Print Job, 1903).

Dornbusch, C. E., *Military Bibliography of the Civil War* (New York: The New York Public Library, vol. two, 1967, vol. three, 1972).

Dowdey, Clifford, *The History of the Confederacy: 1832–1865* (New York: Barnes & Noble Books, 1992).

Driver, Robert J., *52nd Virginia Infantry* (Lynchburg, Virginia: H.E. Howard, Inc., 1986).

Dyer, Frederick H., *A Compendium of the War of the Rebellion,* 3 vols. (New York: Thomas Yoseloff, 1959).

Eaton, Clement, "Henry A. Wise: A Study in Virginia Leadership, 1850–1861," *West Virginia History,* vol. 3, no. 3, April 1942, 187–204.

Ferguson, J. M., "The Battle of Scary, W.Va.," *Confederate Veteran,* vol. 25, 1917, 503.

Fleming, Martin K., "The Northwestern Virginia Campaign of 1861," *Blue & Gray Magazine,* August 1993, 10–17, 48–65.

Flourny, H. W., ed., *Calendar of Virginia State Papers* (Richmond, 1893).

Foote, Shelby, *The Civil War: A Narrative, Fort Sumter to Perryville* (New York: Random House, 1958).

Ford, Ebenezer Hanna, *The Story of a Regiment: A History of the Campaigns, and Associations in the Field of the Sixth Regiment, Ohio Volunteer Infantry* (Cincinnati: Published by the Author, 1868).

Frank Leslie's Illustrated Newspaper, 1861.

Freeman, Douglas Southall, *R. E. Lee* (New York: Charles Scribner's Sons: 1934).

————, *Lee's Lieutenants, Volume 1: Manassas to Malvern Hill* (New York: Charles Scribner's Sons, 1942).

Fry, James B., "McDowell's Advance to Bull Run" *From Sumter to Shiloh: Battles and Leaders of the Civil War–Volume I* (South Brunswick, New York: Thomas Yoseloff, 1956), 167–193.

Fuller, W. G., "The Corps of Telegraphers Under General Anson Stager During the War of the Rebellion," *Sketches of War History* (Military Order of the Loyal Legion of the United States, Ohio, vol. II, 392–404). Cincinnati, Ohio: Robert Clarke & Co., 1888.

Grayson, A. J., *History of the Sixth Indiana Regiment in the Three Months Campaign in Western Virginia* (undated).

Grebner, Constanin, *"We Were the Ninth," A History of the Ninth Regiment, Ohio Volunteer Infantry, April 17, 1861, to June 7, 1864* edited and translated by Frederick Trautmann(Kent, Ohio: The Kent State University Press, 1987).

Griggs, Walter S., *General John Pegram, C.S.A.* (Lynchburg, Virginia: H.E. Howard, Inc., 1993).

Grimsley, Mark, *The Hard Hand of War: Union Military Policy Towards Southern Civilians, 1861–1865* (Cambridge: Cambridge University Press, 1995).

Hagy, P. S., "The Laurel Hill Retreat in 1861," *Confederate Veteran,* vol. 24, 1916, 169–173.

Hall, Granville Davisson, *Lee's Invasion of Northwest Virginia in 1861* (Chicago: The Mayer & Miller Company, 1911).

Hassler, William W., "Henry Heth–Lee's Hard Luck General," *Civil War Times Illustrated,* vol. V, no. 4, July 1966, 13–20.

Head, Thomas A., *Campaigns and Battles of the Sixteenth Regiment, Tennessee Volunteers, In The War Between The States, With Incidental Sketches of the Part Performed by other Tennessee Troops in the same War, 1861–1865* (Nashville, Tennessee: Cumberland Presbyterian Publishing House, 1885).

Hermann, Isaac, *Memoirs of a Veteran* (Atlanta: Byrd Printing Company, 1911).

Heth, Henry, *The Memories of Henry Heth,* James L. Morrison, ed. (Westport, Connecticut: Greenwood Press, 1974).

Horton, Joshua H., and Teverbaugh, *A History of the Eleventh Regiment, Ohio Volunteer Infantry* (Dayton, Ohio: W.J. Shuey, Printer and Publisher, 1866).

Hotchkiss, Jedediah, *Make Me a Map of the Valley: The Civil War Journal of Stonewall Jackson's Topographer,* Archie P. McDonald, ed. (Dallas: Southern Methodist University Press, 1974).

Husley, Val, " 'Men of Virginia–Men of Kanawha–To Arms' A History of the Twenty-second Virginia Volunteer Infantry Regiment, C.S.A.," *West Virginia History,* vol. XXXV, no. 3, 220–236.

Imboden, John D., "Jackson at Harper's Ferry in 1861" *From Sumter to Shiloh: Battles and Leaders of the Civil War–Volume I* (South Brunswick, New York: Thomas Yoseloff, 1956), 111–125.

_____, "Incidents of the First Bull Run," *From Sumter to Shiloh: Battles and Leaders of the Civil War–Volume I* (South Brunswick, New York: Thomas Yoseloff, 1956), 229–239.

Johnston, Angus James, II, *Virginia Railroads in the Civil War* (Chapel Hill: The University of North Carolina Press, 1961).

Johnston, Joseph E., "Responsibilities of the First Bull Run," *From Sumter to Shiloh: Battles and Leaders of the Civil War–Volume I* (South Brunswick, New York: Thomas Yoseloff, 1956), 240–259.

Jomini, Antoine Henri, *The Art of War,* translated by G. H. Mendell and W. P. Craighill, (Westport, Connecticut: Greenwood Press, 1971; originally published in 1862 by J. B. Lippincott & Co., Philadelphia).

Jones, Allen W., "Military Events in West Virginia During the Civil War, 1861–1865," *West Virginia History,* vol. 47, 1988, 39–52.

Kepler, William, *History of the Three Months' and Three Years' Service From April 16th, 1861, to June 22d, 1864, of the Fourth Regiment Ohio Volunteer Infantry in the War for the Union* (Cleveland: Leader Printing Company, 1886; reprinted by Blue Acorn Press, Huntington, West Virginia, 1992).

Klement, Frank, "General John B. Floyd and the West Virginia Campaigns of 1861," *West Virginia History,* vol. VIII, no. 3, April 1947, 319–333.

Kreidberg, Marvin A., and Merton G. Henry, *History of Military Mobilization in the United States Army: 1775–1945,* Department of the Army Pamphlet No. 20-212 (Washington, D.C.: U.S. Government Printing Office, 1955).

Lamers, William M., *The Edge of Glory: A Biography of William S. Rosecrans, U.S.A.* (New York: Harcourt, Brace & World, Inc., 1961).

Lee, Stephen D., "The First Step in the War," pp. 74–81, *From Sumter to Shiloh: Battles and Leaders of the Civil War–Volume I* (South Brunswick, New York: Thomas Yoseloff, 1956), 74–81.

Lesser, W. Hunter, *Battle at Corricks Ford: Confederate Disaster and Loss of a Leader* (Parsons, West Virginia: McClain Printing Company, Inc., 1993).

Lewis, Virgil A., *How West Virginia Was Made: Proceedings of the First Convention of the People of Northwestern Virginia* (Charleston, West Virginia: New-Mail Company Public Printers, 1909).

Lockard, E. Kidd, "The Unfortunate Military Career of Henry A. Wise in Western Virginia," *West Virginia History,* vol. XXXI, no. 1, October 1969, 40–54.

Long, A. L., *Memoirs of Robert E. Lee: His Military and Personal History* (New York: J.M. Stoddart & Company, 1886).

———, "Lee's West Virginia Campaign," *The Annals of the War* (Philadelphia: The Times Publishing Company, 1879). Republished by *Civil War Times Illustrated,* 1974, 82–94.

Long, E. B., with Barbara Long, *The Civil War Day by Day: An Almanac 1861–1865* (Garden City, New York: Doubleday & Company, Inc., 1971).

Lowry, Terry, *September Blood: The Battle of Carnifex Ferry* (Charleston, West Virginia: Pictorial Histories Publishing Company, 1985).

———, *22nd Virginia Infantry* (Lynchburg, Virginia: H.E. Howard, Inc., 1988).

McBrien, Joe Bennett, *The Tennessee Brigade* (Chattanooga, Tennessee: Hudson Printing & Lithographing Co., 1977).

McCabe, James B., Jr., *Life and Campaigns of General Robert E. Lee* (Atlanta: National Publishing Company, 1866).

McClellan, George B., *The Armies of Europe* (Philadelphia: J.B. Lippincott, 1861).

———, *McClellan's Own Story* (New York: Charles Webster & Company, 1887).

———, *Report on the Organization and Campaigns of the Army of the Potomac: To Which Is Added an Account of the Campaign in Western Virginia* (Freeport, New York: Books for Libraries Press, 1970), reprint of the 1864 edition.

McComb, William, "Tennesseeans in the Mountain Campaign," *Confederate Veteran,* vol. 22, May 1914, 210–212.

McKinney, Tim, *Robert E. Lee at Sewell Mountain: The West Virginia Campaign* (Charleston, West Virginia: Pictorial Histories Publishing Co., Inc., 1990).

McPherson, James M., *Battle Cry of Freedom* (New York: Oxford University Press, 1988).

———, *What They Fought For, 1861–1865* (Baton Rouge: Louisiana State University Press, 1994).

McPherson, James M., ed., *The Atlas of the Civil War* (New York: MacMillan, 1994).

Martin, Albro, *Railroads Triumphant: The Growth, Rejection, and Rebirth of a Vital American Force* (New York: Oxford University Press, 1992).

Monfort, E. R., "From Grafton to McDowell Through Tygart's Valley," *Sketches of War History* (Military Order of the Loyal Legion of the United States, Ohio, vol. II, 1–21). Cincinnati, Ohio: Robert Clarke & Co., 1888.

Moore, George Ellis, *A Banner in the Hills: West Virginia's Statehood* (New York: Appleton-Century-Crofts, 1963).

Moore, Robert H., *The Danville, Eighth Star New Market and Dixie Artillery* (Lynchburg, Virginia: H.E. Howard, Inc., 1989).

Morris, Roy, Jr., *Ambrose Bierce: Alone in Bad Company* (New York: Crown Publishers, Inc., 1995).

Morton, T. C., "Anecdotes of General R.E. Lee," *Southern Historical Society Papers,* vol. X, January to December, 1883, 517–520.

National Archives, *A Guide to Civil War Maps in the National Archives* (Washington, D.C.: The National Archives, National Archives and Records Administration, 1986).

Nevins, Allan, *The War for the Union: The Improvised War* (New York: Charles Scribner's Sons, 1959).

Oram, Richard W., ed., "Harpers Ferry to the Fall of Richmond: Letters of Colonel John De Hart Ross, C.S.A.," *West Virginia History,* vol. XLV, 1984, 159–180.

Ordinances of The Convention, Assembled at Wheeling, on the 11th of June, 1861 (Wheeling, Virginia, 1861).

Patterson, Richard, "Schemes and Treachery," *Civil War Times Illustrated,* vol. XXVIII, no. 2, April 1989, 38–45.

Pauley, Michael J., "They Called Him 'Tiger John': The Story of General John McCausland C.S.A.," *Blue and Gray Magazine,* vol. 1, no. 5, April–May 1984, 12–17.

_____, *Unconstructed Rebel: The Life of General John McCausland, C.S.A.* (Charleston, West Virginia: Pictorial Histories Publishing Co., Inc., 1993).

Perret, Geoffrey, *A Country Made by War: From the Revolution to Vietnam–The Story of America's Rise to Power* (New York: Random House, 1989).

Phillips, David L., *War Diaries: The 1861 Kanawha Campaigns* (Leesburg, Virginia: Gauley Mount Press, 1990).

_____, ed., *War Stories: Civil War in West Virginia* (Leesburg, Virginia: Gauley Mount Press, 1991).

Pinkerton, Allan, *The Spy of the Rebellion* (Kansas City: Kansas City Publishing Co., 1884).

Plum, William R., *The Military Telegraph During the Civil War in the United States* (Chicago: Ansen, McClurg & Company, Publishers, 1882).

Potts, J. N., "That Battle at Philippi," *Confederate Veteran,* vol. VI, no. 9, September 1898, 424.

Price, Henry M., "Rich Mountain in 1861, An Account of That Memorable Campaign and How General Garnett Was Killed," *Historical Society Papers,* vol. XXVII (Richmond, Virginia: Published by the Society, 1899), 39–48.

Pryor, S. G., *A Post of Honor: The Pryor Letters, 1861–1863; Letters From Capt. S.G. Pryor, Twelfth Georgia Regiment and His Wife, Penelope Tyson Pryor,* Charles R. Adams, ed. (Fort Valley, Georgia: Garret Publications, Inc., 1989).

Rankin, Thomas M., *23rd Virginia Infantry* (Lynchburg, Virginia: H.E. Howard, Inc., 1985).

Rawling, Charles J., *History of the First Regiment, Virginia Infantry* (Philadelphia: J.B. Lippincott Company, 1887).

Reid, Whitelaw, *Ohio in the War: Her Statesmen, Her Generals, and Soldiers* (Cincinnati: Moore, Wilstach & Baldwin, 1868).

Rice, Otis K., *West Virginia: A History* (Lexington, Kentucky: The University Press of Kentucky, 1985).

_____, "West Virginia," *Encyclopedia of the Confederacy* (New York: Simon & Schuster, 1993), 1699–1703.

Riddle, Thomas J., "Reminiscences of Floyd's Operations in West Virginia in 1861," *Southern Historical Society Papers,* vol. X, January to December 1883, 517–520.

Riggs, Susan, A., *21st Virginia Infantry* (Lynchburg, Virginia: H.E. Howard, Inc., 1991).

Robertson, W. Glenn, "First Bull Run, 19 July 1861," *America's First Battles: 1776–1965* (Lawrence, Kansas: University Press of Kansas, 1986), 81–108.

Rosecrans's Campaigns, extracted from: U.S. Congress Joint Committee on the Conduct of the War. Report of the Joint Committee on the Conduct of the War, 1863–1866 (Millwood, New York: Kraus Reprint Co., 1977).

Ruffner, Kevin C., *44th Virginia Infantry* (Lynchburg, Virginia: H.E. Howard, Inc., 1987).

Savage, John H., "Gen. R.E. Lee at Cheat Mountain," *Confederate Veteran,* vol. 7, 1899, 116–118.

Scott, J. L., *36th Virginia Infantry* (Lynchburg, Virginia: H.E. Howard, Inc., 1987).

_____, *45th Virginia Infantry* (Lynchburg, Virginia: H.E. Howard, Inc., 1989).

Scott, William Forse, *Philander P. Lane: Colonel of Volunteers in the Civil War, Eleventh Ohio Infantry* (Privately Printed, 1920).

Schneider, James J., "Theoretical Implications of Operational Art," in Clayton R. Newell and Michael D. Krause, eds., *On Operational Art* (Washington, D.C.: U.S. Government Printing Office, 1994).

Sears, Stephen W., *George B. McClellan: The Young Napoleon* (New York: Ticknor & Fields, 1988).

_____, ed., *The Civil War Papers of George B. McClellan* (New York: Ticknor & Fields, 1989).

Shaffer, Dallas B., "Rich Mountain Revisited," *West Virginia History,* vol. XXVIII, no. 1, October 1966, 16–34.

Shaw, James Birney, *History of the Tenth Regiment Indiana Volunteer Infantry, Three Months and Three Years Organizations* (Lafayette, Indiana, 1912).

Sherwood, G. L. and Jeffrey C. Weaver, *20th and 39th Virginia Infantry* (Lynchburg, Virginia: H.E. Howard, Inc., 1994).

_____, *59th Virginia Infantry* (Lynchburg, Virginia: H.E. Howard, Inc., 1994).

Sifakis, Stewart, *Who Was Who in the Civil War* (New York: Facts on File Publications, 1988).

Simpson, Craig M., *A Good Southerner: The Life of Henry A. Wise of Virginia* (Chapel Hill: University of North Carolina Press, 1985).

Smith, Edward Conrad, *The Borderland in the Civil War* (New York: The MacMillan Company, 1927).

Speed, Thomas, *The Union Regiments of Kentucky* (Louisville, Kentucky: Courier-Journal Job Printing Company, 1897).

Stewart, D. B., "First Infantry Fight of the War," *Confederate Veteran,* vol. XVII, no. 10, October 1909, 500.

Stokes, J. W., "The Retreat from Laurel Hill, West Virginia," *Southern Bivouac,* vol. III, September 1884–May 1885, 11–16, 61–66.

Stover, John F., *History of the Baltimore and Ohio Railroad* (West Lafayette, Indiana: Purdue University Press, 1987).

Stutler, Boyd B., *West Virginia in the Civil War* (Charleston, West Virginia: Education Foundation, Inc., 1963).

_____, "The Civil War in West Virginia," *West Virginia History,* vol. 47, 1988, 29–38.

Summers, Festus P., *The Baltimore and Ohio in the Civil War* (New York, 1939).

Tanner, Robert G., *Stonewall in the Valley* (Garden City, New York: Doubleday & Company, Inc., 1976).

Taylor, Walter H., *Four Years with General Lee* (New York: D. Appleton and Company, 1877).

Thomas, Emory M., *Robert E. Lee: A Biography* (New York: W.W. Norton & Company, 1965).

Thomas, Joseph W., "Campaigns of Generals McClellan and Rosecrans in Western Virginia, 1861–1862," *West Virginia History,* vol. V, no. 4, July 1944, 245–308.

Thompson, C. L., "The Battle of Scary," *Confederate Veteran,* vol. 26, 1918, 275–276.

Thompson, Robert Luther, *Wiring a Continent: The History of the Telegraph Industry in the United States, 1832–1866* (New York: Arno Press, 1972).

U.S. Government, *The War of the Rebellion: A Compilation of the Official Records of the Union and Confederate Armies* (Washington: Government Printing Office, 1880).

U.S. War Department, *The War of the Rebellion: A Compilation of the Official Records of the Union and Confederate Armies,* 70 volumes (1880–1901).

Van Dyke, Augustus M., "Early Days; or, The School of the Soldier," *Sketches of War History* (Military Order of the Loyal Legion of the United States, Ohio, vol. V, 18–31). Cincinnati, Ohio: Robert Clarke & Co., 1903.

Wallace, Lee A., *A Guide to Virginia Military Organizations 1861–1865* (Lynchburg, Virginia: H.E. Howard, Inc., 1986).

Watkins, Samuel R., *"Co, Aytch:" Maury Grays First Tennessee Regiment or A Side Show of the Big Show* (New York: Collier Books, 1962).

Ward, James E. D., *Twelfth Ohio Volunteer Inf.* (Ripley, Ohio, 1864).

Warner, Ezra J., *Generals in Blue: Lives of the Union Commanders* (Baton Rouge: Louisiana State University Press, 1960).

_____, *Generals in Gray: Lives of the Confederate Commanders* (Baton Rouge: Louisiana State University Press, 1965).

Waugh, Jack, "Long Distance Victory: McClellan's First Battles," *Civil War Times Illustrated,* vol. XXII, no. 7, 10–19, November 1983.

Waugh, John C., *The Class of 1846: From West Point to Appomattax: Stonewall Jackson, George McClellan and Their Brothers* (New York: Warner Books, 1994).

Weigley, Russell R., *The American Way of War: A History of United States Military Strategy and Policy* (New York: MacMillan Publishing Co., Inc., 1973).

Wessler, William L., *Born to Be a Soldier: The Military Career of William Wing Loring of St. Augustine, Florida* (Fort Worth: Texas Christian University Press, 1971).

White, Robert, *West Virginia,* vol. II, *Confederate Military History,* Clement A. Evans, ed., 1899.

Wilder, Theodore, *The History of Company C, Seventy Regiment, O.V.V.I.* (Oberlin: J.B.T. Marsh, Printer, 1866).

Wilkinson, Warren, "West Virginia Operations: Operations of 1861," *Encyclopedia of the Confederacy* (New York: Simon & Schuster, 1993), 1703–1705.

Wilson, Lawrence, *Itinerary of the Seventh Ohio Volunteer Infantry, 1861–1864* (New York: The Neale Publishing Company, 1907).

Wise, Barton H., *The Life of Henry A. Wise of Virginia: 1806–1876* (London: MacMillan & Co., Inc., 1899).

Womack, James J., *The Civil War Diary of Capt. J.J. Womack, Co. E, Sixteenth Regiment, Tennessee Volunteers (Confederate)* (McMinnville, Tennessee: Womack Printing Company, 1961).

Wood, George L., *The Seventh Regiment: A Record* (New York: James Miller, 1865).

Woodworth, Steven E., *Davis and Lee at War* (Lawrence, Kansas: University of Kansas Press, 1995).

Zinn, Jack, *R. E. Lee's Cheat Mountain Campaign* (Parsons, West Virginia: McClain Printing Company, 1974).